ALSO BY RICH COHEN

Tough Jews: Fathers, Sons and Gangster Dreams

THE AVENGERS

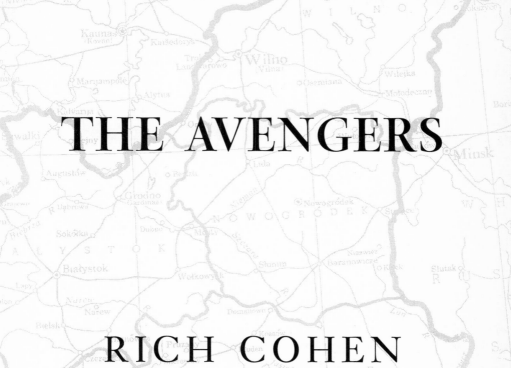

THE AVENGERS

RICH COHEN

JONATHAN CAPE
LONDON

Published by Jonathan Cape 2000

2 4 6 8 10 9 7 5 3 1

Copyright © Rich Cohen 2000

Rich Cohen has asserted his right under the Copyright, Designs
and Patents Act 1988 to be identified as the author of this work

First published in Great Britain in 2000 by
Jonathan Cape
Random House, 20 Vauxhall Bridge Road,
London SW1V 2SA

Random House Australia (Pty) Limited
20 Alfred Street, Milsons Point, Sydney,
New South Wales 2061, Australia

Random House New Zealand Limited
18 Poland Road, Glenfield,
Auckland 10, New Zealand

Random House (Pty) Limited
Endulini, 5A Jubilee Road, Parktown 2193, South Africa

The Random House Group Limited Reg. No. 954009
www.randomhouse.co.uk

The photographs on pages 240 and 248 are by Hayim Goldgraber
All other photographs are used courtesy of Rich Cohen

A CIP catalogue record for this book
is available from the British Library

ISBN 0-224-06001-5

Papers used by Random House are natural,
recyclable products made from wood grown in sustainable forests.
The manufacturing processes conform to the environmental
regulations of the country of origin

Printed and bound in Great Britain by
Biddles Ltd, Guildford and King's Lynn

For Ellen Cohen

CONTENTS

THE AVENGERS

I T IS LIKE no Holocaust story I have ever heard. There are no cattle cars in it, and no concentration camps. It takes place in underground hideouts and forest clearings, and in the ruins of German cities after the Second World War.

I first heard the story in 1977, when my family visited Israel, a trip partly chronicled in the photo album my mother put together when we returned to our house in suburban Chicago. The pictures show a smiling family backed by the usual landmarks: Western Wall, Dead Sea, Masada. I was ten years old. My brother was fifteen. In many photographs, he wears black, sun-absorbing concert T-shirts. In one, he makes a muscle. My sister, who would soon turn eighteen, looks bored, like every minute on this trip is another party missed. There is a shot of my father leaning on an Israeli tank, looking into the distance, as if scanning for Babylonians. My mother was taking the pictures, or else holding her hands over her face so no pictures of her could be taken. When it comes to photos, my mom is a classic case of dish-it-out-but-can't-take-it. Viewed together, these pictures record a middle-class Jewish pilgrimage, a family rite, Christmas in the Holy Land: kids squinting through the glare, searching out a lost connection, a link to a homeland that, after all that air travel, feels like just another country.

If you want to know about the rest of our vacation, those moments when the camera stayed in the bag, feuds, quarrels, threats and fits, you must dig deeper, beneath the old diplomas and hockey-mom patches, to the frayed pages of *The Cohen Daily News,* a news-

3

paper edited and published (by me) during the three weeks we spent in Israel. The paper, which was not really a daily, was handwritten on yellow sheets torn from my father's legal pads. Held together by a clip, the paper was passed from family member to family member. The stories, printed under smudged headlines, set down even the most scandalous rumors. Below my brother's byline ran a piece about my parents: "Herb and Ellen Fool Around." The article talked of a gleam in my dad's eye, of noises on the other side of a wall, of disheveled hair, of laughter. "Ellen was seen under the covers wearing a big smile," the story read. "Talk has it, that was all she was wearing."

Reviews ran in the back of the paper, including my dad's musings on a restaurant in Haifa where every dish was stuffed. "Not only is the food filling," he wrote. "It is stuffing." The last issue of *The Cohen Daily News*, published as my parents packed, tells of a trip we made to a kibbutz north of Tel Aviv, a visit with relatives once thought lost in the Holocaust. In just a few paragraphs of my sister's blocky print, the story recalls the most important evening of our vacation, our first meeting with the Avengers, veteran fighters who slogged out World War II in the gloomy forests of Eastern Europe, later fought for Bible-bleached Middle Eastern wastes, and were the kind of people who inspired Joseph Goebbels to write in his diary: "One sees what the Jews can do when they are armed." In a dozen sentences, my sister set down the moment that fused the lost connection and made the homeland feel like home—an electric moment that lurks just beyond the photos in my mother's album.

We drove to the kibbutz by rental car. The directions given to us by the man at the hotel were useless. Israelis—who knows why—give directions that are both clipped and broad, like every place is the same place, like any street gets you there: only a fool can miss it. "OK, you come out on the road and you are going," the man said, waving a hand. "You are going and going and going all the time. You are seeing a bridge but you are not going there because you are still going all the time. Then you see a tree, a building, and there you are."

We took a map. I had it on my knees. On family trips, I was the navigator. I was fascinated by maps. This one showed a sliver of land along the sea. Brown, blue. The names of the towns were familiar from religious school: Yafo, Jericho, Beersheba. Looking at the map, I began to sense just how abbreviated Israel is. It seemed the map was actual size. Picking out a town, I would say, "We should be in Netanya in two hours." And just as I was saying this, my father would gear down and say, "Here is Netanya."

We turned onto a road that ran through open fields. Little cars would dart up behind us flashing their lights. You could see them in the rearview mirror. Rolling down his window, my father waved them on. And off they would drive, bounding ahead, trailed by dust. We were going to see Ruzka Korczak; we had been sent by my grandmother. In 1920, my grandmother emigrated to New York from a small town in Poland, where she had nine siblings and an infant niece, the daughter of her oldest brother. Though my grandmother was to be just the first of the children to make the trip, the family ran out of money. And the seasons changed. And the politicians fell. And the War started. Several years after Nazi Germany collapsed, my grandmother got a letter from a woman named Sara, who came from her town in Poland. Sara now lived in Israel, where she searched for survivors, trying to put them back together with lost family. She met ships, studied dockets, interviewed passengers. Early in our vacation, we had lunch with Sara. Even if she had something of interest to say, I missed it. Her husband was named Shlomo; I could not move much beyond that.

In her letter, Sara told my grandmother that almost every Jew in their town had been killed. And yet a member of my grandmother's family had survived—the niece. For much of the War, this niece had fought as a partisan in the forest. She was now settled on a kibbutz north of Tel Aviv. "Do you remember your niece?" wrote Sara. "You are her only family. Her name is Ruzka."

The road climbed up a hill. Looking back, I could see the flat brown country below. It was blurry in the dust. We turned onto a bumpy trail. Fields rolled into the distance. The crops were so green they hurt my eyes. The air smelled like Illinois when the farmers sell their vegetables in town. We went around a bend, and there was Ruzka. I had heard stories about her, things she had done in the War. I had expectations. What I got instead was a slight, smiling, gray-haired Jewish woman not so different from my Grandma Esther, who was just then passing her golden years in a retirement complex in North Miami Beach.

When we stepped from the car, Ruzka gave each of us a hug, as if we had met many times before. She had the rugged face of a farm worker—a dramatic backdrop for her eyes, which were warm and youthful. She asked us many questions and seemed to savor each answer, listening as fully as most people talk. As we followed her along the road, she pointed out buildings: "That is the dining hall," she said. "That is where the children live. That is where we keep the guns." In the distance, we could see children, cattle, goats. The kibbutz is a collective, a socialist settlement where you might work in the fields or pick fruit or milk cows. Spotting any cow, a local can say, "That is my cow." The few kibbutzim that still survive are hold-overs, relics from the pioneer days, when such one-for-all communities seemed the best way of coping with scorching summers and marauding neighbors. Looking to the eastern horizon, where the fields turned brown, Ruzka said, "Before we fought the Six Day War in '67, the other side of those fields was Jordan."

Ruzka led us to a white house with a red roof. The windows blazed with light. Inside, the walls were lined with paintings and books. Avi, whom Ruzka married after the War, a handsome, fair-skinned man with white hair and brilliant blue eyes, smiled and said hello. Since emigrating to Palestine in the thirties, Avi had spent much of his life trying to recapture the culture of his youth, the music and literature and food of Austria. "Avi, what are you doing?" asked Ruzka.

He was picking at the tray Ruzka had set out: fruit and vegetables.
"Darling, Ruzka, tell me, why no sausage?"
Ruzka smiled at Avi, and then fixed a plate for each of us.
There was a knock on the door. Then another. The floorboards creaked. The house filled with the smiles and guffaws of old Jews. "This is Abba Kovner," said Ruzka. I had been told Kovner was a

poet, that he had won the biggest awards a writer in Israel can win, that soldiers carried his books to war. He looked like no one I had ever seen, a lost Old World prophet. His shoulders were hunched. His body was steely slender, a piece of modern sculpture, edges and angles. His eyes shone with a dark, secretive melancholy. In any picture, his face recedes, more still and somber than the surrounding hills. At his side, never beyond whispering distance, was his wife, Vitka. She was long-limbed, with dark hair and big eyes. Her face was plain until she smiled and her smile remade her face and then her smile was gone and her face fell again into the blank gaze she must have worn as a girl in Eastern Europe.

Abba, Ruzka, Vitka—this was not an ordinary relationship, not the conventional idea of a married couple crossing the fence to visit a neighbor. These people had met over thirty years before, in the cramped streets of Vilna, the capital of Lithuania—kids caught in the second act of World War II. Some people have tried to cast their relationship in terms of a traditional love triangle. They say Ruzka and Vitka were in love with Abba, or Abba and Ruzka were in love with Vitka, or Vitka and Abba were in love with Ruzka. In truth, all were in love with all. They finished one another's sentences, read one another's thoughts. The things they endured and survived bound them in ways hard for anyone living today to imagine.

For the most part, they did not like to talk about the past, or about their own exploits. They wanted to know about America, or Chicago, or, in my case, the rigors of fifth grade. Only slowly, often from the mouths of other people, did we learn of the underground army they formed in Europe, of the battles they fought with the Germans, of how they escaped Vilna moments before the Jewish ghetto was destroyed. There were also stories of the forest, where they lived and fought for a year, blowing up enemy trains and transports. The forest is where they spent their last days in Europe. It is where the old life came to an end. And it's where the new life began—where Israel was born. The story of Abba, Ruzka and Vitka is, after all, a Middle Eastern story. In the woods they were already fighting as Israelis. The courage and grit they found in the trees was the most important thing they would bring to Palestine. The forest is also where they devised the outlandish plots they would carry out in the chaotic days after the War—plots whereby they visited a measure of vengeance on the men who had killed their families. As they spoke, the sky outside filled with stars. Constellations wheeled. Yellow light glowed in the windows and the room seemed to fall into the past, to the cities and swamps of their youth.

As I grew up, I spoke with Ruzka and Abba and Vitka numerous times, on trips we took every few years to Israel and on their visits to the United States. In my memory, their story plays out before a shifting backdrop—houses by the sea, suburban lawns, crowded restaurants. I once met Abba in Tel Aviv at the Diaspora Museum, which he had conceived and designed. The museum was built to tell the story not just of the slaughter of the Holocaust, but of the years of Jewish life that had come before the slaughter. His hair was long and gray and he wore chinos and kept his hands in his pockets. He led me through halls of documents and photographs. In one room, he stood before a detailed model of the Great Synagogue of Vilna, a graceful network of arches and supports. "How can you know what we lost," said Abba, "if you don't know what we had."

I usually met Abba, Ruzka and Vitka in their homes on the kibbutz, in rooms crowded with books and music and paintings. Abba and Vitka's son, Michael, is a painter, and often I sat looking at his airy watercolors of houses in the Negev desert. As Abba or Ruzka spoke, doors opened and members of the old crowd wandered in, smiling and laughing, filling in the story. To an American, these people seemed an exotic hybrid—rugged intellectuals, fighters schooled only by their experience and curiosity. When Ruzka listened, she let her hands fall to her sides, opened her eyes and drank in every word. I often spoke with her as we walked the narrow lanes of the kibbutz, past houses glowing with life, insects underfoot. She held her hands behind her back and talked in a soft voice.

Our visits to the kibbutz were mostly passed happily with our family, with Ruzka and her children—who are my cousins—Yehuda and Yonat and Ghadi, their spouses, and their children. Still, whenever I found a chance, I steered the conversation back to Europe, their lives before the war, how they survived, what they did when peace came. I suppose I was obsessed. To me, their story seemed to offer a view of history different from what I saw on television or read in books—this was World War II as seen from the East, by those on the bottom, by Jews who, with nothing else to lose, decided to fight.

In 1998, I traveled to Israel to meet with Vitka and the other partisans—those who were still alive, anyway—who had fought with her during the War. By gathering the strands of the story, I hoped to set down a legacy that had been so carefully passed to me. I lived in a guest cottage on the kibbutz and spoke with Vitka each morning, or else she took me to some nearby kibbutz where other former comrades were living. If a person was unwilling to speak of the past, she would tell them I was a cousin of Ruzka's. They would look me over, smile and say, "Ruzka was wonderful. Let us speak in the garden."

Over a period of several weeks, these people told me in greater detail stories I already knew and also told me others I could never have imagined, stories they had never told anyone, the last great secrets of the War. When I asked Vitka why she had kept these things hidden, she frowned. Abba did not want these stories told, she explained. Israel was then living under a terrorist threat and Abba was afraid members of extremist groups might use his actions during the War as an excuse for their own behavior. Even more, he was afraid other Jews would not understand the life he had lived in Europe; removed from the context of war, his actions might seem brutal or cruel.

I asked Vitka why she had decided to tell the story now, and she talked about time and how things change. When Abba and Ruzka died, she realized that, if she did not tell their story, it might die with her.

One evening, on the kibbutz, Vitka led me into the fields, beyond the furthest porch light. A bird rose in the sky. Stars danced on the horizon. We reached a patch of manicured grass, each blade trembling in the evening breeze. Headstones were set in neat rows, dates of birth and death spanning the short history of the nation. On the edge of the cemetery, Vitka stood over two graves: Abba and Ruzka, buried just a few feet apart. To the other side of Abba, there was a third plot, an empty plot, which Vitka was careful not to step on. Vitka placed a small rock on each headstone, closed her eyes and said something under her breath. She looked at the ground, then back toward the kibbutz. "Come," she said. "Let's go home."

THE GHETTO

RUZKA KORCZAK grew up in Plosk, a small village in western Poland. She was smart and lively and alert. She was one of a handful of Jews to attend the public school. When a teacher made a Jew-hating remark, Ruzka moved her desk into the hall, refusing to sit in the same room with such a man. For the rest of the term, she took down as much of the lessons as she could hear. From that day, Ruzka was aware of herself as an outsider. As a result, she turned inward. At fourteen, she was painfully shy, a girl you might see walking on the side of the road in a country town. She was very small, less than five feet tall, with a loping gait and choppy brown hair. Her eyes were the color of her hair, and they were beautifully clear. Even on dark days, they seemed to reflect the sun. Her skin was coppery and her gestures had the ease of a farm girl's. As she got older, she spent most of her time alone. In another age, she probably would have gone from school into a simple life. It was the nature of her times that prodded her, extracting the great qualities she kept hidden. The War was strange that way—it took everything you had and gave back something in return.

When she was fifteen, her father took her out of school. He was a cow merchant, a Jewish profession, and it was hard going. To help the family, she worked at a bakery. At the end of the day, she would walk through the dark, dusty streets of town. In the winter, she could hear the hard-packed snow under her shoes and smell the smoke in the chimneys. She often stopped at the library. She read Tolstoy, Turgenev, Dostoyevsky; Marx, Engels, Lenin. One evening, she came across a book by a Zionist named Leo Pinsker. The book was called *Auto-Emancipation*. It changed her life. "The malign Gentile image of the Jew is fixed in perpetuity," wrote Pinsker. "For the living, the Jew is a dead man; for the natives, an alien and a vagrant; for the property holders, a beggar; for the poor, an exploiter and a millionaire; for patriots, a man without a country; for all classes, a hated rival." For Ruzka, Zionism became almost a religion. It gave her loneliness a context. The small story of the girl in Plosk was now part of the big story of the Exile. She vowed to make her way to Palestine.

Ruzka Korczak, far right, in Plosk with friends before the War.

Ruzka joined a Zionist youth group, HaShomer HaTza'ir—"The Young Guard"—a left-of-center organization dedicated to the sacredness of work. The leaders of The Young Guard believed in sharing possessions, the equality of women, that children belong to the community. They vowed to create a new kind of Jew, to "rebuild ourselves in building the land [of Israel]." There were dozens of such groups scattered in the towns and cities of Eastern Europe, where Jews suffered the most. In these groups were teenagers who spoke Yiddish, Polish and German, took classes in Hebrew and spent summers hiking and singing in the forest. They wore green pants and gray shirts and learned the survival skills they would need in Palestine. They believed in self-defense, that Jews must protect their families. In classes, older boys taught them to shoot guns. They had no illusions about the fate of the Jews in Europe. Though most of these people had never left their own countries—to them, the Holy Land was a dreamscape of camels, dunes and sea—they believed that Palestine was the only chance for a Jewish future.

On August 23, 1939, Hitler and Stalin signed a nonaggression pact, dividing Poland between them. Nine days later, German divisions crossed the frontier. Painted on German supply trains were caricatures of hooked-nosed old men over the words, "We're off to Poland to thrash the Jews." That fall, as the streets of Ruzka's town filled with German soldiers, she decided to go to Warsaw, where she hoped to meet up with the leaders of The Young Guard. She was eighteen. She planned to return to Plosk in a few months, when things had cooled down. It was therefore with a calm ease that she left a world she would never return to, whose mundane pleasures would soon take on the aspect of a dream.

As Ruzka packed, her father talked to her. He said he understood why she was leaving. He would go with her if he did not have to care for his own parents, who were too old to travel. He did not look at her as he talked, not wanting to show any emotion that might shake his daughter's resolve—he knew she must go. Ruzka glanced at her father and swallowed hard. He said he had only one favor to ask: if Ruzka was not back by Yom Kippur, the Day of Atonement, he wanted her to keep the fast. "Promise it," he said.

Ruzka was not religious. Like many Zionists, she had a secular notion of history, a Judaism centered less on God than on the people, the story—the glory, the fall. She believed in the story more than the deity, the story of the Jews and how each person turns it into his or her own personal story. Her father said he respected her beliefs and asked only this one favor.

"I expect to be back home for the holidays," said Ruzka. "But if I am not, I will keep the fast. I promise it."

As she left the house, Ruzka heard her mother say, in a soft voice, to herself, "I will never see her again."

The road to Warsaw was crowded with refugees. Peasants led mules or cows, or hauled carts past run-down farmhouses with sagging roofs. The land was rich and green. German planes passed low overhead. Ruzka could see the black crosses on their sides and the heads of the pilots all looking in the same direction. And she could hear the explosions over Warsaw, ten miles across the fields. The planes would then return, high in the sky, having dropped their bombs. When Ruzka reached the city, it was on fire, a grid of flaming wood buildings. She walked the deserted streets. Her clothes smelled of smoke. By luck, she happened to run into a member of The Young Guard whom she had met at a meeting a few months before.

"Where is everyone?" asked Ruzka.

"They've all gone to Vilna," said the girl.

"Why?"

"From Vilna, maybe they can go to Palestine."

Vilna is almost three hundred miles from Warsaw. According to a Soviet treaty, it was to remain a free city, an island floating in occupied Europe. In 1939, fifteen thousand Jewish refugees flowed into the city. Ruzka went on foot, traveling along an underground railroad set up by Jews for Jews fleeing from Nazi Poland. With ten other people, she walked down frozen country roads and forest trails. In each town, the group was met by a guide who took them as far as the next town. At night, they slept on the floors of synagogues or in cramped living rooms in private homes. They slept side by side in one another's warmth or by a roaring fire, shadows flickering. It was a brutal winter. The wind blew the snow into tall drifts and the temperature dropped thirty degrees below zero. When the snow thawed that spring, dozens of bodies were found, those not strong enough to survive the crossing, their blue ice-burned hands clinging to their satchels.

Ruzka knew only that she must cross the Bug River. On the other side of the river were the Russians. After a week on the road, her group reached the Bug. It is a wide river that meanders through the flats of eastern Poland, full of islands and swamp grass and debris. In the winter, its banks are lined with ice and chunks of ice are carried in the current. The water is black and cold. Off in the distance, Ruzka could see German soldiers. The Jews hid in the fields. That night, they met a Polish peasant with a wooden boat. As Ruzka climbed in, the boat rocked from side to side. Ice clanked against the hull as they crossed the river. On the opposite bank of the Bug, the guides paid the peasant. The group had made it to Russian territory. There were still two hundred miles to cross. Days and nights on the road. After three weeks, they reached Bialystok. A few days later, they wandered into a Lithuanian town across the frontier from Vilna. Polish guides were paid to lead the Jews over the hills. The first night, Ruzka was turned back by the Russian border patrol. The next night, she crossed into Vilna.

Over a rise, Ruzka could see the city tucked into a valley between green hills. The red shingle roofs ran together and the hills were wooded above the town. The streets were twisting and medieval. The sky was filled with church spires. A castle rose on the edge of the forest. The Neris River wound by the buildings like a silky ribbon. On her first day in the city, Ruzka was stopped by the police, questioned and arrested—an illegal immigrant. The members of The Young Guard bribed a local official, buying Ruzka's freedom. With the help of the Zionists, she then settled in a brick building on the outskirts of town. Built in the mid-1800s as a Jewish poorhouse, the building had been taken over by Zionist youth groups; it was now a way station for Jews on their way to Palestine. It was as big as a cruise ship and housed a thousand refugees, young people from Berlin, Munich, Vienna, Cracow and Warsaw, who sat up all night talking, or else argued politics. They were organized into kibbutzim. In Israel, they were to live in these same groups on settlements where they would farm and multiply.

Ruzka slept in a room with fifteen people, none older than seventeen. It was a world of kids. Hometowns, customs, traditions, families—all of it left behind. The world of their parents, of school and work and traditional plans, had vanished the day the Nazis marched in. The old struggles and dreams now seemed like a fantasy. Ruzka had not seen her mother or father in two months; for the first time, she realized that she might never see them again. All at once, she understood her situation—she was alone and she was free.

In those first weeks, Ruzka rarely spoke. She hung on the edge of each conversation, waiting. She was so young and so small, but she was learning. Older people sensed a calm in her, an ability to listen. Ruzka let people tell their own stories in their own way; she never tried to argue someone out of a belief. If there was a disagreement, she was asked to settle it. Almost by accident, she became a leader. Like only the greatest leaders, she had the ability to get people to do voluntarily those things which must be done. The best word for her is righteous.

One morning, Ruzka was sitting in the courtyard reading a book called *Essays on Socialist Zionism*. A young girl walked up to her. She was about twenty, the same age as Ruzka, but seemed much younger. She had a spring in her step and smiled through long lashes. Her eyes were big and dark and her brown hair hung below her shoulders.

"What are you reading?" she asked.

Ruzka held up the book.

"Why such a serious book?" asked the girl.

"The world is a serious place," said Ruzka.

"I think the world is not so serious," said the girl.

"Do you see where we are living?" asked Ruzka.

The girl looked across the teeming courtyard to the brick building, laundry hanging from the windows. "OK, so if the world is serious, all the more reason not to read a serious book."

"What do you read?" asked Ruzka.

The girl said she had read all the Russians but her favorite book was *The Count of Monte Cristo*.

"What's your name?" asked Ruzka.

"Vitka Kempner."

Ruzka and Vitka were at once attracted to each other, brought together by their differences. Vitka was drawn to the character of Ruzka, her integrity, her humility and her strength. In Vitka, Ruzka found the youth she had lost, the fun of childhood. Vitka's silliness was not just frivolous but a kind of philosophy, a response to a situation that was absurd, a determination by a young girl who had already been robbed of home, family, freedom, not to be robbed of life. Ruzka and Vitka shared a bed, sat in the courtyard, walked in the forest. They became inseparable.

One day, a strange young man came to the refugee building. He wore wool pants and a hat pulled over his eyes. He walked the halls, glancing into each face. His hands were behind his back—he was inspecting. He stood for a time in a corner, observing, saying nothing. He was slender, with long arms and long legs. His face was dark and his features so soft they were almost feminine, and yet he exuded a certain raw power. He had big hands. Some of the young women commented on how attractive he was. Vitka did not think he was attractive, just strange.

When he left, people stood together talking.

"Who is he?" asked Vitka.

"He is one of the leaders of The Young Guard," she was told. "His name is Abba Kovner."

Ruzka had arrived in the city in the winter. It was now spring. In the evenings, when the streets filled with farm boys in from the fields, Ruzka and Vitka walked to town. Looking south, they could see trees on a hill and then more hills with more trees. The road ran past houses and ancient fortifications, red brick walls that once protected Vilna from invasion. Since the founding of the city, the Jewish population had been driven beyond the walls five times. Vitka knew the popular songs that year and sang them to Ruzka. The girls talked about the country, its people, its past. Vilna had been built in the 1300s by a prince from a nearby province. Its founding myth is dark and strange: One afternoon, the prince, out on a hunt, found himself in the woods along the Neris River; he killed and ate a deer; he then fell asleep and in his sleep dreamt of a wolf in an iron mask howling with the strength of a hundred wolves. In the morning, an interpreter told the prince the wolf represented a fortified city that would rise on this very spot. He built Vilna. It grew into the capital of Lithuania, the last country in Europe to accept Christianity.

The Jews, who first came to the city from Russia and Germany, worked as cobblers and tinsmiths and merchants. Beginning in the sixteenth century, they were confined to a ghetto in the center of town, a warren of wood buildings and blind alleys. The cellars of the ghetto were three stories deep; some people called them the dwellings of the Devil. Over time, the city gave rise to a great Jewish community, schools of scholars and holy men. In 1812, when Napoleon passed through Vilna on his doomed way to Moscow, he peered into the Great Synagogue, where hundreds of Jews were praying, and said, "Surely this is the Jerusalem of Lithuania." And that is what Jews have called Vilna ever since.

By 1939, two hundred thousand people lived in Vilna, a third of them Jewish. It was a tranquil little pocket of Europe with war all around, Russians in the East, Germans in the South and in the West. The streets were a stream of ancient architecture, collapsing wooden buildings, byzantine corners and vistas of green hills, tin roofs and brick roads curving under the trees in the smoky twilight. The girls walked by storefront synagogues and steamy rooms where the young men argued over Trotsky and Stalin. The Jews were divided into rival factions: there were Zionists, there were Communists, there were Bundists, who believed in labor unions, there were the Orthodox and there were the assimilated Jews, who saw themselves less as Jews than as Poles or Lithuanians or Germans. Each group had its organizations, ideas, way of doing things. Communists distrusted Bundists, Bundists distrusted Zionists, Zionists distrusted the Orthodox and everyone distrusted the assimilated Jews.

Now and then, a breeze blew on the faces of the girls and brought them the smell of the fields. The wind whistled by the river, which reflected church spires and bridges. On weekends, workmen sat on the banks with homemade fishing poles. It was dark and safe under the bridge where Ruzka and Vitka shared lunch and told their stories. Vitka had recently learned by mail of her father's death. Her mother said it was a heart attack, but Vitka knew it was the War that killed him. By telling her story and sharing her feelings, Vitka understood she was giving Ruzka a treasure for safekeeping.

Vitka grew up in a town in western Poland called Kalisch. Her parents were tailors. She was a Jewish girl who could pass as a non-Jew. She spoke Polish without the inflections of Yiddish. For a time, she saw herself as a Polish patriot and hated everyone the Poles hated—

Vitka Kempner before the War.

except Jews. She hated Germans, she hated Russians. When she was twelve, she joined Betar, a Zionist youth group that was a rival of The Young Guard. Betar was very right-wing, and dedicated to a kind of holy violence. Its leader was Vladimir Jabotinsky, who behaved like a Jewish fascist, dressing his followers in brown shirts which symbolized the soil of Palestine. He wrote: "It is the highest achievement of a multiple of human beings to act together with the absolute precision of a machine." In Poland, Betar was led by Menachem Begin, who would later become the Prime Minister of Israel. Vitka quit the group when she discovered *The Count of Monte Cristo*. No matter how hard she tried, she could not be gloomy. She switched to The Young Guard. And though she attended the meetings and sang the songs, she remained carefree and open-minded, unmoved by political dogma. Vitka was on her way to a simple life before the Germans marched into Poland.

When the Germans invaded, Vitka, at the urging of her parents, who had other relatives to care for, took her thirteen-year-old brother to the woods outside of Kalisch, where they would be safe from the bombs; they planned to return in a few hours, when the bombing was over. In silence, they walked along forest trails stamped with tank treads. Now and then, a plane passed so low it brushed the tops of the trees. In the afternoon, Vitka heard the crash of boots. Crouching in the weeds, she could see German soldiers marching down the road. The eyes of the soldiers were as dull as the trunks of the trees, and their boots splashed in the puddles.

"What are you doing here?"

Vitka turned quickly. A German soldier was standing over her. He was about her age, maybe nineteen, and she could see the short blond hair under his helmet. "Get up," he said. He looked her up and down and then at her brother, who had his fists clenched at his sides.

"Running will do you no good," said the soldier. "Your boys are very beautiful on their horses, but they don't stand a chance. We are the strongest country in the world. You are lucky," he went on. "We are the army. We are nice. But after us will come the SS and then you will know what Germany is."

A few hours later, Vitka and her brother were at home in their beds.

One afternoon, about two weeks after the Nazi invasion, the SS issued an order in Kalisch. The town, not far from the German border, was in that part of Poland that was to become *Judenrein*—"Jew-free." The entire Jewish population of three thousand was ordered to assemble the next day in an abandoned church. That morning, Vitka's parents went to town for news. Vitka waited at home all afternoon. Her parents did not return. In the evening, there was a knock on the door. Two soldiers told Vitka to gather her things. They took her to the church, where she met her family and every other Jew from town, rich and poor, believers and atheists, friends and enemies, people who would not have said hello to each other the day before. A Nazi paced before them, cursing, accusing. For Vitka, worse than anything was having to stand still in the face of this man's rage. "He yelled at me," she later said. "That I did not like at all."

Vitka told her parents she was leaving and taking her thirteen-year-old brother. Her father said, "Go," believing they would soon be together again. She made her way through the crowd to a bathroom. She opened the window and climbed out, pulling her brother after her. Skirting patrols through the dark countryside, they walked to their grandfather's house in the next town. The old man told Vitka to continue on, away from the War. "But your brother is too young," he said. "Your brother stays here."

In four weeks, Vitka was in Vilna.

That spring, Ruzka and Vitka took a room in a private house in the city. It had once been a grand estate and there were still sockets for chandeliers and a carved mantel over the fireplace, but the girls were there on the cheap, with dozens of other refugees, sleeping on floors, in halls, in bathrooms. The girls soon found jobs in a hairbrush factory. Vitka separated dark bristles from light bristles. Ruzka worked in the yard, in the rain and snow, scrubbing the bristles clean. By the end of each day, the water had soaked into her shoes, her socks were wet, her toes were numb and her teeth chattered. The girls did not need to work: food and shelter were supplied by The Young Guard. But work was part of their philosophy: without work, a person can have no self-respect. What money they made was given to the group to fund trips to Palestine.

On June 15, 1940, the Russians marched on Vilna. It would be wrong to say that they attacked Vilna. They did not need to. They just walked in, a move in the geopolitical game that Stalin was playing with Hitler. Paris had fallen to the Germans a few days before. Stalin was now scrambling for what remained of the East, the staging grounds and buffer zones of what the realists knew would be the next front in the War. The Russians dissolved the government and seized the radio stations. Soviet troops could be seen on the trains and buses, in restaurants and bars, drinking up their leave; they exuded the brutality of the steppes. The Russians outlawed the Zionist groups, which they said challenged Soviet sovereignty. The Young Guard and Betar went underground, learning to operate from basements and secret rooms, a step ahead of the law.

Stalin ordered all refugees to apply for Soviet citizenship. The Zionist groups held meetings. Arguments raged. If Jews became Soviet citizens, they would no longer be refugees; if they were not refugees, they were not eligible for certificates to emigrate to Palestine. But if Jewish refugees did *not* become Soviet citizens, they could be arrested by the NKVD, the Soviet secret police. Most Zionists decided to refuse Soviet citizenship, steer clear of the soldiers, hope for the best. In the following weeks, dozens of Jews were caught, tried and sent to Siberia. Menachem Begin was among those shipped East. "This seemed terrible at the time but turned out to be a blessing," Vitka said. "Those who were sent to Russia survived the War."

A friend at the police station told Vitka that her name was on an NKVD arrest list. She quickly dropped out of sight, spending day after day in her room. In June of 1941, after weeks of hiding, she told Ruzka, "I want to be free. I want to go walking."

She packed a bag and fixed her hair in the mirror.

"Where will you go?" asked Ruzka.

"Byelorussia," said Vitka. "They cannot have my name in Byelorussia. Who am I? Why should they bother with me?"

"I'll write when it's OK to come back," said Ruzka.

Vitka threw her bag over her shoulder and looked at Ruzka, who was sitting on the bed. Vitka had known Ruzka just over a year but already felt for her something more certain than love.

"What then?" asked Vitka.

Ruzka smiled. "Then we go to Palestine."

Ruzka was startled by the air-raid siren. She was reading a book on the grass in front of the apartment house. It was a breezy Sunday morning. Vitka had left the city a week before. The stores were closed, the streets empty. Ruzka looked into a perfect blue sky. Not a cloud. She could hear birds in the trees. Then she saw German planes flying above the fields. She stood as they passed by and for a moment she was in their shadow and she heard the blare of engines and felt as if she were in the wake of a great ship. The planes went over the city and she could hear explosions by the airport. At 11 a.m., the Soviet Foreign Minister came on the radio and said that the Germans had attacked seven hours before. The enemy was crossing the Niemen River on their way to Vilna. The streets were filled with cars leaving town. In the cars were the dolled-up wives of the Russian officers. Troop trucks were loaded in the city squares. As the trucks climbed into the hills, soldiers hung from the back, cigarettes in their mouths. The few soldiers who remained in Vilna turned desperate that night, waving guns and demanding civilian clothes. In the morning, the city filled with new refugees speaking of the German assault, of ancient towns on fire.

That afternoon, Ruzka started walking east. There were thousands of Jews on the road, families dragging what little they owned. They crossed tiny bridges over streams where horses grazed. Now and then, a farmer gave them water. At night, German fighter planes flew over the refugees, opening up with machine guns. Dozens of people were killed on the road, others made it to the trees. When the pilots flew above peasant huts, they fired their guns until the thatched roofs burst into flame. German paratroopers jumped into the woods in civilian clothes, disguised as peasants. They buried their parachutes and blended in with the refugees. The Russians quickly became aware of these enemy soldiers trying to infiltrate their lines. In the morning, the roads to the east were cut. Like most refugees, Ruzka turned back. Others were stopped at the border.

The streets were empty when Ruzka returned to Vilna, the shutters down. It was like the quiet between storms. As she walked past the brick buildings, a lone soldier flashed by on a motorcycle. He wore leather gloves, black pants, tinted goggles and a helmet with the iron cross. His boots were muddy. He sped down the street and out of sight—the first German she had seen in Vilna. A moment later, she heard the rumble of engines, voices and boots. The German army marched into the city, motorcycles, then infantry, field guns, half-tracks and tanks. The soldiers were dusty and she could tell that they had come from a great distance. The doors of the houses flew open, the girls stood in the windows throwing down flowers and the boys lowered colorful banners. Ruzka walked home through the ancient ghetto, where the poor Jews lived. The windows were shut tight and nothing moved.

Vitka had been in Grodno for over two weeks. She was there when the Germans marched through. A few days later, she heard that Vilna had been captured. She asked herself, "If the Germans are there and if the Germans are here too, why not go back to Vilna? If I have to live under the Nazis, I should be with Ruzka."

She threw her bag over her shoulder and walked out of the city. On the road, she saw a German soldier loading a transport truck.

"Where are you going?" Vitka asked. She was calm and direct.

"I'm going to Vilna," said the soldier.

He was maybe twenty and had the accent of a farm boy.

"I'm going to Vilna too," said Vitka. "Can I have a ride?"

The man looked at Vitka. "Are you a Catholic?" he asked.

"No," said Vitka.

"A Protestant?"

"No."

He let his arms fall to his sides. "What are you?"

In her childhood, Vitka had sometimes been ashamed of her religion. She was a patriot, a Pole, and she wanted to be just like everyone else, a piece of the nation, no better, no worse. She sometimes found the past of her people a burden. It was in the back of every conversation, at the threshold of every door. But since she had seen her family rounded up, had gone on the road, had met Ruzka, she had changed. She was proud of her past, of her people, of her doomed place in Nazi Europe.

"I am a Jew," she said.

The young soldier looked at Vitka, swallowed hard and ran. A country boy filled with lies, stories of bloodsucking Jews, the virus, the mongrel, the origin of disease—and now, alone with a Jewish girl, he got spooked. Vitka hurried into the forest.

She hid there for hours. From the edge of the trees, she could see into a clearing, where a freight train stood on the track that went to Vilna. The boxcars were open, equipment inside. The train started to move, going slow. Vitka ran out of the trees, jogged next to an empty car, tossed her bag through an open door and jumped in. She slid to the back of the car and looked out at the countryside. It was dark and she could see a dark road that wound by peasant towns where life had not changed for a thousand years. The wheat fields bent in the wind and summer was in the air. The clacking of the rails lulled her to sleep. She dreamed of her family waiting around a table, her mother serving dinner, an empty seat where she was supposed to be.

She woke when the train reached Vilna. She jumped from the car and walked across the yard, not fast, not slow, shoulders back, chin up. If you look like you know where you are going, no one stops you—that is what she believed. She was soon on the empty streets of the city. She walked by buildings and stores. It looked the same as before. She found her way to the house where she had lived with Ruzka. It was 5 a.m.

"Ruzka," she yelled. "I'm back! Ruzka!"

A window opened. "Are you crazy?" said Ruzka. "Are you trying to get killed?"

Vitka's smile disappeared.

"Get up here," said Ruzka, and closed the window.

Ruzka made tea as the sun rose over the steep roofs of the city. "You must be crazy," she said.

"Why?"

"Here you are, on the street before curfew, no yellow star, and I look out and see you calmly walking along the sidewalk. Right on the sidewalk! Thank God you are alive."

"I don't understand."

"It's the law for the Jews," said Ruzka. "The Germans made it two days after they came in. It's posted all over the city."

"What is it?"

"Everything you have just done—the opposite."

The Germans came to Vilna with their usual Jewish laws—the yellow star, the curfew and the sidewalk, where no Jew was allowed to walk.

"So where do we walk?" asked Vitka.

"In the street with the animals."

Vitka went to the window. People were on their way to work.

"There is more," said Ruzka.

"Tell me."

"When the SS arrived, they kidnapped sixty of the most prominent Jews in Vilna: rabbis, professors, entertainers, politicians. They said these people were taken to be certain that the Jews obeyed the law."

"And have the people obeyed?"

"Yes, the people have obeyed but we've never seen these men again," said Ruzka. "And then others started to disappear. A man would go off to work and never come back. Or the Germans took them from their houses. Hundreds of men—vanished."

"Where are they?"

"The Germans say they have been resettled in the East."

"What about The Young Guard?" asked Vitka. "What have they done?"

"They have kept our men from the Germans," said Ruzka. "Some live in homes disguised as Aryans. Some are in the convent with the nuns."

Vitka drank her tea.

"What are you thinking?" asked Ruzka.
"Only that I am afraid."

On September 6, 1941, Nazi soldiers fanned out across Vilna. They went to every house and apartment where a Jew was living. They knocked on doors, stood in thresholds. Their boots creaked. They came early, so the bewildered people could not sort their appearance from what they had dreamed the night before. Jews had ten minutes to gather their possessions; they were being moved to a ghetto. Many put on layers and layers of clothes: five shirts, four sweaters, three jackets. They could bring only what they could carry. Some dragged canned goods and sacks of flour. In the street, there were thousands of Jews stumbling along with suitcases and duffel bags. The sidewalks were lined with Aryans, merchants and school kids and professionals, familiar faces. Most just watched the ribbon unfold. It was a hot summer day and some Jews collapsed under their loads. Dishes, clothing and photos spilled. Scavengers scrambled after them in the street. This humdrum avenue of shops and stop-lights had been transformed into a tunnel of noise. Now and then, a Pole jumped into the street and yelled, "You wanted Palestine and you get the ghetto!" The street ended at a wooden gate on Rudnicka Street, marked by the sign: "Plague! Entry forbidden!"

There was a small sign underneath: "Jews are forbidden from bringing in food and heating supplies—violators will be shot!"

Beyond the gate was the ancient ghetto, the byzantine, deep-cellared warren where Jews had been forced to live until the late Middle Ages. Less than a square mile, it consisted of six tiny streets. Before the War, a thousand people had lived here. There would now be thirty thousand. The Germans surrounded the ghetto with a tall wooden fence. The windows that looked over the fence to the free city were boarded. From one street, leaning back on your heels, you could see the top of the Great Synagogue—it was outside the ghetto—the peak of its golden dome, the tablets of the Command-ments. For the Jews of Vilna, the world had been narrowed to a few crooked houses.

The streets of the ghetto were empty. Until just a few days before, it had been home to the poorest people in the city, a neighborhood of cobblers and workshops and jewelry stores. Wealthy Jews would go there to smell the bread in the ovens. When the Germans conquered the city, they closed the ghetto schools and synagogues and sent patrols into the streets. On August 30, a German soldier had been shot at in the ghetto. Most likely, this was a staged act, a bit of theater to justify what was to follow.

A German SS officer posted the following notice:

> Sunday afternoon shots were directed from ambush at German soldiers in Vilna. Two of these cowardly bandits were identi-fied—they were Jews. The attackers paid with their lives for their act. They were shot on the spot. To avoid such hostile acts in the future new and severe deterrent measures were taken. The responsibility lies with the entire Jewish community.

Nazi soldiers stormed the ghetto streets, arresting every Jew they could catch. The dust raised in the ghetto could be seen across the city. Women were dragged down stairwells, beaten and killed. The survivors were led out past the streetlights. A few days later, a peas-ant said she had seen the Jews being led into the woods beyond the city. There was a train depot in the forest; the Germans said the Jews were being resettled in the East. This massacre, which emptied the ghetto, was known as "The Great Provocation." It prepared the ghetto for its new inhabitants.

When an SS soldier told Ruzka and Vitka they had just ten minutes to gather their possessions, Vitka said, "We don't need it." Unlike most of the other Jews of Vilna, the girls had already lost everything. There was no property to protect, no parents to worry about, no brothers to look after.

"We are ready now," she said.

The girls walked in the flaring street, their heavy boots crunching over broken glass. Ruzka's peasant scarf, tied in her hair, moved with the breeze; she did not know where she would sleep that night. A black sedan rolled down the street, honking its way through the crowds. At the gate, a driver in a blue uniform got out. He took a trunk down from the roof, opened the back door and helped out a man in a suit. The man in the suit said a few words to the driver and then dragged the trunk through the gate. "It's a Jew," said Vitka.

Inside the ghetto, Ruzka saw the man sitting on the trunk, smoking. She later wrote of those Jews who set themselves above the others, by wealth, by education: "They stood against the mass, making themselves distinctive, as if to demonstrate their lack of affinity, sometimes smiling contemptuously; this group, full of pride and contempt, seemed more miserable than all the other pitiful people."

The girls lived at 15 Straszun Street, a house along the ghetto wall. A friend of a friend had invited them. It was a trim, square, three-story building with a black slate roof. There were two bedrooms and a living room, a kitchen and a bathroom. The girls lived with ten boys. Over time, modesty became a useless luxury and the girls undressed before the boys the way a girl might undress before her sister. The girls shared a bed in the back of the flat and the bed was pushed against a boarded window which softened the sunlight to a dull yellow blur. Ruzka was shocked to see the traces of the people who had lived in the house before her. "The room is alive," she said. There were pictures of family vacations and letters from relatives and beds unmade and meals half-eaten. Ruzka pretended that these people had just gone away and were now living in another town. But when she looked at the room, trying to build a story from the evidence—he was a loving husband but she was a dreamer, absent-minded, humorous—she believed only the worst and was filled with rage, at the Jews who went on living, at herself, for staying in this home that belonged to someone else, and at the Germans, who made her hate her people and herself.

One day, a man hanged himself in the courtyard. He was cut down and left on the pavement, his hair pushed to one side and his face blue and his tongue showing between his teeth. People stepped over the body when they walked down the street. Ruzka was amazed at how easily those in the ghetto came to live with the dead.

Franz Murer, grasping a pistol, walked the well-lit sidewalks of the city. He wore the black uniform of an SS colonel. At the ghetto gate, he pushed his way through the Jews returning from jobs in the factories. That fall, the Germans had marched east with the hope of destroying the Soviets before the first frost. They had since bogged down in Russia, with winter on its way. Germany had not prepared for such reversals, and the soldiers at the front were short of gear. The Jews were put to work making boots, hats, coats. Each morning, before dawn, they lined up at the gate, waiting to be checked off by Lithuanian policemen who examined their work permits. On the way home at night, the Jewish workers were searched for food and fuel, or whatever else they might smuggle into the ghetto. If a policeman saw Murer, he redoubled his search.

Murer was one of the top-ranking Nazis in Vilna; he was in charge of the ghetto. He had an office in a graceful brick building in the city. He would sometimes leave his desk and walk to the Jewish quarter. He liked to oversee gate inspections. He had steel-blue eyes and dark hair. He was a rabid anti-Semite. "The Jew is the enemy of the German people and is responsible for the war," he said. "He is a forced laborer and is forbidden to be in contact with his employers except on matters relating to work. Anyone maintaining contact with Jews shall be treated as if he were a Jew."

Now and then, if Murer was especially bothered by the look of a Jew, he would tell the policeman to step aside. "I will conduct this search myself," he would say. He once found that a young woman was hiding a piece of bread. He led her to the prison, had her clothes removed and told the jailer to hit her twenty-five times. He then took the cudgel and beat her himself.

His orders were enforced by Lithuanian police, the SS and members of the Einsatzgruppen, the mobile killing units that had followed the German army into the East. There were four squads of Einsatzgruppen, each numbering three thousand soldiers. These squads marched into the just-vanquished countries of Eastern Europe with orders to kill every Jew, every Communist. The squads sometimes posed for group pictures. Side by side in gray uniforms, high collars and soft caps, some smiling, some wearing the curt Hitler mustache, they look as doughy and unremarkable as a bowling team that loses. These were bland psychopaths, squads of nobodies. Before the War, they had been shoe salesmen, bank tellers, telephone operators.

Each member of the Einsatzgruppen, even if he worked at a desk, was required to kill at least one Jew. In this way, no soldier could stand above the others; if the War should be lost, then everyone would be part of the crime. It was the Einsatzgruppen that kidnapped Jews in Vilna. The soldiers served under Heinrich Himmler, the architect of Germany's Jewish policy. Addressing a squad of Einsatzgruppen, Himmler said, "Most of you must know what it means to see one hundred corpses lie side by side, or five hundred, or a thousand. To have stuck this out and—excepting cases of human weakness—to have kept our integrity, that is what has made us hard. In our history, this is an unwritten and never-to-be-written page of glory."

Soon after the conquest of Vilna, Murer appointed a Jewish Council to govern the Jews. The council occupied the biggest house in the ghetto, a four-story brick building set around a courtyard just inside the ghetto gate. As members of the council Murer chose some fifty ordinary Jews: teachers, doctors, electricians, construction workers, engineers. The first head of the council was a former bank manager, Anatol Fried. He was surprised by his selection. He did not think of himself as a Jew. Fried requested permission to go about without a Jewish star and to venture onto the city sidewalks. Murer denied the request. In the ghetto, kids made up songs about Anatol Fried, the Jewish leader who hated the Jews.

Murer also created a Jewish police force to keep order in the ghetto. He named Jacob Gens, a smart, officious forty-year-old, as chief of police. Gens was handsome, with a broad nose, thick, downturned lips, a high forehead and almond eyes. He wore simple suits and striped ties. He was the essence of the modern European gentleman. He subscribed to magazines and read new books, went to concerts and could be seen at the opening nights of the best plays. He believed in progress, science, the decency of the common man. After the First World War, when Lithuania gained its independence, he joined the army. He loved the military discipline and soon became the highest-ranking Jew in the service. To other Jewish soldiers he said, "Never disguise yourself." Because of him, Jews in the Lithuanian army were excused from church services. When he left the military, he married a wealthy non-Jew. He moved in the highest levels of society. When the Jews were driven into the ghetto, he was offered a chance to save himself, to live out the War under an assumed name. He refused, saying he belonged with his people. He went to the ghetto by choice.

Gens built his police of young men, Jews who saw in the force a way to gain privilege, to live outside the law. The police wore white armbands with a blue Star of David. They stood at the ghetto gate as the sun rose, checking the work permits of men filing out to the factories. Each night, they conducted searches and enforced curfew, patrolling streets where babies were born and families said prayers over sparse meals. Several members of The Young Guard—sixty members lived in the ghetto—joined the force. In their police uniforms, these men would act as double agents, giving Zionists a degree of freedom, a way to break curfew and sneak out of the ghetto. At this time, The Young Guard was waging a white resistance, a guerrilla operation to keep Jews clothed and fed. It was based on simple logic: The German invasion is no different than the other invasions—German, Swedish, French—that the Jews have lived through. If we have food and shelter, we will survive the War.

The Young Guard sent a few members to live as Christians outside the ghetto, where they would gather food and blankets. Among the Zionists, such agents were called "our Aryans." They returned to the ghetto on those nights when members of The Young Guard were on duty at the gate. The Zionist agent would conduct a phony search, then wave in the smuggler. It was hard living in the ghetto, and these blankets and food kept people alive. Though the Jews had little contact with the outside world, a ghetto-dweller was actually able to get a letter by the German censors to his family in Brooklyn, New York. It was written in a kind of code: "We are eating as on Yom Kippur, clothed as on Purim, and housed as at Succoth."

From his office at the Jewish Council, Jacob Gens could see the sloped roofs of the ghetto. He would often stay late in the office, going through notes and files, trying to find a way to keep the people of the ghetto fed. If he could save the Jews of Vilna, he might be remembered as a hero, the man who saw his people through its darkest time.

One night, Franz Murer showed up in his office. Murer said he needed several thousand Jews to work in factories in the East. He wanted the Jewish police to round up these Jews. Gens asked where these workers would be sent. Murer said he did not know—the army would decide. Gens said that he could not send people on a train without knowing its destination.

"If you do not help," said Murer, "we will do it ourselves. If we do it ourselves, it will be far worse for the Jews."

Gens was a military man. He had been a captain in the Lithuanian army. He knew about power. As a military man, he believed he understood Murer and the other military men of Germany. He could work with them. He asked Murer if he needed quite so many Jewish workers: could the number be reduced? After some passionate back-and-forth, he convinced Murer to take a thousand fewer Jews than planned. Gens considered this a great victory.

On October 23, 1941, the Jewish police issued yellow permits to all those workers with jobs outside the ghetto. The next morning, the men with yellow permits left for their jobs. The families of these workers—Murer defined a family as no more than a wife and two children under sixteen—were told to report to the Jewish Council, where they were gathered in the courtyard. Lithuanian soldiers then stormed the ghetto. They kicked in windows and doors, dragging off whomever they could catch. Jews hid in cellars and attics, dozens or even hundreds of people jammed into a windowless room. More than one story has been told of the horror of such rooms, of dead, heart-pounding hours, boots on the landing, muffled cries, a baby's tears, a red-faced man or woman saying, "Shut that baby up! It will be the end of us all!" Of a young mother burying the baby under a blanket, the soldiers marching away, silence and the stunned mother holding her baby dead in her arms. In the street, Jews were bludgeoned. If they climbed over the ghetto fence, they were shot. By the end of the day, almost four thousand Jews had been marched off.

When the permit-carrying Jewish workers returned from the factories, the ghetto was like a city after a terrible storm. Everything was quiet and still. People came out of hiding to stand dumbly in the streets. The Jews had been skillfully divided between haves and have-nots, those with permits and their families—who were sheltered in the courtyard of the Jewish Council—and the others, who were condemned. Those with permits might feel sympathy for those without, but they were not willing to give up their permits. "This was the method," Ruzka later wrote. "To cause a division between people being prepared for the same fate. To release the animalistic impulses at the bottom of the human soul."

In the weeks that followed, Murer came again and again to see Gens. Now he needed a thousand Jews, now three thousand, now five thousand. Jewish police issued permits; Lithuanian soldiers stormed the streets. The roundups were called Aktions, which gave them the sound of official policy. The Yellow Pass Aktion. The Blue Pass Aktion. The Pink Pass Aktion. By December, the ghetto population had been halved. Ruzka and Vitka, and the other members of The Young Guard, survived in hiding places or with forged passes or beyond the ghetto gate, living as Christians. When Ruzka went to see a member of the Jewish Council—she was asking after a missing friend—she was told that the Jews had been resettled in the East, where they were working and eating well. Some people even received letters postmarked Estonia or White Russia, a curt message in familiar handwriting: "Plenty of food, easy work, hope you meet us soon." In reality, these letters, which Nazi officials hoped would calm Jewish suspicions about German intentions, were written at gunpoint. To the people in the ghetto, the very term, "resettled in the East," quickly became a kind of code, like saying someone had been sold down the river or had bought the farm. It meant another

Jew was in the mysterious nowhere at the end of every German road. A group of rabbis went to see Gens, to tell him he had no right to select Jews and bring them to the Germans. By resettling the few, said Gens, he was protecting the thousands. A rabbi asked Gens to remember the words of Maimonides: "Better all be killed than one soul of Israel be surrendered."

Vitka was living in a house outside the ghetto. The Young Guard had asked for volunteers to move into the free city, where they would act as couriers, returning to the ghetto with information and supplies. Equipped with fake papers and fake names, the couriers were to look for work and shelter. A few times each week, they would have to pass from the ghetto to the free city, from the Jewish world to the world of Aryans, from the street to the sidewalk. Those arousing the least suspicion were shot. The couriers were almost always girls—partly because the Germans were less likely to notice a girl, who was not seen as a threat, partly because these Jewish girls were unaccountably brave, and partly because girls could not be caught with the simple command "Take down your pants." The faces of these girls, seen on identity cards and forged passports, skin smooth and unlined, suggest a secret society composed of those who believe in both their immortality and their fast-approaching death. Many left the ghetto and were never heard from again.

Vitka, who spoke excellent Polish and carried herself like a peasant, was perfect for the job. She thought she might have trouble fooling Poles, but not Germans. Germans believe what they are told, she said. If you tell a Nazi that you are a Polish peasant, he says, "Ah, a Polish peasant." Germans could not distinguish between Poles, who were Slavs, a slave race, and Jews, who were subhuman, a race marked for extinction. Poles, on the other hand, could pick out even a blond-haired, blue-eyed Jew. It had less to do with race than with class—Jews were from different neighborhoods, went to different schools. When Vitka became a courier, Ruzka helped her dye her hair. She found a bottle of solution in the trash. Vitka held her head over a bucket as Ruzka massaged her scalp.

When Vitka's hair dried, Ruzka stood her in the sun.

"What do you think?" asked Vitka, whose dark hair was now a bright, frightful red.

"I think we need help," said Ruzka.

For a small fee, a Jewish barber bleached Vitka's hair with peroxide. She left the ghetto wearing a long coat and a hat.

Vitka went out of the ghetto with the workers. On her chest was a scrap of a Jewish star connected to her coat by two threads. When she was beyond the gate, she pulled off the star, shoved it in her pocket, stepped up onto the sidewalk, turned a corner and took off her hat, revealing her blond hair. Through her hair you could see the dark roots. Her heart raced as she walked into the hushed city streets.

She found a job with a middle-aged woman in the suburbs, cleaning house and tutoring the woman's daughter. Vitka lived in a second-floor maid's room. From the window, she could see trees in the backyard. On one wall of the room there was a cross, whose presence Vitka could feel even at night when the lights were out. The woman was very religious and she prayed before each meal. She asked Vitka to pray with her. Vitka said no thank you and gave no explanation. Each night, Vitka went to bed thinking of the ghetto, of what was happening to Ruzka and the others. She was not where she belonged.

Two or three times each week, at sunset, Vitka returned to the ghetto. Stepping from a side street, she pulled on her hat and put a yellow star on her coat. Once, she forgot her star and, in a panic, stuck a yellow leaf to her coat. A Zionist working as a policeman at the gate, looked at the leaf, smiled and waved her through. She then met with members of The Young Guard, receiving instructions from them and passing on news from the city.

In late December of 1941, at one of these meetings, Vitka was given an important mission. She was to walk to a convent in the fields beyond town, where the leader of The Young Guard was hiding. Vitka was to bring him back to the ghetto, where he was to meet a young girl. When Vitka asked about the young girl, a Zionist waved her off, saying, "People think she is insane."

A few nights before, the girl, who was about seventeen, had been found in the forest by Jews out foraging for food. The girl was bruised and bloody, and was wearing no clothes. She had been walking for two days. She said she had seen the Jews of Vilna killed in the forest of Ponar.

The girl was taken to see Jacob Gens. She told him she had seen the Jews of Vilna lined up and shot; she told him how she had escaped. Gens looked at the girl. Her name was Sara. He did not believe her story. She was crazy. Very clearly. It was sad, but how could what she said be true? No. He could not believe it. It threw into question his very sense of the world. Gens saw himself as a realist; like all realists, he believed that man is motivated by self-interest. Killing the Jews of Vilna could not be in the self-interest of the Germans. Many of these Jews were able-bodied young men; surely they could be used to build bombs, make coats. No. This girl was crazy. And it was his duty to stop her from spreading panic. An unruly ghetto would be dangerous to the Germans and it would then be in their self-interest to kill Jews. "Do you want your father to live?" asked Gens.

"Yes."

"Then don't tell anyone what you think you saw," said Gens. "I will help you get work, just keep quiet."

Sara was sent to the hospital, where her wounds were closed and she was heavily sedated. It was there that members of The Young Guard first heard her story.

Now and then, Vitka took a map from her pocket and studied the spidery roads. She had grown thin, cheekbones sharp beneath her pale skin. She had been walking for two hours. When the moon rose, the farms looked frozen in the light. At last, from a hill, she could see the Benedictine nunnery, candles burning in the windows. A nun met her at the side door. The nun was young and pretty and in her smock and habit she looked like a tomboy.

"Can I help you?" she asked.

"I am here to see Abba Kovner," said Vitka.

"We are only nuns here," said the woman. She thought a moment, then asked, "And who are you?"

"A Jew from the ghetto."

The nun looked at Vitka's dark skin and the dark roots of her blond hair. "Of course," she said. "I am the Mother Superior."

The Mother Superior was thirty-five, a college graduate from Cracow. There were seven other nuns at the convent. When the Germans invaded, she offered to shelter as many Jews as possible. Eight Zionists were living in the convent. In the fall, the Mother Superior dressed these men as nuns, in gowns and habits, and sent them to work in the fields. In the afternoon sun, they could be seen picking their way through the rows.

"Why have you come to see Abba?" asked the Mother Superior. Her voice was lilting and she stood back on her heels like a seasoned farmhand. Each morning she worked in the fields, and in the afternoon she prayed and read the Gospels. She looked in the Bible for answers to her own troubles, for the strength to see her through the War. She believed that God was involved in human affairs, that everything was a test.

"I have come on a mission from the ghetto," said Vitka.

Vitka was led to the room where Abba Kovner slept. He was sitting on his cot. "Excuse me," said the Mother Superior. "This girl is here for you."

Vitka wore a peasant dress. It was late at night and she was so young he must have thought to ask if she had permission to be out so late. "Come in," he said. He asked Vitka why she had come. She told him about the girl who was found in the woods. "I have come to bring you to the ghetto," she said.

In a moment, Abba was ready to go with Vitka. On their way out, Vitka thanked the Mother Superior, saying, "You have done so much for the Jews."

The Mother Superior said, "In this situation, a Jew is the only decent thing to be."

Abba and Vitka walked in silence. The moon was over the fields. In the last few months, Abba's world had turned upside down. His father had been among the Jews resettled in the East; his mother and broth-

Abba Kovner before the War.

ers lived in the ghetto. Abba was only twenty-four years old, but the War made him feel like an old man. He was born in 1918 in Sebastopol, where his family, on the way to Palestine, had been stopped by World War I. When the fighting ended, the Kovners, out of money, returned to Vilna, where their family had lived for generations. Abba grew into a devout Zionist. By eighteen, he lived in a state of pure possibility— as only a man without a country can. Lithuania was not his home. Palestine was still a dream. Though not religious, he read and reread the Bible. He liked best the stories of battle, Jewish armies sweeping through the desert, brutal setbacks followed by stunning victories. In his private mind, he saw himself as a kind of biblical figure, a young man waiting for the call.

The Kovners lived in a modest house in Vilna. The father urged his sons to find a practical way to earn a living, but Abba insisted he was an artist. Before the War, he had been known as a sculptor. The bohemians of the city respected his textured work and the power of his words. He was charismatic, a stirring speaker, a young man who could excite the crowds. And yet there was something solitary about him. He was like a captain alone on deck, steering his vessel through a turbulent sea. It was this quality that made him a leader. It was why, on the day of the German invasion, with planes lighting up the hills, the older leaders of The Young Guard left him behind, saying, "There are hundreds of Zionists in Vilna. You will lead them."

At first, Abba had felt betrayed, abandoned. As the storm gathered, the most important Zionists fled to Palestine or found shelter in Russia, leaving kids like Abba and Vitka to find their own way. He soon realized that yes, he had been abandoned, but he had also been set free. No longer did he need to seek anyone's approval. There was no one left to give it. In those first weeks, he witnessed things that would forever separate him from the old leaders and from his own youth. He was in the city during the Great Provocation, the day the Germans rounded up the Jews of the old ghetto. As Abba hid in a stairwell, he saw a Nazi soldier pull a baby from its mother, swing the baby by its feet and dash its head against a brick wall.

Though Abba and Vitka went through the country in silence, it was not awkward or unpleasant. Vitka felt good just walking next to Abba. Almost too soon, she heard her shoes clatter on the paved streets. For Abba, walking by the old haunts, every corner told a story. The sun was rising when he reached the ghetto. The Jewish workers were leaving. A Zionist smuggled Abba and Vitka into the ghetto. Abba went to see his mother. When he was a boy, he and his mother had been extremely close. He was older now, responsible for more than just his family. She tried to control her emotions when she saw him. She asked how he was eating. Just before he left, she said, "What will happen to us?"

Abba and Vitka then walked to the hospital, where the sick slept three to a bed. Dr. Sedlis had been one of the most respected doctors in Vilna before the War, but he now had few supplies and the conditions in the hospital were far from sanitary; he often operated without anesthetic.

When Dr. Sedlis saw Abba and Vitka, he said, "You are here for the girl."

He led Abba and Vitka to a room that looked out on a courtyard. Sara was sitting up in bed, an ashen, ghostly figure. Her hair had been combed, her arm bandaged. Abba told the doctor he wanted to talk to the girl alone. Sara looked out the window as she told her story:

A week before, she had been rounded up in the action of the yellow passes. Her father had a permit but there were three children in the family and he could protect only two. Sara hid with her mother and a dozen other Jews in a secret room in the ghetto. It was dark in the room and all morning she could hear shouts and cries in the street. In the afternoon, she heard a voice say, "They are in here." The door was kicked in and the room flooded with light. Sara saw her mother dragged out, then she was dragged out. She could see the Jewish policeman who had given up their hiding place. She was marched out the ghetto gate and into the back of a covered truck. The engine started and the truck rumbled off. The Jews had no idea where they were going. For a time, the road was smooth and then the truck geared down and the road got bumpy. Through a gap in the tarp, Sara could see trees rushing by. "We are in the woods," she said. At last, the truck stopped and the tarp was pulled back. The Jews found themselves in the forest of Ponar. They were led down a path, beyond a barbed-wire fence and into a clearing. An old man raised a prayer book and said, "Dear Lord, comfort my people." A soldier hit him with a club and the book fell from his hands.

There were about a hundred people in the clearing and the men were separated from the women. They were divided into groups of ten. Soldiers came for the first group of men. They were led into the woods. A few minutes later, Sara could hear shooting. The soldiers came for the next group. It was late in the afternoon when they came for Sara's group. The women were led to a hill. On the ground were piles of shoes, shirts, coats, socks, underwear. The women were told to add their clothes to the piles. Sara undressed. She stood next to her mother on the cold forest floor. The naked women were marched into a tunnel made of canvas. It was dark in the tunnel and it smelled like a tent. Stepping out into the light beyond the tunnel, Sara found herself on the edge of a pit filled with dead bodies. When the Russians occupied Lithuania, they dug these trenches for fuel tanks. The bodies were moving—a few people on the bottom were still alive.

A voice said, "On your knees."

Sara looked straight ahead. There were gunshots. She felt a pain in her arm and passed out. When she came to, she could hear crying. She was in the pit. It was very cold and the bodies beneath her were frozen and she could see legs broken so that the bone showed and arms doubled-back and everywhere the faces of the old and young, ice forming around their lips. She turned away and found herself looking into the stunned blue eyes of a corpse. Her mother. She cried out. Someone grasped her hand. "Shut up," a woman whispered, "or the Nazis will come back to finish us. Keep quiet. When it gets dark, we'll get out."

Sara lay still for many hours. She listened to Lithuanian and German soldiers on the edge of the pit. They were drunk. When it got dark, the voices went away. The woman squeezed Sara's hand.

"Now," she said.

They crawled over bodies, backs, arms, faces. Sara pulled herself from the pit. The woman did not have the strength to pull herself out. Sara tried to lift her out but could not do it. She tried again and again. Then she heard a German voice.

"Go," said the woman. "Go now."

Sara crawled into the trees. Pine needles stuck in her hands. She dug at the mud under the barbed wire fence and crawled beneath. It cut her arm. She could hear soldiers searching the woods. She crawled into the brush. She lay there for two days. When she stood, her legs were weak. She walked in the direction of Vilna, stumbling and crying, until at last she was found by Jews in the forest.

Sara was quiet for a time, then said, "I have no more to tell."

A few days later, Abba called a meeting of The Young Guard. The leaders of the group met in a cellar beneath the Jewish Council. The room was low-ceilinged and lit by candles. It had been many weeks since the Jews in the ghetto had seen Abba—they were surprised by his appearance. His face was cold and sharp and his body was as tough as wire. He wore dirty work pants. He had not shaved. There were maybe a dozen people in the room, including Abba, Ruzka and Vitka.

Abba stood before them, hands trembling. "Our dear ones have been sent to their deaths," he said. "We must settle accounts with our consciences now, and not in the future. The truth in all its nakedness has been shown to us—our friends have not just been deported. I am sure of that. And yet many still do not see the truth clearly. What is that truth? That our friends and families, those who were deported, are no longer alive. They were taken to Ponar—to death."

Each person in the room had friends and fathers, mothers and sisters who had been "resettled in the East." No one wanted to believe what Abba was saying.

"And even that is not the whole truth," he went on. "The whole truth is much greater. The extermination of thousands is just a prelude to the extermination of millions. Their death means our complete annihilation."

Abba was the first Jew in Vilna to see the scope of the Nazi plan. How had he come to such a terrible conclusion? He had no more information than Jacob Gens and the members of the Jewish Council. Yet, unlike them, he was an outsider, not tied to the civilization of Europe. He had always believed the worst was possible. And so when he thought of all the Jews who had disappeared, of the story the girl Sara had told him, of what he had seen with his own eyes on the day of the Great Provocation, the soldier dashing the Jewish baby on the bricks, the picture fell together. These were not random atrocities committed by a crazy local commander; these crimes were part of a plot to wipe out the Jews of Europe. Abba understood this not as an educated man deduces but as a prophet sees—a flash of insight, a glimpse of a terrible truth. After all, what is a prophet, any prophet, even a great prophet like Moses, if not a man who, for a brief moment, detaches himself from history, so he can glimpse the road, and how it descends into the wood.

"It is still beyond me why Vilna is wounded and dripping in blood, and yet Bialystok is serenely peaceful," he continued. "I do not know why things have happened as they have. But one thing is clear to me: The lessons we learn here do not apply only to Vilna. Ponar is not just a passing phase. The 'Yellow Pass' is not an isolated invention of the local commander. It is part of a complete system. We are faced with a well-thought-out system to which we cannot, as yet, find the key...."

"Is there any escape?" he asked. "No. If this system is a consistent one, then flight from one place to another is an illusion and, like every illusion, it is stupid. For who will flee from the Vilna ghetto to Bialystok or to Warsaw? The young, the quick, the healthy. The weak and the old and the children will remain in the city, doomed to destruction. And when the tragedy finally reaches those cities where the young people have taken refuge, then, by that time, they will be broken in spirit, rootless, unready and confused. Therefore, our first answer must be: There is no flight in flight."

He looked around the room. "Is there any chance of rescue?" He asked. "We must give the true answer, cruel though it may be. No. There will be no rescue. Perhaps tens or hundreds of Jews will be saved; but for our people as a whole, for the millions of Jews in the areas of German occupation, there is no chance. Is there any way out? Yes. Revolt and armed self-defense. This is the only way which promises any dignity for our people."

A young man named Jacob got to his feet. He spoke in the calm voice you use when trying to get a man in off a ledge. He reminded Abba that they were Zionists; Europe was not their problem. Why risk ourselves to defend a way of life we consider a dead end? "We have always negated the Exile and the Diaspora in all its manifestations," he said. "European Jewry is now undergoing a catastrophe. Yes, we are in the thick of this catastrophe. But it is only an accident that we are here at all. Our place is in the Land of Israel. It is our reason for being. We must save as many of our members as possible. Yes. We believe in struggle. But in the Land of Israel. Not here. A struggle in the ghetto would just be a kind of theater....

"What is more, we have no support," he continued. "By ourselves, we are weak, defenseless. The Germans are immensely strong. In such circumstances, staging a revolt is the same as committing suicide."

"What are you saying?" Ruzka asked calmly. "Are you saying it's good if the Jewish people is wiped out so long as our little group survives? If you save yourself, will you be able to look into the eyes of a child in Israel when that child asks, 'What did you do?' When that child says, 'What did you do when thousands or millions of our people were murdered?' Will you tell that child, 'I saved myself alone'? Will you tell that child, 'I hid myself and did not let them take me to be helplessly murdered with all the others'?"

The books Ruzka had been reading, and all that she had been thinking, had crystallized into conviction. "It's our duty to fight for our people," she said. "It does not mean we've forgotten about Israel. We do it because we love Israel. Every people has its stories of heroism. It is these stories that give you the strength to go on. But these stories cannot remain only in the past, a part of our ancient history. They must be a part of our real life as well. What will the coming generations learn from us? How good will they be if their entire history is one of slaughter and extermination? Our history must not contain only tragedy. We cannot allow that. It must also have heroic struggles, self-defense, war, even death with honor."

A man named Israel stood up. "What about collective punishment?" he asked. "What about the German policy of killing a hundred Jews for every dead Nazi? No one has mentioned that. How can we talk about a struggle when you know it will bring about the slaughter of so many people in the ghetto? Do we have the right to put the lives of these people in danger? Won't we be accomplices in their death? And none of the Jews in the ghetto will support us. Maybe they will even blame us for their catastrophe."

Vitka shouted something and Jacob shouted something else and soon the cellar was awash in noise, everyone on their feet cursing and yelling in the candlelight.

Abba raised his hand, a gesture crisp and full of authority that settled everyone into their chairs. "No matter what we do, we will die," he said. "If we are cowardly, we will die. If we are courageous, we will die."

"What does that mean?" asked Jacob.

"It means we can decide just the one thing," said Abba. "We can decide that, whatever happens, we will not go the way the others went."

"You don't know if any of this is true," said Jacob. "All of it is a guess. You don't know anything for sure."

"That's right," said Abba. "I don't know for sure. And no one will ever know for sure. No. Let me change that. One person will know for sure. When they come to take the last Jew in Europe to Ponar—he will know for sure."

Abba moved out of the convent. He told the Mother Superior he could no longer live in safety as the Jews of Vilna perished. To be a leader, he must share the suffering of his people. The Mother Superior said she wanted to go with Abba. "Your fight is a holy one," she said. "Let me come to the ghetto to fight by your side, to die, if necessary. You are a noble people. Despite the fact that you are a Marxist and have no religion, you are closer to God than I."

For a week, the Mother Superior slept in the ghetto, sharing in its squalor. But in the end, after talking to Zionists who worked for the police, Abba asked her to leave. By staying in the ghetto, she endangered the Jewish community. "If they find out about you, they will kill us all," Abba told her. "Besides, you will be of far greater help to us on the outside. Here we are so isolated that we need to keep open every possible link to the free world."

Vitka also moved back to the ghetto. She lived with Abba and Ruzka in her old room at 15 Straszun Street. In historical maps of wartime Vilna, the house is shown over the words, "Underground Headquarters." But really it was just the broken-down flat where Abba, Ruzka and Vitka shared a bed. The relationship of these young people was the cause of much sensation and gossip. Seeing them walking arm in arm down the ghetto streets, Jews, with little else to entertain them, would smile and say, "Abba and his women." Their affair grew into one of the great romances of the War, fighting apart, meeting again each night. A young man recruited to the movement still talks of his first meeting with Abba. "Vitka brought me to the flat where they lived," he says. "I saw this tiny room with a bed on the floor and I asked who slept there. Abba said, 'The three of us. I sleep in the middle.' "

On December 31, 1941, Abba called a public meeting. That morning, Ruzka had wandered through the ghetto streets, pulling aside just the toughest kids, those ready to believe the worst. She invited them to the meeting, promising a great event, a landmark. "Get there before midnight," she said. Abba wanted the meeting to culminate as the New Year rang in, when the Germans would be drunk and celebrating their victories. The sentries would be too far gone to notice the gathering. The meeting was held on the ground floor of the Jewish Council. Vitka told Gens the group needed the room for a party celebrating the coming year. If he had known the meeting was to be a call to arms, he would not have allowed it; Gens was committed to a policy of working with the Germans. At the meeting, Abba would try to wake the young people from this reverie, a policy based on faith in the oppressor. "The youth, which is confused and depressed after the latest German Aktions, must have its faith in itself restored," he said. "It must have national pride and hatred of the enemy instilled into it."

It snowed all afternoon and into the night. The flakes whirled in the sky. The snow was high in the streets. In the snow, the guard post looked like a ruin. Ravens stared down from the rooftops. They had blue-black feathers and shiny eyes and studied the dumps for corpses. Kids wandered the alleys, their coats full of patches. As they came into the meeting room, they stamped their boots and shook the snow from their shoulders. Water pooled on the floorboards. The room was crowded with the winter steam of bodies. It was lit by candles. Each time someone came in, the candles flickered, the shadows danced. Men and women sat on chairs or leaned against walls. One hundred and fifty kids. Everywhere you saw their desperate faces, lost and searching, not speaking, not thinking. Waiting. The room was backed against the edge of the ghetto. Through the wall, the kids could hear muffled laughter and music, clinking glasses. Nazis celebrating. Now and then, a shout or peal of laughter sent a shiver through the room.

A few minutes before midnight, Abba came in. The floorboards creaked under his boots. People whispered. Many of the kids had heard of Abba, but few had actually seen him. Just looking at him—a Zionist leader who had not gone to Palestine or Russia, who was living here, suffering with them—brought a degree of comfort. He wore a work shirt and looked tough in a three-day beard. He stood before them like a seer, his dark eyes full of visions, of the flames at the end of every street. His voice was low and steady. "Jewish youth—do not believe your deceivers. Of the eighty thousand Jews of Vilna, only seventeen thousand remain. Our parents and brothers have been slaughtered before our very eyes.

"Where are the hundreds of men who were deported recently? Where are the naked women and children who were taken away on the night of the Great Provocation? Where are the Jews taken on the Day of Atonement? None of those who were taken through the ghetto gate have returned. All of the Gestapo's destinations are Ponar, and Ponar means death.

"Destroy your illusions. Ponar is not a transit camp. Everyone there is murdered. Hitler intends to destroy the Jews of Europe, and he has begun with the Jews of Lithuania.

"Let us not go to the slaughter like sheep. We are not strong, but the butchers can be answered in only one way: self-defense."

He paused for a moment, then went on.

"It is better to die as free men fighting than to live by the grace of the murderers. Let us defend ourselves to our very last breath."

Abba stepped back. He looked at the room. In one motion, the young people were on their feet. Some were crying. Jaws twitched. Shadows jumped. Through the wall came the muffled cry of German voices. The soldiers were singing "The Horst Wessel Song," the Nazi anthem, which calls for a time when "Jewish blood shall flow from the knife." The voices rolled in a drunken rhythm. There was silence in the meeting room. Then one of the Jews started to sing. Others picked up the tune. An old Zionist song. Everyone was soon singing, faces gleaming with sweat. *Withdraw not in despair, endure the torturing pain. As long as there is a spark of hope, bright days will dawn again.* And the two songs ran together, words and melodies flowing through the wall, until it was one song, a single lyric blazing into the future.

One day, as Abba was sitting in his ghetto flat, a young man came in the door, nodded and handed him a note. A month had passed since the meeting on New Year's Eve. Many of the young people of the ghetto had heard Abba's call and had pledged themselves to the cause, but there were so few weapons and it was very difficult to find a safe place to train recruits. At this stage, Abba was just another rebel leader trying to outfit his army. He tore open the note. It read, "We must meet, Wittenberg." A message from Isaac Wittenberg? Unthinkable. Wittenberg was a mysterious, shadowy figure, a Communist with direct ties to Moscow. He lived underground. Few people knew what he looked like, how old he was, where he was from.

Before the War, Wittenberg considered the Zionists his enemies. To the Communists, even Jewish Communists like Wittenberg, the Zionists were reactionaries, foes trying to seduce the people from the true path. But if a Communist is anything, he is pragmatic. A temporary alliance with the Zionists might benefit their fight against the Fascists. Besides, Wittenberg was smart—he knew the Germans wanted him dead not just because he was a Communist, but because he was a Jew. Wittenberg had also contacted Betar, the right-wing Zionist group. He wanted to form a common front, an army of Jews to sabotage the Germans.

The Jewish leaders met on January 21, 1942, in the ghetto. The leader of Betar was at the meeting, Joseph Glassman, a handsome young man with a long Roman profile and dark, sappy saloon-singer eyes. After the Germans invaded Poland, Glassman had been sent to a work camp. He had escaped and made his way to Vilna. In the ghetto, he joined the Jewish police, where he could pick up information and keep an eye on Gens, whom he considered the greatest threat to the Jews. Glassman came from a solid, career-oriented middle-class family. He was the kind of kid who seems ordinary until trouble starts. He was moved by flights of passion. He once told a room filled with people, "No surrender to fate, no acquiescence to annihilation."

Abba had a way of looking at people, studying each feature of each face, gathering impressions—an artist's habit. He was surprised by Wittenberg, who looked less like a revolutionary than a broad-cheeked, thick-necked peasant. Wittenberg was born in Vilna in 1902. As a young man, he worked in a shoe company. He went on to head the leather workers' union. He then joined the Communist party. He was forty years old, fifteen years older than Abba, and his experience made him a leader. His voice was hardly more than a whisper but he had the steady calm of a veteran. He knew how to survive on the run. Over time, Abba, Ruzka and Vitka came to see him as a father, someone to trust at even the bleakest moment.

The three leaders—Wittenberg, Kovner, Glassman—had a great deal in common. Each was a Jew who had given up Judaism, who had left God for some modern system of belief. Yet still they clung to the core of Jewish belief, a faith in a better world, a promised land. In other words, they saved the promise and ditched the promise-maker, exchanging the Messiah for Marx or Herzl or whomever. They disagreed only on what the promise would look like. To Wittenberg, it was a Communist paradise for every worker in the world, from each according to his ability, to each according to his need. To Kovner and Glassman, it was ancient Israel reborn as a modern democracy. The men agreed to set aside these differences and take them up again only if they survived the War. In the ghetto, they would fight not as Zionists or as Communists; in the ghetto, they would fight as Jews. "Hitler has made us one people at last," said Abba.

Together, these leaders formed a new group called the United Partisans Organization (UPO), which would be led by Wittenberg, with Kovner and Glassman serving as his lieutenants. Each man selected a code name. Wittenberg would be known as Leon; Glassman as Abraham; Kovner as Uri, a name he took from a great historian of Jewish Vilna. The UPO would acquire weapons and train troops, sabotage the German war machine and spread the battle call to other ghettos. Couriers were soon sent with Abba's manifesto to Bialystok and Warsaw, where it would ultimately inspire the uprising in the Jewish ghetto. And the UPO pledged that when the Germans came to liquidate the Vilna Ghetto, to take away the last of the Jews, they would fight in the streets.

As the meeting ended, Wittenberg took out a bottle of vodka. He filled several glasses. "We must toast our new enterprise," he said.

Wittenberg raised his glass, saying, "May we someday drink together in freedom."

Abba took the vodka in one gulp.

"Where will we get our first gun?" asked Glassman.

Abba reached into his coat and pulled out a German pistol. He set it on the table with a clank.

"Where did you get it?" asked Wittenberg.

"A friend stole it," said Abba. "There are plenty of guns. We just have to take them from the Germans."

One morning, in the winter of 1942, three weeks after the first meeting of the UPO, a truck parked outside the ghetto gate. On the back of the truck was the logo of the Vilna waterworks. A man stepped out of the truck in a jumpsuit and a worker's cap. His walk was quick and determined. He crossed the street to a manhole alongside the ghetto fence, surrounded it with road-horses and strung it off with electrical tape. He set up a sign: "Men Working." He went to the truck and returned with a flashlight, a pipe wrench and a crowbar. He was followed by men in work clothes carrying a wooden crate. You could tell it was heavy from the way they strained. The Lithuanian soldier guarding the gate said, "Such work so early in the day."

"We have to lay twenty feet of pipe," said the man with the flashlight. Stepping over the electrical tape, he pulled up the manhole cover. It clattered on the street. He held aside the tape as the other men carried the crate into the hole. He turned on his flashlight and followed the men into the sewer. The weekday traffic flowed easily around the road-horses. An hour later, the men emerged grime-covered from the hole, gathered the road-horses, electrical tape and sign into their truck and drove off. That is how the first shipment of guns was brought into the Vilna Ghetto.

The man with the light was a Communist named Shmuel Kaplinsky. It was his idea to bring in guns this way. He had been a plumber before the War and worked for the city waterworks, which is where he got the uniforms. His face looked like a map of the region, crossed by hills and ridges, the red lines of access roads, the blue lines of highways. He was simple, optimistic, trusting. In later years, when talking of the War, he would shake his head and say, "But the Poles liked me. I was a Pole myself." He would tell the story of the day he went swimming in a river in the country and was caught in the current and pulled under. A Polish soldier swam to his rescue. "He saved my life," said Shmuel. "If he hated me, why did he save my life?" Even on the black days, he never lost his stubborn trust in people. If only he could make his situation known, the Poles would swim to his rescue.

A few days after being moved to the ghetto, while wandering around a cellar three stories below the street, Shmuel happened upon an ancient wash drain. He pulled up the grill and climbed into the hole. An iron ladder carried him down into the cramped, putrid sewer tunnel. He crawled through the dirty water. It was a short trip beneath the ghetto to the manhole where he brought in the guns. Over the next several weeks, he spent hours mapping the tunnels. In the spring, when the snow melted in the hills, it was a swift, clear underground river. After a rain, it was a wretched swamp. To pass through it, a man would have to tilt his head back to suck at the few inches of air along the ceiling. Some tunnels were only shoulder-wide, and the presence of even one man meant a dangerous rise in water level.

In those first months, Shmuel often sent Jewish ghetto soldiers on long, soggy rambles under the city to record the location of each manhole cover and each drain. They walked miles in halls full of echoes and water-drip shadows, silence and night. Some lost their way, dark tunnel leading to dark tunnel, until they went howling mad. They starved or disappeared or drowned. When a man did not return, Shmuel went after him. A corpse might block a drainage and cause a sewage backup. If city workers found the Jew, it would alert the Germans to the use being made of the tunnels. For underground fighters, the sewers had become a parallel universe, a network of secret rooms and corridors that could carry a Jew out of the ghetto and safely across the city.

Shmuel found the bodies caught in overflow drains and pipes, bloated and blue, gnawed at by rats, eyes wide with fear. He would drag them along the corridors, up the ladder and out through the subcellar wash drain, which was beneath a building controlled by the Jewish underground. He then sent for the undertaker. A few hours later, a coffin would arrive from a shop outside the ghetto. Shmuel would remove the lid, pull out the nails and carefully open the false bottom built into the coffin. Inside the compartment were guns and ammunition. He would then replace the guns with money—the remains of family fortunes, cash fetched from black market deals—and reseal the coffin. Before the body was buried outside the ghetto, the undertaker would retrieve the money. In this way, even in death, underground soldiers served the cause.

One afternoon, an unassuming young woman passed through the gate into the ghetto. She wore a tattered coat and the yellow star—another poor Jewess home from the rattle-stink factories. She went to Abba's apartment. He came to the door, smiled, frowned. "Mother Superior," he said. "What are you doing? It is dangerous."

She reached into her pants and took out, one after another, three pear-shaped grenades. "I've heard you will fight," she said. "I want to contribute."

Abba picked up the grenades.

"From the Lowlands," she went on. "Pull the pin down, then up, very fast. You have ten seconds before it takes off your arm."

Weapons often came from unlikely places—from a Polish merchant especially pleased with a Jewish slave worker, from bits and pieces found in a German metal shop, or even from the belt of a dozing Lithuanian guard. Each night, Abba sent Jewish partisans into the city to cut deals, bribe locals and buy equipment. That winter, the Germans caught a teenager in the rail yards breaking into a freight car loaded with machine guns. He was sixteen. In Gestapo headquarters, Zalman Tiktin was questioned by Murer and a sadistic Gestapo officer named Bruno Kittel. When asked whom he stole the weapons for, Tiktin said, "I stole them for you, because you killed my parents."

Abba received reports from Jewish agents living and working outside the ghetto. One of these agents was a young man named Lebke Distel, who lived as a Christian on the outskirts of the city. To Germans, he seemed the Aryan ideal. He had blue eyes and blond hair and walked with a pigeon-toed, barrel-chested swagger. He worked in a munitions factory packing bombs, a jumpy existence. He volunteered for overtime, saying he needed the money for his family. He told the other workers that his father was in a Russian prisoner-of-war camp. Late at night, he smuggled out weapons one piece at a time. He passed the pieces to a courier, who gave them to the undertaker to carry to the ghetto. In 1942, a detonator exploded in Lebke's hands. He lost four fingers on his right hand, three fingers on his left. The factory sent for a doctor, who closed the wounds. Lebke was assigned to a month of easy work. Looking back, he says, "The Germans, they took real good care of me."

Abba had been working with the underground for several weeks, gathering weapons, training recruits, preparing for combat. His scouts were scattered in lookouts across the ghetto, reporting back even the smallest development. Abba wanted to know everything. One day, a German officer, in a long gray overcoat and knee-high boots, stepped through the ghetto gate. Germans were not allowed in the ghetto, not even high-ranking officers. It was one of the ways the Nazis isolated the Jews, casting them as dangerous, diseased, inhuman; the sign on the ghetto gate read: "Plague! Entry forbidden!" As the officer walked down the street, crowds scattered, kids ducked into alleys. His face was stern, angular, tight-lipped. He grabbed a young man by the collar. "Take me to Abba Kovner," he said.

The young man led the soldier to the street outside Abba's building.

"Wait here," said the kid.

When Abba heard a German officer was waiting to see him, he flushed. Vitka suggested he go out the window, over the ghetto roofs and into the city.

"I must see what it's about," said Abba.

He walked out of the building in shabby pants and torn clothes.

"What do you want?"

"Are you Abba Kovner?"

"Yes."

"I am Anton Schmidt," said the officer, "of the accursed German army."

Schmidt was forty-two years old. He had been born in Austria and had gone to fight for Germany when the War started. He was then a sergeant-major. By 1941, he was in charge of a group responsible for rounding up lost soldiers and returning them to their units. He commanded men and transport trucks. His operation was based in buildings near the railroad station. There was a radio, a phone and a desk. On the wall, a map with pins marked the positions of the German army, which then controlled Europe from the Atlantic Ocean to the Volga River. When Schmidt marched east, he was shocked by the slaughter, by what was happening to the Jews. Through stray conversations he found his way to the resistance. A rebel soldier told him to find Kovner.

Schmidt dreamed of mass escape, of spiriting the Jews in fishing boats across the Baltic Sea to the safety of Sweden. Like Abba, he was driven by visions of a better world. The two men—Jewish partisan and German officer—decided to work together.

When Schmidt heard of a Nazi plan to kidnap Jews from the ghetto, he told the leaders of the underground. He then filled his trucks with Jewish rebels and carried them to Belorussia. A few days later, when things quieted down, he drove them back. Other Jews hid in the basement of his office. One afternoon, he said, "There is a man, a dog named Adolf Eichmann, and he is organizing all this." He told Abba to remember the names of the criminals—that one day the War would be over and then it would be time for revenge. He gave the members of the underground German uniforms and transit documents. In those months, he saved the lives of many partisans. Warned of the risks he was taking, Schmidt said, "I will outlive them. They will never take me alive."

Schmidt disappeared in February 1942. Abba later learned that he had been arrested and was tortured by the Gestapo. He gave no information. In the end, he stood before a firing squad. The shirt he had been wearing was delivered to his wife. It had twenty-seven bullet holes. After the War, when the Gestapo files were captured, she was given a note her husband had written a few minutes before his death. "Every man must die once," Schmidt wrote. "One can die as a hangman, or as a man dedicated to helping others. I choose to die helping other men."

Abba had lost more than a truck and a place to hide. Schmidt had been a reason to hope, to again see the world as a collection of individuals, each with the possibility to choose good over evil. "I'm Anton Schmidt," he had said, "of the accursed German army."

On some afternoons, Ruzka walked to the little ghetto library, where, for a few hours, she lost herself in the sad, ruinous smell of mildewed books. She felt as if she were wandering in the sacked remains of the library of Alexandria, picking through the remnants of a lost civilization. There were popular novels and city histories, studies of the Franco-Prussian War and World War I, Zionist books and stories by Cervantes and Dickens, and bound volumes of the Talmud, Biblical commentaries and commentaries on the commentaries, the ceaseless hairsplitting of the Diaspora sages. One day, in the spring of 1942, Ruzka came across a pamphlet that had been published two years before, when Finland was fighting back a Russian invasion. It urged the Finnish people to revolt and gave a quick course in guerrilla warfare. Using a Finnish-Polish dictionary, Ruzka carefully translated the pamphlet and brought it to Abba, who used it to build cheap, effective bombs.

There were then about a hundred members in the underground, young men and women who had yet to see combat. Abba wanted the soldiers trained and prepared for the terrible odds they would face. Several times a week, he met the fighters, in groups of eight or ten, to display each new weapon in his arsenal. He told rebels how to make grenades: unscrew the metal heel of a lightbulb, fill the bulb with gasoline, screw it back together; throw the bulb, the filament ignites the gasoline—boom! Or: fill an empty pipe with nails, pack it full of powder, run a fuse through the powder, light it, throw it—bang! The air fills with nails! The fighters were also taught to shoot. Instruction was given by Shmuel Kaplinsky, drawing on his years in the Polish army. In these sessions, the fighters shared a single snub-nosed revolver, which was passed hand to hand like an icon. In a cellar three stories below the street, they aimed at a wall of packed mud. There was a blue pistol flame and the teeth-rattling report. The bullet would then be prised from the mud, with hopes of using it again.

Perhaps the most important work was done by Ruzka, who each day recruited fighters. Some of the kids were referred to her, some she found on her own. These Jews, few older than twenty, living without families or hope, were a ready audience. They had no school, no job, no synagogue. There was no future, so they lived in the present. Years later, when asked how they survived, many say, "Ruzka." Or they call her "little Ruzka," or "little sister." They remember her ghosting through the ghetto, a petite and soft-spoken young girl, talking to kids in apartments, on the street, standing in line for work. She asked after their welfare with an empathy that made everyone trust her. If one of these people showed even a spark of defiance, Ruzka spoke of the underground. If a kid wanted to join, she brought him or her to see Abba, then to be questioned by the other leaders of the UPO: Isaac Wittenberg and Joseph Glassman. The leaders sat behind a table in a candle-lit cellar. On the table were a Bible and a pistol. If the recruit was accepted, he or she swore an oath, one hand on the Bible, one hand on the pistol.

One day, Ruzka questioned Rachel Glicksman, a girl who lived in the ghetto with her mother and sister. Rachel had grown up in Vilna, where she belonged to a Zionist youth group. In school, she had known Abba as a charismatic older boy. She wanted to join the underground. Before Rachel met with the leaders, Ruzka told her, "No matter what they ask, act determined, like you will do anything. They want to see if they can trust you, if you are committed."

The leaders asked Rachel dozens of questions. Where are you from? What do you believe in? What do you read? Why do you want to fight? At the end of the meeting, Wittenberg narrowed his eyes, his features hard in the smoky light, and asked, "Are you willing to leave your mother behind?"

"What do you mean?" asked Rachel.

"If it is necessary," he said, "will you leave your mother to die?"

Why hadn't Ruzka told her about this? Leaving her mother behind? Ruzka had spoken only of fighting, of honor. How could she leave her mother? Her father was gone, she was the oldest. She was not alone in the world. She was responsible for more than herself.

"I could not leave my mother to die," said Rachel.

And so Rachel was turned away by the underground.

In the spring of 1942, Ruzka hosted a Passover Seder. The table was set with mismatched silverware. One of the girls had smuggled wild-flowers into the ghetto. They looked beautiful and out of place on the table. A boy brought beets. For dinner, the fighters ate beet salad and drank pulpy beet juice, which stained their mouths. The youngest of the fighters, just fourteen, read the Four Questions, which evoke the explanation of the meaning of Passover.

"Why is this night different from all other nights?"

"Why *is* this night different?" Ruzka asked herself. "Is it where we are that makes it different? The ghetto? Or is it what has happened? Ponar?"

She looked at Vitka. Her fingers were long and slender and everything they touched seemed to shimmer. She looked at Abba, who was at the head of the table. At twenty-five, he was the oldest person in the room. His sleeves were pushed up, his arms marbled by veins. "No, it is us," she thought. "We are different. If we fall, we shall fall fighting. We shall fall as free men and women and our blood will bring redemption to that blood which cries out for revenge."

One July evening, five months after the underground was formed, Vitka left the ghetto at sundown, pulled the yellow star from her coat and walked into the streets of the city. It was a quiet summer night, and the streets were filled with people. Vilna was wreathed in the acrid smoke of factories. Church bells chimed in the dank air. Vitka was leading a patrol of two boys and one girl, underground fighters who, beneath their jackets, carried grenades and pistols. Vitka carried a bomb built by Abba. One of the boys had the detonator. Vitka was doing her best to guide the patrol through the city unobserved, studying each face with her quick brown eyes. In her mind, she went over each detail of the mission. She had been chosen for it by Abba, who explained it one night in the flat on Straszun Street.

"You will be the first to go," he said. "The mission is yours."

Ruzka was in the room. She must have known what this meant: Vitka was now, without a doubt, Abba's girl. It was the custom in the underground movements of Europe: the commander sent his girl on the most dangerous mission. It was his way of saying, "I am the toughest man, I have the toughest girl."

Vitka was to blow up a German train as it made its way east, carrying soldiers and supplies to the Russian front. For two weeks, she had left the ghetto each afternoon and spent the night wandering alone along the train tracks, which passed through the forest seven miles south of Vilna. She was scouting for a place to blow up the train—somewhere far from the ghetto and far from the forest camps where Jews were used as slave labor. The Nazis met each rebellious act with collective punishment, killing a hundred Jews for one dead German. The underground leaders did not want to give the Germans reason to blame the explosion on Jews. But everywhere Vitka went, she found Jews—draining swamps, breaking rocks, building roads. Or else there was a farmhouse where a barking dog might give her away.

One night, as she walked along the edge of the forest, she felt that she was being watched. She turned quickly. A wolf was staring from the trees. It had blue fur and yellow eyes. It growled and Vitka could see its pointy teeth and its arched back and its pink tongue. Behind it was the forest night. Slowly, step by step, she moved backwards—only to hear sharp voices and a dozen guns going off. Across a field, she saw German soldiers on their bellies or else standing in a crouch, sighting rifles and pistols. The guns went off and in the flash she could see the faces of the soldiers, pale with sharp jaws.

Someone shouted. The soldiers stopped shooting. Vitka heard boots on the dry ground. A soldier ran up to her, out of breath, red-faced.

"Did you not see the signs?" he asked.

"What signs?"

"This is a shooting range," he said. "It is off limits."

Time after time, when Vitka was in a dangerous situation, when the wrong choice meant death, she was overtaken by an icy calm. She would later say it was like an out-of-body experience. There was danger, yes, but she felt as if she were outside of it, viewing the scene from above. She was able to read such situations, to tell the enemy the one thing that would make him see things in a new way. "I am sorry," she said. "I was out walking and I got lost. I am from Vilna. Please, help me."

The soldier no longer saw a spy. He instead saw a woman in need. She appealed not to his reason or to his charity. She appealed to his vanity.

"Of course," he said, taking Vitka by the arm. He walked her to the road and called to a peasant passing in a cart. "This girl is lost," said the German. "Show her the way to Vilna."

When the German had gone back to the woods, the peasant said, "Get back to your ghetto, Jew."

A few nights later, Vitka found the perfect spot for the explosion. It was some twelve miles from the city, where a trestle carried the train tracks over a gorge. As Vitka led the Jewish rebels to the spot, her mind wandered to the past, to her mother and father, and the distance she had crossed. She thought of her hometown, quiet streets at sundown, lights in the windows, chimney smoke mounting in the crisp winter sky. They reached the trestle just before midnight. There was no moon and the sky was washed in stars. Leaving the fighters under the trees, Vitka scrambled onto the train bed. Stepping tie to tie, she walked out on the trestle. The gorge was dark. She sat on the tracks and took out a powder-packed pipe. She worked in silence. Now and then, she looked up the tracks to the trees. She hooked the pipe onto one of the rails. From a distance, it looked like a part of the train track. She ran a fuse from the bomb, along the rails, to the detonator, which she set across the rails. When the train crushed the detonator, it would set off the bomb.

Vitka then hid with the other fighters in the woods. Each kid held a gun and a few grenades. "I hear something," one of the boys said.

Vitka saw the light of the train sweeping across the trunks of the trees. Smoke from the engine climbed into the sky. The windows were yellow. The train got bigger and bigger. "It must've gone over the detonator," she thought. There was a blast, then a brilliant flame. Dirt was thrown into the air. For a moment, it was as bright as day in the woods. Vitka saw the grassy forest floor and the shadows of the trees and the faces of her friends. Debris rained down. The train was moving in slow motion. The engine went into the gorge. The cars lay smoking. Vitka ran along the wreckage, lobbing ghetto grenades— tin cans filled with nuts and bolts set off by a splutter fuse.

German soldiers climbed out of the train and began firing pistols. They did not follow the partisans into the woods. One of the Germans set up a machine gun and fired into the trees. Vitka led the patrol to a swamp a few hundred yards from the wreckage. One of the Jewish fighters—a young girl—had been shot dead. Vitka buried her in the forest. The patrol started back before dawn.

The leaders of the UPO were waiting in a ghetto cellar. Vitka told them about the explosion, the gunfight, the girl who died. This was the first time Vitka met Wittenberg and Glassman. She was impressed by Wittenberg, who was strong and simple. "You are very brave," he told her.

Ruzka hugged Vitka and said, "You have done a wonderful thing."

Abba laughed in a way that said everything.

Wittenberg had a bottle of vodka. "It is time we have a celebration," he said.

He took a swig and passed the bottle to Glassman, who took a swig and passed it to Vitka. "I don't drink," she said.

Wittenberg shrugged and passed the bottle on to Abba.

They began to sing. Though many fighters would go on missions over the next few months, blowing up trains and trucks, Vitka's mission had been the first such act of sabotage in all of Occupied Europe—a fact they learned from Wittenberg, who had read intelligence reports from Russia. The fighters sang all morning and the people in the street who heard their drunken laughter must have wondered what anyone could find to celebrate in the ghetto.

A few days later, Abba saw the story in an underground newspaper: It said that Polish partisans had blown up a German train transport. Over two hundred German soldiers had been killed. The SS then marched into the nearest Polish town and killed sixty peasants. "This is not something I felt guilty about," Vitka later said. "I knew that it was not me killing these people—it was the Germans. In war, it is easy to forget who is who."

Then came the blue days of summer. A strange, haunted peace settled on the ghetto. During the previous winter, the Germans had bogged down in Russia. Short of manpower, the Germans now found it wasteful to simply shoot the Jews. They would instead work them to death. Jews made coats and bombs, graded roads, dug trenches.

For the time being, the Aktions came to an end. Jacob Gens, the head of the Jewish police, took credit, summing up his policy in a phrase: "Work to live." If the Jews wanted to survive, he said, they must make themselves indispensable to the Germans. "We must prove that, contrary to the accepted assumption that we cannot succeed in any craft, we are in fact most efficient, and no substitute for us can be found under present wartime conditions," he wrote. "Work for the Wehrmacht is the command of the hour."

In these months, a society grew up in the ghetto, a self-contained little world of fighting and backstabbing and double-dealing, but also of charity and kindness and dignity and love. There were aristocrats and bourgeois, haves and have-nots. The richest man in the ghetto was Weisskopf, a tailor whose shop employed two hundred workers. His contacts with the German army brought him blankets and firewood. Poor Jews called him "The King of the Ghetto." The nouveaux riches were the sooty, blue-collar chimney sweeps. They worked on the rooftops, the ceiling of the world: from the rooftops, with the help of the locals, who, for a price, might pass baskets up from their windows, they could sneak food into the ghetto; from the rooftops, they also had a view of freedom, Vilna drifting in the morning fog, the roll of the river, avenues and parks, forests in the distance. There were reports of rebel armies forming in the forest, which, to young people, suggested another way to live.

Gens called this brief period of calm "The Days of Civilization." He encouraged cultural activity. Once a week, he hosted "The Club," a gathering of scholars to discuss the great topics of the past. At the first session, which he called "A Nation and a People," the experts spoke until three in the morning. *The Ghetto News*, a newspaper printed with the approval of Murer, began to appear on the streets. There were articles, editorials, reviews, listings. Gabik Sedlis, who forged documents for the underground, showed his watercolors. Abraham Sutzkever, a ghetto fighter, read his poem "Kol Nidre." An orchestra performed Beethoven's *Leonora Overture* No. 3, Chopin's Piano Concerto in E Minor and Tchaikovsky's Fifth Symphony. An athletic association led the Jews in gymnastics, rhythmics, running, jumping, boxing. When the library loaned its one-hundred-thousandth volume, a party was held. On display in the lobby was a scale model of Vilna, built, from memory, by an obsessive, starving Jewish architect. It showed every corner and building of the city. Jews stood around the model, looking at the hills and rivers, the patterns of a lost world.

A theater company formed in the ghetto. A sign above the stage read, "Within the walls, yet young." Some of the actors had been famous before the War. The company performed *Corn and Days of Wheat, You Can Never Know, Green Fields, The Man Under the Bridge, The Flood* and a musical comedy called *The Treasure*. The audience wore their best clothes and the men smoked cigarette butts between acts. In the front row sat Jacob Gens. He waved and smiled. In his glad-handing, you could see the superficial concern of the city politician, the man who sees people in numbers. "We can only save the many by sacrificing the few," he often said. Now and then, Murer came to the theater with visiting Germans. They stood in back, drinking and laughing.

On opening night, members of the underground walked through the crowd, handing out flyers that read, "Theatrical performances should not be held in cemeteries." Abba said that plays and symphonies filled Jews with illusions, a sense of stability. In other words, the culture of the ghetto did the work of the Nazis. People must not be allowed to forget, he said, where they were and where they were going.

In a manifesto, he wrote:

In the face of tomorrow, which will arrive with the horror of deportation and murder, the hour has struck to dispel the illusion. There is no way out of the ghetto except by way of death. Illusions otherwise only shatter our unity in these moments before death. Before our eyes they have led away our mothers, our fathers, our sisters—enough!
Comrades!
—Don't give the foe the chance to ridicule you!
—When a German ridicules a Jew—Don't help him laugh!
—Don't play up to your murderers!

—Denounce the bootlickers at work!

—Denounce the girls who flirt with Gestapo men!

—Work slowly, don't speed!

—Show solidarity! If misfortune befalls one of you—don't be vile egoists—help him. Be united in work and misfortune!

—Jewish agents of the Gestapo and informers of all sorts walk the streets. If you get hold of one such, sentence him—to be beaten until death!

Gens responded in *The Ghetto News*. "We wanted to give the people the opportunity to free themselves from the ghetto for several hours, and this we achieved," he wrote. "We are passing through dark and difficult days. Our bodies are in the ghetto, but our spirit has not been enslaved. It has been said that concerts should not be held in graveyards. True, that statement is true, but all of life is now a graveyard. Our hands must not falter. We must be strong in body and soul."

The days of civilization lasted through the fall and into the winter. The underground continued to fight against the Germans outside the ghetto and to plead with the Jews inside, but it seemed an impossible struggle. To the ghetto Jews, the logic of the underground proved to be flawed. After all, the killing had ended and there was still life in the ghetto.

In February 1943, a young Jew named Isaac Kowalski was returning from a mission in the forest, one of a dozen or so assignments the Jewish underground had safely carried out. He walked down the frozen streets as the sun rose. There was no one on the bridges. As he neared the ghetto, he saw a group of German soldiers with black armbands on their sleeves. In the ghetto, he learned that the soldiers were in mourning. After a five-month siege and the death of over a million troops, the German army had surrendered at Stalingrad. There were stories of bitter house-to-house fighting, of Germans hunkered down on a few rubble-strewn streets, soldiers freezing in bloody rags. The underground greeted the stories with relief. The flood had crested. It was now only a question of time. One year? Two years? If the Jews could just hold out, they would be rescued by the Russian army. At Gestapo headquarters, the flags flew at half-mast.

In his office at the Jewish Council, Jacob Gens had similar thoughts. He looked at maps and counted days. The Russians could reach Lithuania within a year. More than ever, he was dedicated to his policy of cooperation. This was no time to be seduced by the apocalyptic hysteria of the underground. Jews who lived to see the return of the Russians would survive. "We shall feel the pain of all this only after we leave the ghetto," he wrote. "For today, we must have strength. Those who believe in God should pray: the Almighty will help us. The nonbeliever should say the spirit of society and of Jewish patriotism will help us endure all this and, after the ghetto, remain human, for the sake of the great future of the Jewish people."

In a cellar in the ghetto, Abba listened to the radio. The radio had been smuggled from the free city, where it was purchased on the black market. The Germans forbade Jews to own radios and telephones, or anything that might break their isolation. Each night, Abba would sit for hours before the receiver, his cigarette glowing as he searched for a voice or a melody, a hint of life beyond the walls. The announcers spoke English or French or Russian or German, the great frenzied babel of the wartime night, of soldiers on roads and blacked-out cities, of mail-call in barracks and screeching air raids, of Winston Churchill fading in—"Everyone thinks if they feed the crocodile, the crocodile will eat them last"—then fading out. Abba sometimes picked up songs broadcast by the BBC, Gershwin or Coward or Porter. He danced with Vitka and Ruzka in the glow of the dial, three floors below the street. They had little to eat in the ghetto and were hungry to the point of weakness and yet, at such moments, the radio crackling like a fire, Vitka felt a sweet, pure joy. To find happiness in such a place filled her at once with guilt and with a belief in the holiness of life.

Abba often listened to SWIT, an underground radio station which was thought to broadcast from Poland. SWIT announcers told of the real war, the one the Germans kept out of their newspapers. The Gestapo searched for the station, raiding basements and torturing suspects. SWIT, it was later learned, actually broadcast from a studio in London. After he listened to reports on the station, Abba would write a newsletter and distribute it to the underground. In April 1943, during a break in a regular SWIT program, a voice shouted: "Hello, hello! The Warsaw Ghetto has begun to resist." As Abba sat trembling, the announcer spoke of a Jewish revolt, fighting in the streets, Molotov cocktails, incandescent bolts of flame, German deaths. The revolt had begun on April 19 and would continue for twenty-seven days. In his diary, Joseph Goebbels wrote: "Heavy engagements are being fought which even led to a Jewish supreme command issuing daily communiqués. Of course, this fun won't last very long. But it shows what is to be expected of the Jews when they are in possession of arms."

Abba had been the first person to urge the Jews of Warsaw to rebel. A year before, he had sent a messenger to meet with Zionists living in the city. The messenger told the Jews of Warsaw about Ponar and about the underground that had formed in Vilna. She then read the speech Abba had given on New Year's Eve:

It is better to die as free men fighting than to live by the grace of murderers. Let us defend ourselves to our very last breath.

In Vilna, the partisans thrilled with the news of revolt and walked in the street with fiery eyes.

In the summer of 1943, Jacob Gens was named the ruler of the Vilna ghetto—a position he already held in all but name. Fried, the banker who had reluctantly taken on the leadership of the Jewish Council, had been forced out. Murer, saying Fried had been smuggling food into the ghetto, removed him from office; he would die in a death camp. Yitzhak Rudashevski, a twelve-year-old boy, recorded the reaction of the people in his diary. "Murer visited Fried and found him in possession of four kilograms of candy," wrote Rudashevski.

"The entire ghetto is enraged at the old despot who used to sit in his office as though on a throne with candies at his side!"

Gens ran the ghetto by decree. He allowed no disobedience. "The basis of our existence is labor, discipline and order," he explained. "We must not have among us people who recoil from labor, behave improperly or commit offenses." If a Jew committed a crime, he was locked in the ghetto jail, which was run by Gens. A few days later, the offender would appear before the ghetto court, where Gens sat as the judge. One June afternoon, six Jews who had been convicted of murder stood on a scaffold in a ghetto lot. A few hundred people had come to see the hanging. The shadow of the scaffold fell across the crowd. The convicts wore dirty work clothes. Each had a thick twist of rope around his neck. Gens climbed the scaffold. "Sixteen thousand out of the seventy-five thousand Jews of Vilna have survived," he said. "These sixteen thousand must be good, honest, diligent people. Anyone failing to uphold these precepts must expect the same as these men. We shall eliminate them with our own hands. Today, we apply the death penalty to six murderers, Jews who killed Jews."

One day, in October of 1942, the underground received a tip from a Jewish policeman: The Germans would soon liquidate the Jewish town of Oszmiana, a rural settlement a few dozen miles from Vilna. Abba sent a girl named Liza to warn the Jews of Oszmiana. She walked through the forest to the town, where she met people on the streets. She told them that the Nazis would soon destroy Oszmiana, that the Jews would be sent on trains to die. She asked the people to flee with her into the forest. Only a few people followed her. Torn by guilt—she had failed in her mission—Liza returned to Oszmiana to plead with the town leaders. She was still pleading when the soldiers stormed the streets. Liza was never heard from again. In Vilna, the rebel fighters spoke of her bravery, of how she had given her life to save the lives of others. In the future, when the underground leaders wanted to call their soldiers to arms, wanted to tell them, "This is it! Gather the guns and grenades, get ready for the final fight!," they would use the phrase "Liza is calling!" Calling you to revolt, to rebel, to fight. Liza is calling you to die.

In Oszmiana, German and Lithuanian soldiers were joined by

members of the Jewish police of Vilna. The Jewish police were given special uniforms for the occasion. The presence of the Jews put the people of Oszmiana at ease, making it possible to believe the German assurances—the train will take you to a new home, to a better job. "One bright day, the Jewish police donned official uniforms," Yitzhak Rudashevski wrote in his diary. "Leather jackets, boots and green round hats with glossy peaks and Stars of David. It is said the reason for the uniforms is that thirty of the policemen are riding to end the life of a neighboring town. The Gestapo thus kills two birds with one stone: first they carry out another bloody piece of work. Second, they demonstrate that Jews in uniform will drive their brothers from their homes, distribute certificates and keep order with the knout."

If Jacob Gens had any doubts, if, for even a moment, he saw the terrible truth, that he was working not for the Jews but for the Nazis, he never said so, at least not in public. Such thoughts would have been too awful to entertain. Such thoughts would have turned his leadership into a crime. Gens was not a bad man. He was a man who made a bad decision and that bad decision led to other bad decisions, until he was too far down the road to find the way back. He believed that the Germans would be true to their self-interest. And it was not in the self-interest of the Germans to kill a perfectly good workforce. Gens did not have the Holocaust as a point of reference; he did not know the unimaginable was at that moment being imagined. We look at him from the other side of a great divide, an after-photo where everything seems inevitable, where the past leads in one direction—to Ponar. He was a sophisticated European gentleman whose best qualities were used against him. He did not understand the nature of his own times.

In Vilna, every Jewish child had lost parents or siblings or cousins. Life was just shock after shock. There was no recreation, no school. Now and then, an adult organized an activity for the children, something to structure their days. On one occasion, the children took part in a mock trial, performing as judge, jury, defendant, lawyers. The trial was held in a basement. Adults sat against the walls. On trial was King Herod, the last monarch of ancient Israel, whose leadership led to the destruction of the Second Temple. Trying Herod was a way— the only way—to try Gens, who seemed to prosper as the ghetto suffered. Herod was charged with crimes against the Jewish people. At the defense table, a boy in a flowing robe looked on with disdain. The prosecutor, Yitzhak Rudashevski, paced back and forth before the jury. "I accused Herod of a policy of ambiguity, of playing the role of the Roman agent, of murdering the people," he wrote in his diary. "The defense showed Herod's positive deeds and explained that Herod lived in a tempestuous time and that many of his deeds were for the benefit of the Jewish people." The jury returned with a guilty verdict, then the argument was taken up by the adults. It raged through the night. There were shouts and threats. As the sun rose, one of the men said, "If Herod had supported the rebellion, it would have only hastened the catastrophe."

One morning in April 1943, Lithuanian soldiers posted a notice in the Vilna ghetto. Jews who wished to go would be transferred to the Kovno ghetto, where many of them had relatives. In Kovno, they were promised work and food. Three hundred and sixty Jews volunteered. Jewish police were to escort them to the train and ride along with them to Kovno. The police, whose presence offered comfort, marched the Jews to the depot beyond the ghetto gate, where a freight train waited. The police helped the Jews up into the boxcars, then locked the doors. The police were seated with Gens up front in a passenger car.

After a while, the whistle blew, the train jerked and the streets glided backward out the window. The engine picked up speed in the country. The train seemed to be following a strange route. Gens asked a railroad man how they were traveling to Kovno.

"No, not Kovno," said the railroad man. "We are traveling to Ponar."

Gens talked to a Lithuanian soldier. Murer was contacted. The train stopped at a station in the country. Gens and his police, abandoning the other Jews to their fate, were taken back to the ghetto. The train waited all night at the depot and in the morning went on to Ponar. When the boxcars opened, the Jews saw they were not in Kovno. Gens and the Jewish police were nowhere in sight. Panic swept the crowd. The Jews attacked the Germans and Lithuanians. Some soldiers were ripped to shreds. The Germans opened fire with machine guns. The forest was strewn with bodies.

The next morning, an SS officer named Weiss went to the Vilna ghetto and ordered twenty-five Jewish policeman to travel with him back to Ponar to bury the bodies. In Ponar, Weiss led the Jewish police past soft mounds covered with moss and weeds, narrating what had transpired on this killing ground. "Here are the dead Soviet prisoners," he said. "Here are the dead from the Second Aktion," "Here are the dead from the Aktion of the Yellow Passes." The police were the first Jews to be shown Ponar. They carried the dead from the woods and buried the bodies in the pits. Germans photographed the Jews at work. The Germans were losing the War in the East. Rather than bringing salvation to the Jews, as Gens believed, the German defeats were ushering in the last act. The Days of Civilization had come to an end.

A few months after the liquidation of Oszmiana, Gens was ordered to help the Germans destroy another Jewish town. He sent his policemen to the town to assure the people that no harm would come to them. Joseph Glassman refused to go. Glassman was a double agent, an officer in the police who was also a leader of the underground. Even so, he believed that keeping his police position was less important than protesting a Jewish role in a German massacre. He was arrested. Gens decided to ship Glassman to a work camp, where he would drain swamps. A few nights later, Glassman was led from the Jewish Council building with his hands tied behind his back. He was put in a flatbed cart and wheeled toward the ghetto gate. He was guarded by a Lithuanian soldier and a Jewish policeman. Two German soldiers waited to arrest Glassman beyond the ghetto gate.

As the cart rumbled down the street, a kid, leaning in a doorway, ran a comb through his hair. A moment later, with the cart still a few dozen paces from the gate, the street filled with members of the underground. Standing just out of sight, Ruzka orchestrated each move: the cart was surrounded, fists and shouts filled the air. One of the fighters, a seventeen-year-old girl named Cesia, dug her fingers into the neck of the Lithuanian soldier and pulled him to the ground. It was an epiphany. Before that, she felt that if she ever struck a soldier, the blows would glance off or fail to register, as in a dream. "When I saw him stretched out in the street I could not believe I had done that," she later said. Once freed, Glassman was rushed into a cellar, where he would hide until a decision was made. This was the first time the people of the ghetto had seen the Jewish underground in action.

A few hours later, Wittenberg and Kovner were called to a meeting by Gens. Sitting in a stiff-backed chair in his office, Gens looked like a sculpture, all ledges and lines; it was the face of the last generation, marked by deals and compromises, a veneer of sophistication protecting a stubborn refusal to see. Gens knew of the Jewish underground. He did not disagree with many of their sentiments. "We both want to save Jews," he said. "You want to fight and I know how you feel. But for the time being, the way to help Jews is to be essential to the Germans. If we appear unruly, we will give the Germans reason to kill us. Do you know why Oszmiana was liquidated? Because the town was a home to forest partisans."

Gens said he knew that the underground was hiding Glassman. Gens had arranged to transfer Glassman to a work camp. If the Germans believed Gens could not deliver this Jew, who had been held under arrest, Gens would be removed from office. The ghetto would suffer, he said. It might even be liquidated.

Wittenberg could judge Gens as a contemporary. He was the same age and had grown up in the same culture, an assimilated home sunk in the chaotic days of prewar Lithuania. The two men had made wildly different choices. Gens had gone inside the system, trading his accent and his history for a life of cafes and barracks, as much a European as a Jew. His life was built within the society that was destroying him. Wittenberg had gone the other way, outside the system, underground. A serious man in a serious fight. He believed in the forward drive of time. Like Gens, he was playing for history, trying to imagine how even his smallest decision would be read at the end of the century.

Abba Kovner asked Gens to please understand what he was asking of the underground. Glassman was one of their leaders. How could they turn over one of their leaders? After all, they had to retain some control over their own fate.

Gens made a promise: If the underground turned over Glassman, he would be sent to a nearby work camp and would be back in the ghetto in two weeks.

Wittenberg and Kovner agreed.

Gens was as good as his word. In two weeks, Glassman was back in the ghetto. Perhaps it was his ability to perform such tricks, to get a Jew out of a work camp, that convinced Gens he could manage the future of the Jews.

On July 7, 1943, an eighteen-year-old Communist was arrested in Vilna. His name was Saul Kozlowski. He was taken to Gestapo headquarters on Vilnius Street, a beautiful tree-lined boulevard of restaurants and clothing stores and women in silk dresses. He was led to a basement with desks, phones, maps on the wall, pictures of Hitler. The secretaries looked no different than secretaries in real estate offices or insurance concerns. In the back of the office there was a windowless room with tables and restraints, trays full of knives. After the War, this office would be taken over by the KGB, like an old restaurant under new management. Kozlowski was strapped to a table and tortured. The Gestapo wanted to know the identity of a Communist called "The Lion," a member of the underground. After several hours, Kozlowski broke. He said "The Lion" was another name for Isaac Wittenberg, a ghetto Jew. As the Germans stepped aside to talk this over, Kozlowski got a knife off a tray and cut his own throat.

The next day, the Gestapo visited Jacob Gens. At midnight, Gens called Wittenberg, Glassman and Kovner to his office—they had not yet learned of Kozlowski's arrest. Gens, speaking in the tone of a bedtime story, talked about the War, how the Jews had survived the Spanish Inquisition and the Cossack hordes and would survive this too. As Gens spoke, a Jewish policeman was walking toward the ghetto gate: Salek Dessler, who served as Gens's chief deputy. Dessler was even more hated than his boss, who at least acted on a kind of principle, even if misguided. Dessler acted on self-interest alone: for position, for privilege, for power. His nose was blunt, his eyes were cold and resentful. From the shadows across the street, an underground scout watched Dessler walk to the gate and return with two soldiers. On their collars were the double lightning bolts of the SS. Seeing this, the scout ran through the ghetto, into the bedrooms and dives, shaking the fighters awake, whispering, "Liza is calling."

When the SS soldiers stepped into his office, Gens stopped talking. He nodded toward Wittenberg. The Germans asked Wittenberg to stand. They clapped shackles on his wrists and ankles. Wittenberg was marched out of the office. Abba looked at Gens. "You betrayed us," he said.

"They did not want him as a member of the underground," said Gens. "They wanted him as a Communist. If I hadn't turned him over, the Germans would have destroyed the ghetto."

"You tricked us into coming here," said Abba.

"If I had told you everything, would you have come?"

"No."

"And then what would have happened?" Gens put his shiny boots up on the desk. "I'll tell you what would have happened. The Germans would have liquidated the ghetto. Thousands of Jews would have died. And for what? Fighting for their lives? Fighting for the Jews? No. They would've died to prolong the life of a single Communist."

Wittenberg was marched toward the ghetto gate, where a car was waiting. His steps were abbreviated, shackles dragging on the ground. German soldiers walked on either side of him. As they marched past an alley, a Jew leapt from the darkness. It was Shmuel Kaplinsky, the Communist who had mapped the sewers. He grabbed one of the SS soldiers by the collar and hit him twice, very fast. As the other soldier reached for his pistol, he was hit from behind. From a distance, the whole attack sounded as harmless as rustling leaves. A few moments later, when the Jewish police arrived, the Germans were stunned and groggy. Wittenberg was gone.

Shmuel cut away Wittenberg's shackles with a hacksaw in a cellar workshop. Several other partisans soon arrived: Vitka and Ruzka, Kovner and Glassman. The fighters decided to hide Wittenberg and put the underground on full alert. If the Germans stormed the ghetto, the rebels would fight, urging the people to fight with them.

Vitka was to hide Wittenberg, telling no one, not even Abba, where he was. That way, even if Abba was captured and tortured, he could not give anything away. To sneak Wittenberg through the streets, which were filling with Jewish police, Vitka put him in a peasant dress and wound a scarf in his hair, traced his eyes with pencil and lipsticked his lips. His shoulders looked big in the dress and his face heavy and full of lines and not unlike the face of an old Yiddish balabusta you might see opening the back door to throw out a tray of fish heads. Vitka hurried Wittenberg past crowds of men and women speaking in shrill voices about Wittenberg's escape. It was 1 a.m. No one cared about curfew.

In the morning, German soldiers surrounded the ghetto. The chimney sweeps could see them from the rooftops: infantry with machine guns, trucks and field guns, soldiers on tanks. Abba met Gens on the ground floor of the Jewish Council building. Gens was very angry. "Murer has given us just a few hours," he said. "If we do not give him Wittenberg, he will liquidate the ghetto."

"What makes you think he won't liquidate the ghetto anyway?" asked Abba.

"Your mother lives in the ghetto," said Gens.

"Do you have something to tell me about my mother?"

"Do you want her to die? Because that is what will happen. She will die. For Wittenberg. Those soldiers out there—that is no joke."

"What do you want me to do?" asked Abba.

"They only want Wittenberg. Give up Wittenberg, and this ends."

"I can't do that," said Abba. "Is there something else I can do?"

"There *is* nothing else."

"I will go to the Gestapo," said Abba. "Take me instead."

"They don't want you."

"Tell them that I am Wittenberg."

"They have an informer, you fool. They know what Wittenberg looks like. You think I haven't thought of that?"

It was the first time that Abba had seen Gens lose his temper. He was sweating and his body looked hollow—the life had gone out of it.

"I am sorry," said Abba. "I cannot give them Wittenberg."

That night, the Jewish police ran through the streets, shouting, "The ghetto is in danger. All men must gather at once in the yard of the Jewish Council." The people walked over in ratty clothes, their faces emaciated. It was a strange summer night. The sky was full of constellations and planets and comets and shooting stars. The wind carried the rumble of tanks and German voices. The Jewish police leaned against the walls. The most respected men of the ghetto were there, the rabbis and poets, politicians and scholars. Off to the side stood a few dozen men in dark suits, men with scarred faces, big shoulders, big hands, cracked knuckles. These were Jewish gangsters who, before the War, had made their living in Vilna's criminal underground. Gens relied on them in emergencies. In the ghetto, they were called "Di Shtarke"—"the strong ones."

Gens wore his police uniform. His expression was stony, hardened by the decisions he had made. "In a raid in the city, the Gestapo captured a Polish Communist named Kozlowski," he told the crowd. "During his interrogation, Kozlowski confessed that he was in contact with a man named Wittenberg, a Jew living in the ghetto. The Gestapo is therefore demanding the surrender of Wittenberg alive within two hours. If he is not surrendered, the German tanks and planes will demolish the ghetto with bombs."

"What shall we do?" Gens asked the crowd. "Shall we surrender Wittenberg and save the remnants of the Vilna ghetto?"

People shouted, "Save the ghetto! Give up Wittenberg!"

"But we don't have Wittenberg," Gens continued. "Wittenberg is being hidden by a few children who call themselves the underground and endanger all of us. We have set up workshops that are economically important to the Germans. You have been given a chance to live and work in peace—and work is our only guarantee of staying alive. As for them, the so-called underground, not only do they have no part in all of this, in our life, they even try to keep us from our jobs. They have separated themselves from the community, and they try to force us to do things that will be the end for us."

As Gens spoke, his voice grew louder, his eyes widened, his breath quickened, a lock of hair swung across his forehead. "We must stamp out this evil in our midst," he said. "We must not feel sorry for the members of this underground, just as they don't care about us, our wives and children. Wipe them out, because your lives are at stake. The Gestapo wants just one man. As soon as we hand him over, we will again have peace. If we don't, it will be the end of us."

Gens dropped his voice and said, "This man or the whole ghetto?"

Someone said, "Save the ghetto."

Someone else said, "Get Wittenberg."

"The ghetto is alive and flourishing," said Gens. "There is no reason to fear it will be dismantled. But only under one condition: Wittenberg is given to the Gestapo. Search for Wittenberg and we will be saved. We owe it to our children and to our wives."

Gens looked at the crowd. "This man or the whole ghetto?"

The crowd answered in one voice, "Get Wittenberg."

"Wittenberg is in hiding," said Gens. "Go find him!"

Jewish police ran ahead of the crowd, shouting, "Find Wittenberg. Save the ghetto."

The members of the underground, who were meeting in their upstairs headquarters on Straszun Street, could hear the cheers go up from the yard of the Jewish Council. A few minutes later, they were visited by rabbis and other leaders; the old men told the rebels they had no right to put their heroics over the safety of the Jews.

"Give up Wittenberg," an old rabbi said. "Save the ghetto."

Abba, who still hoped to make his case for revolt to the people, asked, "What makes you think that giving up Wittenberg *will* save the ghetto?"

The rabbi told Abba to trust Gens, who was, after all, looking out for the interests of the Jews.

The rabbis left. As the underground soldiers talked together, there was a bang and the building shook and more bangs and a rock came through the window and more rocks until the room was filled with stones and the rebels covered their heads and someone crawled to the window and looked out. The street was filled with gangsters, waving ax handles and shouting, "Give us Wittenberg! Give us Wittenberg or come out and fight."

A dozen rebels went down into the street. They fought under the weak ghetto light as the evening fog rolled in. The haze was silky and made everything strange and new and the fighters could see only flashes of pipe and fists and faces that came in and out of the haze and teeth and boots and rings and the thud of blows and the sting of blood and two or three or four gangsters on the ground and someone gasping on the street. The gangsters took their wounded and ran off and the fighters stood in the fog, lost and weary, wondering what would come next.

The mob came howling down the street.

There were old men and young men and old women and children and friends and cousins and teachers. Underground fighters were shouted down, attacked. "Why won't you let us live? Why must we die for you?" The mob raced up creaky wooden stairways, tearing through the ghetto room by room, ripping out false walls and passages, searching every rat hole for Wittenberg. They were doing again what the Germans did when they came for Jews to fill the quota—only this time it was a quota of one. Ruzka never forgot the hysteria of the mob. That long night, she learned something new about ugliness and violence and fear.

In the early morning, the mob burst into the attic where Wittenberg was hiding. He dashed out the back door and ran into the street. There was a herky-jerky chase through the ghetto courtyards. As

Wittenberg ran around a corner, he was met by Jewish police. They walked toward him slowly, step by step, closing the net. The sun had come up and dazzled off their boots. They carried clubs. Wittenberg took out a pistol and fired over their heads. He ran into an alley. He could see the mob. Someone pulled him into a cellar. It was Vitka, her eyes clear and steady. She said, "I have found a place for you to hide."

Abba spoke to the people in the street, sometimes off in a quiet corner, sometimes in the midst of the mob, so he had to yell to make himself heard.

Give us Wittenberg.

"This is the German plan," said Abba. "The Germans are pitting us one against the other. That way, we do their work for them."

Give us Wittenberg.

"What if we give them Wittenberg?" said Abba. "What does it get us? One more week of life in the ghetto? Don't you see? No matter what we do, we die. So let us die fighting. If we fight, we die with dignity."

To these people, Abba was a fanatic. They cursed him and spat on him. He walked to an empty street that ran along the ghetto fence. On the other side of the fence were the Germans. If the soldiers stormed the ghetto, Abba would have to fight the Jews to get to the Germans. That is, he would have to kill Jews before he could kill Germans. He had promised himself he would never do the work of the Nazis. He would never kill Jews. He had always counted on a spontaneous uprising, a struggle on the lip of the grave. But the Jews were not with him. What could he do? Could he lead a people in a war that they refused to fight? Abba found Vitka and said, "Take me to Wittenberg."

Isaac Wittenberg belonged to that great tradition of peasant soldiers that sprang up in the East at the end of the nineteenth century, to a generation, now extinct, of amateur revolutionaries who, seeing only the forward drive of history, what physicists call time's arrow, fought with blind will and faith in the inevitable. He believed he was in the right fight at the right time and that he was part of something bigger than himself and, for this reason, each sacrifice was easier to make. If he did the right thing and did it well, he could not help but make his story a part of the story of his era. Sitting in a cellar with his girlfriend—she was maybe twenty—he listened to Abba's report about the ghetto. Glassman was there too, and so were Ruzka and Vitka and the other leaders of the underground.

"The people will not fight," said Glassman.

"But the ghetto is going to be destroyed anyway," said Wittenberg. "The Gestapo means only to kill the resistance leaders first and afterwards the rest of the people."

"There are Jews in the streets," said Abba. "We will have to fight them before we get to the enemy."

Abba paused, then said, "Give the order and we will fight."

Wittenberg looked around the room: at Glassman, at Ruzka, at Vitka. He understood the situation. He said, "We will not kill Jews."

Wittenberg asked Abba if a deal could be worked out with Gens. What if Gens told the Gestapo Wittenberg had escaped? That way, he could make a run for the forest. Otherwise, Wittenberg could kill himself. Gens could give the body to the Nazis. Wittenberg did not want the Gestapo to take him alive.

Gens said No, the Gestapo would not accept an escape story, nor would they accept a corpse. They wanted Wittenberg for questioning.

Wittenberg pulled on an old military coat and strapped on his pistol. It was heavy and it made his pants sag. His girlfriend sat behind him on the bed, sobbing. As he paced the floor, the muscles in his shoulders moved. For Abba, Vitka and Ruzka, this was one of the great scenes of the War, a moment of terrible sacrifice. When remembering this night, they could not help thinking of what might have been. What if Abba had convinced the people? What if he had forced a crisis? Think of the poems that might have been written, the stories that might have been told. If more Jews had resisted, if every German truck were met by a bomb or bullet or rock . . .

"What should I do?" asked Wittenberg.

"You must decide," said Abba.

Wittenberg turned to his fellow Communists.

"What do you think?" he asked.

A girl named Sonia said, "You must give yourself up."

Wittenberg looked at the ceiling, hugging himself. He then took a deep breath, grasped Abba's arm and said, "Tell Gens I will surrender to him personally so that he can bring me to the Gestapo. That way, the Germans will see that Gens is working with them."

Wittenberg took off his gun, held it a moment, feeling its weight, then gave it to Abba. "You are now the leader," he said.

Wittenberg's girlfriend cried out, "You're worse than the Germans. You are killing him."

When Wittenberg surrendered, Gens told him, "If you don't break after the first interrogation, I will activate my contacts and try to have you released." Gens then gave Wittenberg a capsule of prussic acid. "Hide it in your ear," he said. "In case it gets too rough."

Wittenberg walked out through the ghetto streets. It was getting dark. The Jews stood along the buildings. The fury had gone out of the crowd and the mood was now the hangover after the binge, the passion of last night just a hazy memory. As Wittenberg passed through the gate, he looked ahead, a sacrificial lamb upon whom the people had loaded their guilt and sin; he was being sent into the wilderness. The next morning, Wittenberg was found dead in his cell. He had swallowed the prussic acid.

Abba sent a note to the underground:

As a result of the tragic situation in which we are placed, the organization's commander, Wittenberg, gave himself up to the Gestapo with his, and our, consent. It is likely that history will blame us for it. It is likely that no one will know exactly what our situation was, for a long time, and that our act stemmed from the great responsibility that we have towards the ghetto and the masses, with whom we could not—dared not—fight. The shock within our organization has been tremendous. Wittenberg's name will be tied to the life of our people and for us he will always serve as a noble symbol of heroism. The first company of fighters going out into the forests will be named after him. We shall honor the memory of our commander in the fight with the enemy.

Abba had a natural gift, the ability to anticipate the next development, the coming shift in the action. He knew it was all over in the ghetto. He could feel it. He had appealed to the people and the people had rejected his appeal. And yet he decided to wait in the ghetto for the liquidation he was certain would come. He hoped the Jews, when faced with the trucks and boxcars, would at last follow him into revolt. Jewish rebellion had been his dream and his reason to live and he was not yet ready to give it up. He also knew it was time to send the first of his fighters to the forest. He told his troops, "We have seen what the Jews are and now we have to leave the ghetto." These men were to build a Jewish presence in the woods and blaze the way for other rebels to follow. Abba was, in essence, dividing his forces. Abba, Vitka and Ruzka, and around a hundred troops, would stay to fight in the ghetto. The rest of the underground—about two hundred soldiers—would flee to the forest.

That first group was named Leon, which had been Wittenberg's code name. It was made up of twenty-one underground fighters who had run afoul of Gens and the Jewish police, and also of the wild, fancy-free young men who were desperate to get into the open, where they could live and fight and die. This group—it included Abba's shy, dark-eyed kid brother, Michael Kovner—was led by Joseph Glassman. The fighters were to walk to Narocz, a pine forest fifty miles north of Vilna, where they would meet a Soviet soldier named Markov, who commanded forest partisans. Markov had sent several notes to the Jewish underground, urging them to join the fight.

On Friday, July 27, 1943, the Leon Group left the ghetto disguised as a unit of woodcutters, in work clothes and peasant hats. Under their coats were guns and grenades. It was a dusty afternoon and the dust caught the sun and the wind kicked up the dust and turned their hats. They followed the river through the folding green landscape. The sun went down and the stars came out. They reached a bridge where the fields began. The river was fast and clear and they could see fish jumping in the cold water. They went over the bridge one at a time. The road led into a tangle of trees. There was a click and boots in the brush and a shout in German and German soldiers emerged from behind the trees shooting. Bullets clipped the leaves, and the Jews shot off a few rounds before scattering into the woods. Nine rebels died on the road. In the pockets of the corpses the Germans found identification papers with names and addresses.

The next day, the Nazis arrested the families and neighbors and friends of the men killed on the road. These people—there were thirty-two of them—were taken to Ponar. The Nazis posted a notice on collective punishment:

> The family of everyone who escapes to the forest will be executed. If the family cannot be found, the escapees' roommates will be executed; if these cannot be found, all the tenants of his building will be executed.

Gens responded in *The Ghetto News*. "It is clear that the sacrifices were unnecessary," he wrote. "The deaths of these people lie on the consciences of those who, by their irresponsible behavior, made the innocent pay with their lives for a crime not of their making."

Abba continued to send soldiers to the forest. He believed this was their only hope of survival. But he now sent small battalions, eight or ten fighters who left the ghetto at sundown, walking single file down the city streets, never losing sight of the person in front of them. They climbed a twisting road to the old Jewish cemetery. It was dark by this time and the evening mist moved over the headstones. One of the rebels cupped his hands and issued a sharp animal cry. A blond-haired girl came toward them through the mist. It was Vitka, who had been sent hours before by Abba. No one knew the city like Vitka, no one was as brave. She led the fighters to a fresh grave. Beneath the soil, they found guns and grenades. Vitka kissed each fighter and pointed to the road which would lead to a farm.

From there, a scout would take them to the partisan base in the forest.

It was a long journey to Narocz. The fighters walked all night through the fields, stopping at peasant huts, stealing meat and potatoes, sleeping in groves. After seven days, they reached the cathedral cool of the deep forest. There were signs nailed to the tree trunks: "Danger! Partisans!" When the fighters reached the base, they were lined up before Markov, the Russian commander. He told the Jews to turn in their guns, which, he said, would be given to those who could make better use of them. The Jews were to serve the base as tailors, cobblers, cooks.

"That is not what we came for," said Glassman. "We came to fight the Germans."

"There is more than one way to fight the Germans," said Markov.

At the end of August, Stuka bombers screamed over the trees. Tanks rumbled down the trails. Thirty thousand German troops stormed the brush, trying to flush out partisans. Russian, Lithuanian and Polish partisans fled to the forests north of Vilna. They did not take along the Jews, nor did they tell the Jews which way to travel. The Soviets feared the Jews might be followed. Left without guns, some of the Jews tried to follow Markov; his troops fired over their heads. Two hundred Jews were left in Narocz; seventy lived through the sweep. The survivors, hungry and desperate, broke into small units and tried to crash through the German lines.

A group that included Joseph Glassman and Michael Kovner stole food and guns from country houses and set off across the fields. On October 8, as they walked through a stretch of farmland, they were attacked by Polish peasants. The Germans had promised a kilo of sugar for every dead Jew. It was autumn and the wheat had been cut—the field offered no cover. The peasants fired from behind rocks. Glassman told his men to run for the trees across the field. Only one of the Jews made it, a girl who later told the story to Abba. In the future, whenever Abba came upon a peasant who had turned in or killed one of his soldiers, he shot the man and left a note: "Killed for betraying a Jew."

In August 1943, Jacob Gens was ordered by the Germans to supply three thousand Jews for work camps in Estonia. Gens urged the people of the ghetto to volunteer, saying the move would bring a better life. Though some agreed to go, Gens fell short of the number of people that had been requested. One morning, when hundreds of Jews arrived for work at a nearby airfield, they were surrounded by Estonian troops and forced onto trains. Gens was allowed to go to the depot, where Jews called his name and reached through the boxcar slats. He touched their hands and gave them water. He promised that everything would be all right. When the quota was met, the Germans demanded another five thousand Jews, which would leave just five thousand people in the ghetto. Hundreds of Jews went into hiding. Gens could not fill the quota.

On Wednesday morning, September 1, 1943, German soldiers marched through the ghetto gate to seize two thousand Jews for the work camps. With fixed bayonets, they set off down Rudnicka Street, into the squalor of muddy lanes. The sun was coming up over the rooftops. It was 5 a.m. The streets were quiet, the people hiding. Soldiers kicked in walls and dragged out Jews. An underground scout ran through the courtyards, in and out of windows, shaking people awake, whispering, "Liza is calling." Young men and women jumped from their beds and raced into the street. The underground was divided into two battalions. When a soldier got the order—"Liza is calling"—he was to join his battalion at the mustering point.

The Second Battalion gathered at 6 Szpitalna Street, near the ghetto hospital. There were a hundred kids, tense, excited. *This is it!* Vitka was in the battalion, and so was Lebke, the blond-haired Jew who had lost his fingers to a faulty detonator. They stood in a vacant lot, waiting for their weapons, which a courier would bring from a hiding place. Two, three, five minutes went by. Vitka saw a Jewish policeman talking to a German officer. Then, before anyone knew just what was happening, the Second Battalion was surrounded by enemy troops. A spy had told Gens the mustering point; by turning over the rebels, Gens would help fill the quota and also thwart a confrontation. More than anything, Gens feared violence. If the Jewish underground fired on German soldiers, he would lose control of the ghetto.

The battalion commander gave the order to scatter. The rebels pushed through enemy troops, swinging, kicking. In some instances, one crazed Jew fought four or five soldiers. Others were beaten to the ground. Lebke made it across the road to a courtyard. Lying on the ground, he could see the members of the battalion with their hands on their heads. He could see broad-backed Estonian soldiers. He could see Jews marching toward the gate. Lebke thought of his parents and grandparents, the living and the dead, friends in the battalion. He belonged in the street. What happened to his friends happened to him too. He walked out of the courtyard with his hands up. A soldier shouted.

Lebke said, "I surrender."

The soldier hit him across the face. Lebke looked up smiling.

The First Battalion mustered at 6 Straszun Street. A courier handed out guns and grenades. Abba stood before them. "Our aim is not the defense of the ghetto's last wall," he said, "but the act of self-defense in itself."

As Abba spoke, Vitka appeared around a corner, walking fast.

"Why aren't you with your battalion?" asked Abba.

She told him what had happened.

He asked how she got away.

She told him how, when the battalion was surrounded, she had just walked off, her strides carefree and confident, like she had somewhere else to be. No one stopped her.

Abba looked at his soldiers—they awaited his command. He told them what had happened. Then, before they had time to think, he was giving orders.

"We have guns," he said. "We are ready to fight."

Abba divided his soldiers into three units. The forward unit took up its position at 6 Straszun Street, on the third floor of the building. The unit was led by Yeichel Scheinbaum, a tough young man who formed his own resistance group and called it "Yeichel Scheinbaum's Struggle Group." Ruzka would serve as Yeichel's second-in-command. Abba's unit, which included Vitka, set up in his flat at 15 Straszun. The third unit set up in a house just across the street. Once ready, the rebels would wait for the enemy to wander into Straszun Street. When the Germans marched past the forward position, the Jews would open fire. The Germans would then be caught in a cross fire, with the Jews shooting from the front, the rear and the flank.

Abba had turned his apartment into a fortified bunker. Stacked in the windows were volumes of the Talmud and the Pentateuch, the only books thick enough to stop bullets. The books blocked the sun and made patchy shadows. The walls were piled with stones and bottles of sulfuric acid. Boys sighted rifles through makeshift turrets and girls boiled water to pour down on the Germans. This was the moment the rebels had been waiting for—the blue room at the end of the War. Abba had a typewriter in the apartment, a battered machine bought on the black market. That afternoon, he wrote a letter, which was copied and passed to the Jews hiding in the ghetto.

Jews! Defend yourselves with arms. The German and Estonian hangmen have arrived at the gates of the ghetto. They have come to murder us! Within a short while, they will lead us, group after group, through the gate. Thus they led our brothers and sisters, our mothers and fathers, our children. Thus were tens of thousands taken out to their death! But we shall not go! We will not stretch our necks for the slaughter! Jews! Defend yourselves with arms! Do not believe the reassurances of the murderers. Do not believe what the traitors say. Anyone who goes out the gate goes to only one place—Ponar. And Ponar means death. Jews! We have nothing to lose, death will take us in any event. The hand of the hangman will fall on every person. Flight and cowardice will not save your life. Only armed resistance can save our lives and honor. Brothers! Better to fall in battle than to be led like sheep to the slaughter. And know ye: There is an organized Jewish resistance in the ghetto that will rise with arms. Lend a hand to the revolt. Do not cower in the hideouts. Your end will be to die as rats in the grip of the murderers. Go out into the street. Whoever has no weapons, take a hatchet; and whoever has no hatchet, take a pipe or a stick. For our fathers! For our murdered children! To avenge Ponar, strike the murderers! Strike at the dogs! Jews! We have nothing to lose! Death to the murderers!

Then he waited. For the people, for the masses. But nothing happened. Putting his ear to a window, he heard only silence broken now and then by a gunshot. The masses did not find their way to Straszun Street. And neither did enemy soldiers. The morning shaded into afternoon and the evening shadows began to climb the buildings. Gens had done his best to steer the soldiers clear of Straszun, saying there were no people on that street. He knew that the underground was at Straszun and he was trying to short-circuit the conflict he believed would bring ruin to the ghetto.

A few minutes after sundown—there was still enough light to read by—a German troop marched toward the rebel stronghold. Yeichel Scheinbaum could see the men from his window, maybe twenty soldiers in gray uniforms. They were on Oszmianska Street, which curved as it turned into Straszun. As they walked past buildings, the soldiers banged their rifle butts on the narrow facades, calling, "Come out, or we will blow you up."

"No one shoots until the enemy is in the trap," said Scheinbaum.

So he could not be seen from the street, Scheinbaum leaned against a wall beside the window. The other rebels peeked through turrets or loaded their guns. Scheinbaum looked out the window. He could see the enemy soldiers moving up the street with the ease of men who can shoot without risk of being shot at. He leaned back. He breathed. He looked out the window. He could hear the boots of the soldiers and see their faces. He stepped back. When he again looked out, the enemy had stopped in front of the building next door. They were looking up at the windows, shouting, "Come out, or we will blow you up."

A German walked into the building carrying a black case. He had a mustache and looked older than the other soldiers. A moment later, he ran out of the building. He shouted something and the soldiers ran down the street. Some stood in doorways, others crouched on the ground. Ruzka saw one of the soldiers grimace and then heard a click and then a blast. Fire came out of the building and debris peppered the street. Scheinbaum looked out the window. The building next door was gone and there were bodies in the rubble and Germans standing on the wreckage and one of them turned and looked at Scheinbaum and there was a moment when they were looking at each other and then Scheinbaum gave the order and the Jews in the windows opened fire. The enemy returned fire and bullets went into the books in the windows. There was a pause in the shooting. Scheinbaum looked out the window. There was a single gunshot. Scheinbaum slumped to the floor. He had a neat hole in his neck. Ruzka was in command.

Through the window, Ruzka saw the German with the case and mustache walk into her building. She ordered the unit to retreat. They raced down the stairs and jumped through a window into the courtyard. Ruzka twisted her ankle. Getting to her feet, she remembered the bag of ammunition in the bunker. She pulled herself through the window and started back upstairs. Her ankle ached. She could not find the bag. The German with the mustache ran out of the building. The soldiers sprinted down the street. Ruzka found the bag and ran downstairs. As she hit the landing, she heard a click and dove through the window. While she was still in the air, she felt the explosion and its violence went through her and then Vitka was dragging her into 15 Straszun.

When Yeichel Scheinbaum shot at the Nazis, Gens became hysterical. He pleaded with the Germans, promising that if they left the ghetto, he would round up the quota. The Germans, perhaps having learned from the Warsaw Ghetto revolt, did not want to fight on terms set by guerrillas. It would soon be dark and the soldiers would be lost in a maze of ghetto streets. After blowing up the building, the enemy soldiers marched out of the ghetto.

For years, some veterans of the battle blamed Ruzka for the outcome, for the fact that the fight never became a full-scale revolt. They say that Ruzka hesitated, that rather than order a retreat, she should have attacked. If she had attacked, some say, the German bomber would never have made it into the building. Others say that Scheinbaum ruined the plan, ordering his soldiers to hold fire until the Germans were in the trap, then disobeying his own order. Of course, such arguments are beside the point. The first shot was to call the ghetto to revolt. But by the time Scheinbaum opened fire, it was clear that the ghetto was not listening—there would be no revolt.

The *Ghetto News* reported these events a few days later: "To our joy, the head of the ghetto, Gens, and the chief of police, Dessler, succeeded in persuading the representatives of the German administration to withdraw their troops from the ghetto and to assign the conscription of labor forces for Estonia to the Jewish police."

When the Germans withdrew, Abba went into the street, slouched in the courtyards and cursed. It wasn't that he had killed no Germans—though he wanted very much to kill Germans—it was that the people of the ghetto had not answered his call. He felt ignored and cut off, and this feeling grew into resentment. To Abba, the War was a test that many Jews failed. Those people who behaved with the least decency were often the most respected citizens, religious and political leaders. "Who saw Vilna as we did," Abba wrote, "with thousands choosing to be sent to concentration camps and passing by the barricades and looking at us with pity?"

Ruzka was devastated. For months, she had been living for one thing—Jewish revolt—and now that one thing was gone. "All our plans, our expectations, our prayers, went up in smoke," she wrote.

Vitka saw things differently. "That was the one time I looked at these people, Abba and Ruzka, who carried me through the War, and said to myself: 'They will not make it. They have begun to die,' " she said. "It was the look you saw in the eyes of those who had given up. And it was I, who believed myself the weakest, who said, 'The story cannot end this way. We have lived not just for one battle but for a war. You must go on.' It was a low moment, yes, maybe the lowest, but at last they came out of it and got back to work. I was so happy that I wept. Abba wept too. Ruzka did not weep. She kept everything inside. It is how she survived. She never wept. Then Abba ordered the fighters to flee for the forest. They would go out one group at a time. We would help each group get out, then we would be the last to flee the ghetto."

Gens swore in two hundred new Jewish policemen: an auxiliary force. These officers were to round up the Jews Gens had promised to the Germans. Less than ten thousand people were still living in the ghetto, the remnant of a community that, a year before, had numbered eighty thousand. The auxiliary police made promises and threats, shouting in the rain and tangle of the mob. If a Jew had family that had already been resettled, the police might say, "Go to your family." If a Jew was out of work, the police might say, "Go work for the Germans. A Jew with a job is a Jew with a future." If such arguments failed, the police simply pulled Jews from their hiding places and marched them to the gate. "At the time of liberation, if the ghetto survives, though few may live in it, I shall know I completed my task," said Gens. "I can then announce, with a quiet heart and a pure conscience, that I did my duty to the future of my people."

Gens fell two hundred Jews short of quota. The ghetto was a lake that had been fished out. Gens found a solution. He sent his auxiliary police to the gate, where he said they would meet the person who would lead them to the additional Jews to fill the quota. When the auxiliary police arrived, with their clubs and green uniforms and peaked caps, they were surrounded by German soldiers. At first confused, the police soon understood the Gens solution: the auxiliary police themselves would be sent to Estonia; they would fill the quota. Some of the police, full of panic and fear, broke from the soldiers and turned back to the ghetto. In their path stood the Jewish gangsters, the hard-faced men Gens called on in emergencies. Swinging clubs and pipes, filling the air with curses, they drove the auxiliary police out through the ghetto gate.

Gens issued a statement:

The transport of people for work in Estonia is completed. I call upon all the ghetto inhabitants to return quietly to their homes, maintain order and carry out all of my instructions.

WARNING!

Those guilty of stealing property will be punished by death.

A few days later, Jacob Gens stepped through the ghetto gate in his police uniform. That morning, a German contact had told him, "The Gestapo will arrest you. Leave at once for the forest." But Gens said his disappearance would harm the ghetto. Even with his own life at stake, he believed in the greater good. He was a kind of monomaniac, fixated on the preservation of the ghetto, which, to him, was the Jewish people.

Gens was arrested in the afternoon. "If I am not back by eight p.m.," he told his brother, "assume I will never be back." He said nothing as he was led through the streets. With him was Dessler, his lieutenant. Gens was guarded by German soldiers. Before the Nazi invasion, this had been his city. He knew its avenues, its hideaways, its faded rooms. Now he was a stranger, the ghetto at his back. To save the people of the ghetto, he had rounded up the old and sick, destroyed the rural towns, marched hundreds to their deaths. In a better time, he might have been a decent man. In a better time, he might have been a hero.

The Gestapo sent Dessler back to the ghetto.

A German told Gens, "There is a nest of Jewish partisans in the ghetto who fought us. You, as chief of the ghetto, did not turn them over. I arrest you for this."

Gens was brought to a jail on Rosa Street. In the back, beyond a row of cells, was a doorway filled with light. Gens walked into the courtyard. A hole had been dug. He stood next to the hole. He was blindfolded and shot. A few days later, Dessler, who had been named chief of the Jewish Council, gathered his family and fled the ghetto.

.   .   .

On September 23, 1943, the Jews of the ghetto were told to gather in the courtyard of the Jewish Council. It was an overcast summer day. Black birds turned in the sky. A Gestapo officer named Hans Kittel stood before them. In curt German, he read a document written in the bureaucratic language of divorce notices and tax reforms. "In the name of the Reichskommissar, I order that the Vilna Ghetto, which has been in existence for two years, be liquidated. The inhabitants of the ghetto will be removed today, partly to Estonia and partly to Latvia. The population is urged, for its own good, to obey the order quietly, pack its belongings before twelve noon, and leave the ghetto gates in an orderly manner."

On the other side of the ghetto, Abba was planning the escape of the Jewish fighters. Most of the members of the underground had already quit the ghetto. The lucky ones had made it to the woods; the unlucky had died in the fields or in the streets of Vilna. Several days before, Abba had received a note from a Soviet partisan named Yurgis, a few sentences scratched on a piece of paper. It said there had been a tragedy in Narocz, that the Germans had swept through the forest, that many of the Jewish partisans were missing, that Abba should bring his troops to Rudnicki, a forest about twelve miles south of Vilna, where Yurgis was in command. For Abba, going to Rudnicki meant losing touch with the fighters he had sent to Narocz, dividing again his already divided troops, finding his way to a strange country. It also meant a much shorter trip—twelve miles instead of fifty.

Abba sent two scouts—young Jewish girls—to travel to the Rudnicki forest, mapping a route. The girls were then to return to the ghetto and lead the fighters back to the woods. A week later, when the liquidation order was posted, the scouts had not yet returned. German and Estonian troops had surrounded the ghetto. Abba could hear the trucks idling beyond the gate. He worried that he had waited too long, leading his soldiers into a trap. One or two rebels might sneak past enemy lines. But how could thirty armed Jews get by the Germans?

With the ground blocked, Abba began to search for alternatives—covered trucks or stolen cars or disguises. He at last remembered the sewers. He sent for Shmuel Kaplinsky, who had mapped the tunnels. Shmuel was not sure the tunnels were big enough to carry the entire underground, nor did he know where the rebels would surface.

"Make a plan," said Abba.

Hours later, Shmuel emerged from the tunnels covered in filth. In the streets, he looked like a visitor from the netherworld. He went to 15 Straszun, where Abba was looking out a window, a cigarette between his knuckles. Jews were dragging their bags through the muddy streets to the ghetto gate.

"It is terrible in the sewers," said Shmuel.

"Can we make it?" Asked Abba.

"It won't be easy," said Shmuel. "The tunnel we must take is narrow in places, and we'll be lucky if the water doesn't rise and drown us. There won't be room for family or friends; there will hardly be room for us."

"Where will we come up?"

"Behind the headquarters of the German Security Police," said Shmuel. "It is the only place. It's a quiet yard."

Abba stubbed out his cigarette "I don't know if I like it."

"It's perfect," said Shmuel. "The one place the Germans never see is just under their own nose."

Abba told Vitka to be waiting in the yard behind the headquarters of the Security Police early the next morning. She said good-bye and went into the street, where the Jews gathered in the shifting overcast. It began to rain. Squeezing through a hole in the ghetto fence, Vitka pulled off her star and put a scarf over her hair. She was to find a place for the rebels to hide while waiting for the scouts. Step by step, Vitka slid into her role, changing her walk, her face, her smile, until she was just another peasant girl.

Abba went to see his mother in her dirty little ghetto flat. He told her he would flee and that only rebel fighters would be brought to the sewers, a decision that condemned thousands to the trains. It would be a hard journey, he explained. In the sewers, only those with guns and physical ability had a chance of survival. Abba's mother listened carefully. What she looked like is a mystery. No painting or picture of her survives. In the coming years, Abba's only image of her was a picture he carried in his mind, a picture that changed with his mood and the hour of the day. Sometimes he saw her as a young mother, in the peaceful days before the War, sometimes he saw her as the gaunt woman of the ghetto, and sometimes he could not see her at all. In such moments, he feared that the picture had faded from overuse. But then she would appear to him as she was on that last day, when she realized she was to be left behind. In a voice Abba could barely hear, she said, "What will become of me?"

In the afternoon, the Germans began marching Jews out of the ghetto. Pale-skinned and thin-bodied, with skinny legs and blank faces, eyes rolling, they stumbled in silence. The line snaked down a street framed with soldiers. In the back of the line, there was talk of another way out. Several people ducked into the empty streets, walked to a small building and followed steps down to a cellar where Jewish troops were cleaning their guns. Abba stood before the entrance to the sewer. Thrust in the waist of his pants was the revolver that had belonged to Isaac Wittenberg. Again and again, he told frightened Jews that they could not follow the partisans into the tunnels. Only trained soldiers could survive the ordeal. If someone argued, he rested his hand on the butt of his pistol. At one point, Rachel Glicksman turned up, the girl who, having said she could not leave her mother behind, had been rejected by the underground. Having indeed left her mother, she now begged Abba to make an exception for her and her sister.

"The sewer is closed," said Abba. "But you can go over the rooftops. It can be done. Vitka has done it many times. If you make it, meet us in the yard behind the headquarters of the German Security Police."

A short time later, a young girl came into the cellar. She had blond hair with dark roots and you could see she was scared and when she saw Abba her eyes got wide and she smiled. She had been walking in the rain and her clothes clung to every curve in her body. Abba at first did not recognize her. Then he saw that it was Vitka.

"What are you doing here?" he asked.

She told him she had been sitting on a hill on the edge of the city, from where she could see the Germans rounding up Jews and blowing up houses. "I thought it was the end," she explained. "I did not want to be alone at the end. It took me three hours to sneak back through the lines."

"You will ruin everything," said Abba. "Is that what you want? You are to meet us and lead us into hiding. Who will do that now?"

"I did not think of that," she said. "I thought only that it was the end."

"You've run a terrible risk," he said. "A senseless risk. Now, for a third time, you must get through enemy lines into the city. You must be waiting when we come up from the sewers. Do you understand? Otherwise we come up into God-knows-what."

"I just wanted to come back and see you," said Vitka.

"Well, you've come back and you've seen me and now you must go."

The library was already a piece of the past, a ruin. Shelves had been turned over, books scattered. Going through the wreckage, reading title pages and files, Ruzka was searching for evidence, something to save from the ruins. In the distance, she could hear Jews being marched through the ghetto gate. Now and then, she tossed a book into one of her canvas bags.

For hundreds of years, Vilna had been the literary home of the Jewish Diaspora, of writers who told the story of the Jews in exile; who, in dozens of books, watched Vilna rise from its green plain and fill with steeples and red roofs; who survived attacks by the Swedes and Poles; who survived Cossack hordes and the Black Hundreds, galloping across fields, burning synagogues and casting out Jews; who saw the rise of the czars, of Nicholas I, the Iron Czar, who conscripted twelve-year-old Jewish boys for thirty-year tours in the

Russian army; of Czar Alexander, who tried to convert the Jews of Vilna to Christianity.

Vilna was the home of the Yiddish theater, that great earthy forum of crass jokes and simple truths; it was the home of modern Hebrew, a language that, for over a thousand years, lived only in the Bible but then went from the synagogue to the street. It was the home of schools of philosophy and religion, political leaders and scoundrels, frock coats and beards, worsted suits and peasant smocks, buggies and sports cars and jazz and mystics and gangsters. It was, in short, a world. In his later years, Abba was troubled by the way young people, Jews and non-Jews, were taught about the Holocaust. He believed too much attention was given to the slaughter, to the gas chambers and death camps, as if this gruesome landscape rose from nothing, from nowhere. He thought that the coming generations should learn of those centuries, some of them golden, that had preceded the massacre.

Ruzka gathered maps, birth records, death notices and also copies of the manifestoes Abba had written in the ghetto. In the future, such documents would be as rare and evocative as a vase from Troy or a papyrus scroll from ancient Egypt. Ruzka left the library. She carried the bags through the streets and down to the cellar, where Abba was waiting. The other fighters had already gone, in groups of two, into the sewers, led by Shmuel Kaplinsky. Abba and Ruzka would bring up the rear, helping those who got lost in the tunnels.

Ruzka gave one of her bags to Abba and put the other bag on her back, took a last look around the cellar and climbed through the grate.

The Jews of Vilna walked from street to street, along a route lined with German security police. In the city, the windows of the buildings were misty. Rain clung to the leaves of trees. The wind, which had been blowing all afternoon, seemed to pick up as the hours went by. It turned the collars of coats as the Jews were driven to Rosa, a square with lamps and shrubs and storefronts shuttered in the rain. Jewish men were separated from women and children. Men who struggled to stay with their families were beaten. The women and children were marched into the courtyard of a monastery, where they stood all night in the rain.

In the sewers, a fighter carried a miner's lamp and Ruzka followed the flickering light. The rain coursed through the tunnels. Ruzka was sometimes on her feet, crouching through chambers, sometimes on her knees, crawling through pipes. Sometimes, face down in sewage, she had to turn her head for air. When the rebels went beneath the ancient part of Vilna, the tunnels were channels of stone. Ruzka bruised her ribs. At dinnertime, when people fixed their meals, used their faucets and flushed their toilets, the sound of water was everywhere and Ruzka felt as if she were in the circulatory system of a great animal.

When the lamp went around a corner, the darkness was unbroken. At such moments, Ruzka had to feel her way in the tunnel. She could often hear moans or sobs or a voice speaking its own name. Each sound broke in echoes. If she fell behind, her hands went numb. Abba would touch her and whisper, "You will make it, Ruzka." When she reached the others, they were stalled like a train on a siding and word came back: "Someone has fainted. Someone is blocking the sewer." At such times, the fighters were so close together they were like one being, each shiver moving from body to body. Some of these kids had been dandies on the boulevard, with parrot-colored clothes, smiles full of teeth. They were leaving on their bellies, in the rat-stink and waste, with the shit of the city, as the shit of the city.

"What's happening up there?" Ruzka whispered.

"The boy is still passed out. Maybe he is dead."

Ruzka did not know if she had been in the sewer for hours or minutes. There were times when she felt she would never again see the surface of the earth. Then she heard voices. The walls narrowed. She was climbing, her legs threatening to give way. Shmuel Kaplinsky was standing against a stone wall, face dirty, mud on his glasses. He had gone into the sewers at noon; it was now 7 p.m. After twisting and doubling back, the tunnel brought the fighters just two miles beyond the ghetto fence. Shmuel took Ruzka by the arm and pulled her up. She looked out a grate and into a courtyard. She could see grass and she could smell fresh air and summer rain and she could hear the city, and it was like climbing out of a grave.

Across the courtyard, Ruzka was met by Vitka, who was with other members of the underground. A moment later, Abba emerged from the sewer, his jacket torn and dirty. Years later, Vitka was asked how the fighters looked as they came up from the sewers. With that understatement that is so much a part of her, she said, "How did they look? Not good."

The fighters waited in the trees behind the headquarters of the Security Police, a building on Subocz Street that had once been the retreat of Pushkin, the great Russian poet. Abba divided his fighters into two groups, each of about fifteen men and women. He then led his group through a side door of the Security Police building and down a back staircase which was rarely used. Through the wall, he could hear the muffled voices of Germans. The Jews settled into the cellar, where they would hide until ordered to move out. Abba did not know the way to Rudnicki and was still awaiting the return of the scouts, who would be led by couriers to the new hiding place.

The other fighters went through the streets to Kalis, a fur factory where Jews continued to work as slave labor. Vitka had arranged for rebels to hide in the factory houses. In the streets, the fighters walked in pairs, a boy and a girl, young lovers out for a stroll. Each couple followed the couple ahead, keeping about a hundred yards apart. That way, if one couple was caught, the couple ahead or behind would have a chance to get away. Two couples were stopped by the Security Police that night. When the Germans asked to see everyone's papers, the Jews reached for their guns. A German was killed. The Jews were quickly captured. One of them was the son of Isaac Wittenberg. With hands tied behind their backs, the captured partisans were marched to Rosa, the square where the Jews of the ghetto were gathered in the rain. A German told the crowd that here were four Jews, caught with guns. The rebels were strung from the lamp-posts. They gasped and their arms fell to their sides and their tongues came out. They wore hats and heavy work shirts and were covered with mud from the tunnels. One of the girls had long blond hair and as she struggled her hat came off and her hair fell around her shoulders.

In the morning, Ukrainian soldiers walked through the Rosa square, beating the Jews of the Vilna ghetto. Women and children were then marched to a ravine, where a German, with a wave of his hand, separated healthy young adults from the children, the old and the sick. In the afternoon, fifteen hundred women were sent to Kaiserwald, a work camp in Latvia; five thousand women and children were sent to Majdanek, a death camp in Poland; several hundred sick or elderly Jews were sent to Ponar. The men had been divided into groups of seventy and loaded on trains for Klooga, a work camp in Estonia. Hundreds of country people saw the train go by, the Jews closed inside. In a Lithuanian town called Shavli, the Jews threw notes from the cars; peasants found the notes, which read, "The Vilna Ghetto is no more."

After Abba and his fighters had been two days in hiding, the scouts had still not returned from the forest. Each night, Abba studied a map, running his fingers over hills and valleys, swamps and rivers. He did not like the idea of going into the forest without a guide, but he liked the idea of staying in the city even less. On September 26, 1943, he gave the order: Abba would lead the partisans to the forest himself.

That evening, after sundown, the fighters, disguised as couples, walked past the parks and markets of the city. They smiled and laughed but beneath their skin their hearts beat with the panicked rhythm of the ghetto. It started to rain and the lights came on in the cafes. They felt like the only Jews left in the world, the last of a species. Some fighters had guns under their shirts or pistols in their pants, some carried pipes and screws that were part of a big weapon they had taken apart for the trip, some carried rifles across their backs. If these guns were hidden, the police would see something and get suspicious; but this way, the Germans would see only a peasant boy on his way to hunt in the forest.

The Jews walked past the run-down buildings at the edge of the city and into the country. The rain made streams in the road. Ahead there was a bridge that on most nights was guarded by enemy soldiers. Abba told Vitka to flirt with the Germans. The Jews would then attack the soldiers from behind. But when the Jews reached the bridge, it was raining so hard that there were no soldiers and the Jews spoke of the rain as a blessing.

In a cave a few miles beyond the city, the fighters sat out of the rain and smoked as they put together the machine gun they had broken into pieces. The rain stopped and they walked in the fields over soft swells of earth, and below they could see villages sunk in the night. In the morning, a fine mist moved on the ground and when the mist burned off they could see the fields green and glistening like etchings in an old book. The fighters stole goats and chickens, cut their throats and cooked them on a fire. At night, they slept in the wheat and barley.

Abba noted each town and river on the map. On the second day, they reached a village of small houses with open windows and laundry hung out to dry. There were sheep in the road.

"This must be Tartaki," said Abba.

Tartaki had been founded in the 1500s by Tartars who followed the hordes from Asia. It was a relic from another time. Abba asked a young Tartar if he knew the way to Rudnicki. The boy, not knowing or not caring that these were Jews, said yes, and offered to take the fighters to the forest.

He led the Jews into trails and gullies. The sky was tremendous. Some of the fighters kept their guns pointed at the horizon. In the afternoon of the third day, the fighters crossed a field and could see black birds circling. When they got closer, they could see the birds working on something in the grass. It was a body, a girl, one of the missing scouts. Her eyes had been pecked out and her throat cut. Up ahead, the road plunged into the trees.

THE FOREST

THE RUDNICKI FOREST is on the plains of southern Lithuania, a swampy, mosquito-ridden area that to locals is the backside of nowhere. Some twelve miles south of Vilna, the country, with its brooding skies and sudden storms, feels forsaken. In fine weather, the woods are pleasant. Abba would often stand on a hill in the forest, the clouds moving fast overhead, as below him paths ran to the ruined cities of Europe. He stood for hours in the hum of the deep woods, drowsy winds, afternoons skating by. Though he had been in the forest for only three weeks, already he had the warlike bearing of a partisan. His clothes were ragged, and only his gun was well kept. He lived on the forest as a gull lives on the sea. He hid in swamps and ravines. With Vitka and Ruzka at his side, and his soldiers gathered before him, Abba was part of the wilderness.

When the Jews reached Rudnicki, they could not find the way to the partisan base. They followed a trail for miles over branches and streams. The forest was so thick in places that no sunlight came through. Signs nailed to tree trunks read: "Beware! Partisans!" The muddy path ended in a swamp. There were frogs in the swamp, and snakes and bugs. Across the water, the rebels could see the smoke from the partisan fires. Abba sent Vitka to find a way around the swamp.

She was like an explorer, coasting the murky shore, hacking through brush and vine. If she stepped too close to the swamp, her boot disappeared. Mosquitoes swarmed. She realized the base was on an island in the swamp, which made it very hard to reach. At one point, she walked into the swamp, hoping it would be shallow enough to wade. A few steps from shore, weeds gathered about her and the water rose above her arms. After searching for eight hours, Vitka found a kind of bridge, a network of logs lashed across the swamp. She returned with the Jewish fighters, and they crossed one at a time.

On the other side of the swamp, as the fighters walked along a path to the partisan base, they were surrounded. There were soldiers on the ground and in the trees, guns drawn. Someone called for the Jews to halt. For a long, tense moment, the two groups were locked in a standoff. Then one of the soldiers lowered his rifle, smiled and said, "It's Abba." The other soldiers cheered and laughed. These were survivors from Narocz, those Jews who had made it out of the German trap and into Rudnicki. Vitka could not believe her eyes—Jews from Vilna but already part of the forest, gaunt and steely.

One of them said, "We will lead you into camp."

Abba's soldiers, tired and dirty, having neither showered nor shaved, nor eaten a real meal in months, marched, in parade formation, to the base, where guerrillas were gathered around fires, holding bottles of vodka by the neck, taking quick, head-clearing slugs. Some were Russians, some were peasants straight from the fields. A man in a Lithuanian police uniform led the Jewish fighters to a clearing on the edge of camp.

"You've made it to the forest," he said. "But you have come late. Until now, you have been collaborating with the enemy, doing the work of the Germans. Now we give you the chance to wash away this sin of collaboration. Now we give you the chance to fight."

The first partisans drifted into the Rudnicki forest in 1942. Some were Russian soldiers trapped behind German lines, some were Communists who fled the enemy presence in the towns and cities of Lithuania, running all the way to Moscow, where they organized a brigade. Volunteers from this brigade—the Lithuanian brigade—were dropped by parachute into the forests, where, dressed as civilians, with fake documents, counterfeit money and explosives, they harassed German supply lines, organized stranded Russian soldiers and recruited partisans. They built their base in Rudnicki around the lodges and makeshift bridges of what had once been a hunting camp for the Polish royal family.

When the partisans first reached the forest, they hacked paths in the brush and built barracks, a map room and a radio room, where officers tuned in the distant voice of Moscow. Orders were given around the fires in the center of camp, which burned night and day. Partisans left for missions at dusk. On nights when they were not on a mission, rebels danced and sang and drank wine, a home brew stolen from the local farmers. Each peasant made his own wine, so partisans might one night grow joyous with drink and the next night see visions or collapse or die.

Over time, a network of bases sprang up in the forest, turning Rudnicki into a dark place on the German map, where over a thousand partisans lived. There were two Russian camps, two Lithuanian camps and several outposts of the Polish Home Army, which took orders from the Polish government-in-exile in London. These partisans were supplied by airdrops from Moscow, or else lived off the land, stealing from peasants or from the bodies of dead Germans. Each partisan carried at least one gun, and some had three or four: two pistols, a rifle, a machine gun. The most successful partisans hid a full load of stolen gear under their greatcoats, which made them look fat and prosperous. Without a gun, a partisan was a civilian in need of protection. In the woods, losing your gun in battle was a capital offense. Each morning before sunup, the woods away from the camp filled with the curt sound of rifle fire, signaling the end of the line for offending partisans.

On their first night in the forest, the Jewish soldiers slept by the fires in the center of camp. The base was quiet and the fires burned to embers. The Soviet and Lithuanian partisans were in their barracks. Only the sentries were about. In the center of camp, a man sat over a fire with a frying pan, his face reflecting the flames. Ruzka walked over and looked in the pan, which was filled with grease and curled pieces of meat. Coming from behind, Vitka put her hand on Ruzka's shoulder. The girls sat down and watched the man. He was engaged in a sacred task, preparing meat just as his grandparents and great-grandparents had in these same woods. He gave a piece of meat to Ruzka. She looked at it and took a bite.

"Is this how everyone eats?" she asked.

"Not everyone," said the man. "Some don't have meat."

"One can live very well in the forest," he went on. "You only need to know how to manage. You are city girls, but you will learn."

"We are not here to live well," said Ruzka. "We are here to fight."

The man started to laugh. "The innocence of young girls," he said. "So ready to get yourself killed. Life should not be risked."

He looked at the fire, then said, "Survive and enjoy life."

Ruzka and Vitka went back and lay with their friends on the ground. Vitka turned over and her breath came at regular intervals. Ruzka could not sleep. She was thinking of the battles she would fight, skirmishes on country roads. She might not win these battles, but she hoped to leave evidence, a piece of scorched earth, that people could look at and say, "Here there was a fight." An hour before dawn, as partisans came in from their missions, she fell asleep.

The sky was high and clear in the morning, and it was a fresh crisp day in early October. Abba and some of the other leaders went to talk with the officers in the Soviet camp. When Abba returned, he told the Jewish fighters that they would be organized into four divisions, each with its own name. Today these names sound like parodies of the ideological age: Death to Fascism, led by Jacob Prenner; Struggle, led by Avrasha Rasel; To Victory, led by Shmuel Kaplinsky; the Avenger, led by Abba Kovner and including Vitka and Ruzka. There were fifty fighters in each division, and the four divisions together formed the Jewish Brigade, of which Abba Kovner was commander. Speaking of Abba years later, in different countries with long lives behind them, onetime partisans still frown and say, "The Commander."

The Soviet officers had told Abba to build a family camp to house the Jewish girls, who did not fit the profile of fighters. Abba refused, saying he recognized no real distinction between men and women. In these times, when there were just a handful of Jews left in Europe, and every Jew was marked for extinction, he could not afford the old prejudices. Everyone who could fight would fight. The Soviets might not understand the value of the Jewish girls, but Abba had witnessed the girls' heroism and courage in the ghetto. "The Jewish camp will be a combat camp," he said. "Military law and military discipline will apply the same to everyone."

Abba's division looked for a place to build a camp. After a short hike, they too found an island in a swamp. The partisan camps would now form an archipelago as far-flung and interdependent as the Canary Islands. Trees on the island grew at different angles and there were weeds with purple flowers that bent in the breeze and bushes of prickers and burrs. Here and there, the trees fell away and the sun was brilliant in the clearings. The fighters dug trenches, each about five feet deep, in which they built barracks, or dugouts, of pine trunks. Each dugout housed one hundred fighters who slept, side by side, on a wooden platform. To get inside, you walked down a muddy slope and ducked into the damp, earthy room, in which an average-size man could just stand. There was a door at one end and a window at the other. At night, the wind blew from the door to the window. There was a wood-burning oven made of steel drums, with a tin flue to carry the smoke through the roof. The roof was slanted so the rain and snow would run off. From a distance, these dugouts, rising a few feet above the ground and camouflaged in dirt and grass, looked like scrubby forest hills.

In the following weeks, more and more Jews were brought to the camp by Vitka, and other women fighters, from the fur factory still operating in Vilna. To Vitka, the prime mission of the partisans was to save those who could still be saved. By the autumn, over three hundred Jews were living in the forest. On wet mornings, they picked mushrooms with pale undersides and meaty caps. On dry afternoons, they crushed leaves and rolled them into Russian news-papers. The cigarettes were strong and acrid. On the edge of the camp, they dug a hole and filled it with water. Rocks heated in the campfires were dropped into the hole, creating a hot, bubbling bath.

As many of the new arrivals did not have guns, a caste system soon developed. Abba, who, with the other partisan leaders, lived apart from the soldiers in a dugout where he wrote his poems, devised a solution: Those leaving on a mission or about to go on duty as sentries would check weapons out of an armory, which they would then return on completion of the mission or tour of duty. In this way, hundreds of people could participate in the partisan war, which, Abba believed, was the only way to restore the self-respect of the ghetto Jew.

One afternoon, a Soviet officer walked into the Jewish camp. He was short, with sturdy shoulders, a broad chest and a bushy mustache. His face was brown and windburned, and his white teeth dazzled with the contrast. He could have stepped from the pages of Tolstoy. He asked to see Uri, the code name Abba had gone by in the ghetto.

A sentry asked, "Who is here to see Uri?"

"Yurgis."

Yurgis was a forty-year-old Communist. A schoolteacher before the War, he had also edited a local party newspaper called *Truth*. When Vilna fell, he fled to Russia, where he joined the Lithuanian Brigade. As one of the first men to parachute behind enemy lines, he was the commander of the Soviet camps, a leader of the partisan war in the East. He ducked into Abba's dugout and welcomed him to the forest. He then said that the Jewish Brigade must be disbanded; the Jews would be merged into the Lithuanian Brigade.

"I disagree," said Abba. "We are killed as Jews, we should fight as Jews."

"Are you a Communist?" asked Yurgis.

"No."

"You are a Zionist."

"Yes," said Abba.

Yurgis thought a moment, then said, "If there is a Jewish brigade in the forest, the peasants will come to see the partisans as a Jewish movement. The peasants will never support that. They don't like Jews."

"Who cares if they like me?" asked Abba.

"Be pragmatic," said Yurgis. "The peasants might give us food or guns; but if they think we are Jews, they will fight against us. We want to win a war—not stand on principle. Why make life more difficult?"

"We must fight as we died," said Abba.

"It is not only the peasants who will resist," said Yurgis. "You will also have trouble with the other partisans, the Russians and Lithuanians."

"We must fight as Jews," said Abba.

"Do Jews have a different goal in their war against the Nazis?" asked Yurgis.

"We have a special desire to avenge the things done to our families," said Abba. "It was not the citizens of Lithuania who were annihilated. It was the Jews, and the desire for revenge is so powerful that it must be held in high regard."

"You're from Lithuania," said Yurgis. "You are a Lithuanian. You must fight with the Lithuanian Brigade."

"When they were pushing us into the ghetto, were we Lithuanians then?" asked Abba. "No. We were not Lithuanian. We are not Lithuanian because the Lithuanians would not have us. They see us as Jews. The Germans see us as Jews. We are Jews."

"What is it you want?"

"We want to continue in the forest what we started in the ghetto," said Abba. "We want to prove that you cannot wipe out a people, that some of the people will fight on. And as for the other partisans—it makes no difference whether or not a separate Jewish unit exists. If Jews were to meet with non-Jews in mixed units, they would face the same danger, the same hatred."

Yurgis never again questioned the existence of a Jewish Brigade. Abba liked to believe his arguments had swayed Yurgis, but he knew the Russian must have had reasons of his own.

Several days later, Yurgis visited the Jewish camp to congratulate some of the partisans, who had just returned from a successful mission. He shook Abba's hand and looked at the Jewish soldiers, who swayed around the fire, singing Yiddish songs. Yurgis had tears in his eyes. "I cannot believe it," Abba said to himself. "Yurgis is a Jew."

One evening, Vitka walked to the Soviet camp, where the partisans were preparing for a mission. The sun was down by the time she reached the base and there was a chill in the air. Winter was coming. She stood by the fire, touched by the sight of the soldiers leaving for battle, filling packs and loading rifles. A broad-faced man, carrying three guns and a bottle of vodka, asked her to drink with him.

"I do not drink," she said.

"It's for luck," said the soldier.

"Good luck," she said. "But I don't drink."

The soldier filled a glass. "To your health and life," he said, tossing back the vodka.

He refilled the glass and handed it to Vitka.

"No," she said.

"I drink to you," he said, "you must drink to me."

As Vitka raised the glass, an officer said something to the soldier, and, as he turned to answer, Vitka tossed the vodka on the ground. The Russian looked at the pool of vodka. "Always I've defended the Jews," he said. "Now I know why people hate them."

In the forest, most of the partisans were poor country people, raised to hate Jews. For the Jews, fighting was the only option. It was fight and die, or don't fight and still die. The Polish and Lithuanian partisans had chosen to fight—for adventure, plunder, ideology—but mostly to rid their country of a foreign enemy. Yet to many of these partisans, Jews were an even more odious foreign presence than the Germans. And so, even though the Lithuanians and Poles now shared a common enemy with the Jews, they did not consider Jews friends, or even allies. At their campfires they sang anti-Semitic songs. Russian partisans offered to trade weapons for Jewish girls, who were among the only women in the woods. If Jewish and Polish partisans met on a path away from camp, there might be a fight. The next day a Jew would be missing, or else he would stumble into a roll call dazed but triumphant, a Polish pistol in his pants. For Jews, every exit was an entrance to another trap.

As the partisans in the Jewish camp were having dinner one night, there was a scream and gunfire. The soldiers ran to the edge of camp, where a Jewish girl stood next to the bathing hole. A Russian partisan was holding her wrist and waving a pistol. He was covered in water. "I will kill you," he said. On the ground was an empty bucket. The man was a famous fighter, known for single-handed assaults and all-or-nothing attacks. On some nights, he would drink an entire bottle of vodka and his voice would echo in the trees. He had served for a time in the south, near a camp of Jewish refugees. It had been his habit to go to the camp, pick a Jewish girl and rape her.

"What do you think you are doing?" asked Abba. "This girl is a human being."

The Russian had lived in a world where Jews could be abused without consequence. "Leave now," said Abba, "and you won't be killed."

When Yurgis heard the story, he told Abba, "This is a terrible thing, but you must take a lesson from it. This is a bad man, but he is a very good fighter. I think the Jews must learn to be a little cruel like this man."

In a clearing on the edge of camp, Abba went over the details of one of the partisan missions. The Jews would hike across the river to Drogozha, a village where a pro-German peasant family was said to be hiding pistols and rifles, which the Jews were to capture. Only a few of the partisans had guns for the mission. Joseph Harmatz, who wore a khaki jacket swiped from a Lithuanian officer and wool pants taken from a dead German, carried the camp's most prized possession, a Kalashnikov submachine gun. Abba had the pistol that Isaac Wittenberg had given him. Ruzka and Vitka, and many of the others, carried wooden cutouts, which Abba hoped would in the dark look like real rifles.

Abba led the fighters—there were about twenty of them—out from the camp at night, when the moon was on the horizon. At his side was a scout from a nearby town, a young boy who was to guide the Jews through the network of forest trails. Because the peasants did not like Jews, it was hard to recruit guides. The boy, who was risking his life and the lives of his family, was promised a share in the spoils of the raids. He led the partisans out of the forest. The evening mist was settling. The Jews followed a dirt road for miles, through valleys and scrub, across a single-lane bridge, into a town of steep-roofed houses. They stopped at a house in the fields. Through a win-

Abba Kovner.

dow, Abba could see splintered floorboards and a table with a family sitting at dinner. Grandmother. Father. Mother. Two sons. A shotgun leaned against a wall. Abba sent Vitka around to the back of the house. "If you see anyone," he said, "shout." He told two of his men to wait at the front door, while the others watched the road.

Abba took a deep breath and walked into the house, passing through the rooms with swift, confident strides. As the floorboards creaked, the family looked up from the table. Abba, who had his pistol trained on them, picked up the shotgun and tossed it to one of his soldiers.

Abba told the family that he was a Jewish partisan.

The father said he supported the partisans; the mother burst into tears; the grandmother kept on eating.

Abba told one of his men to send a courier, get the troops, secure the perimeter. "I want this town surrounded," he said.

When the partisan asked how many troops to deploy, Abba thought a moment, then said, "Two thousand."

The partisan marched through the door where the Jewish guards stood in silhouette, their phony rifles against the dark sky.

Looking at the father of the family, Abba said, "We have come for your weapons."

The old man said there were no weapons.

Abba cocked his gun. "Hand them over."

The woman sobbed. "Someone has tricked you," said the man. "There are no weapons."

The woman wiped her eyes, then asked the partisans to sit down to dinner. "Please," she said. "Please, eat with us." Abba and a few other fighters sat down. The woman passed plates of meat and bread. The Jews ate quickly, wiping their plates clean with the bread. Abba thanked the woman. He had almost decided that the old man was telling the truth, that he should leave, when he heard Vitka shout. He jumped from the table and ran outside. A man was racing across the yard. He was a young man, probably a friend of one of the sons. Abba chased him into the barn, where the man had pulled up a trapdoor and taken out a rifle. He was trying to get a shell in the chamber. Abba ordered him to stop. The man dropped the gun and raised his hands. Abba marched him to the house.

Abba told one of his soldiers to take the father outside. The mother asked Abba what he wanted with the old man. "Give us the guns," said Abba, "or we will shoot him." She told Abba that there were no more guns; he now had everything. Abba called out the order to kill the old man. A single shot came from the fields. Abba told his men to bring one of the sons outside.

"Where are the guns?"

"You have the guns," said the woman.

Grabbing the woman by the arm, Abba dragged her across the yard and into the barn, where a broken-down old horse was tied up.

"Saddle the horse," said Abba. "We will take the horse."

The woman said she would not survive the winter without the horse.

"Saddle the horse."

With slumped shoulders, the woman led Abba back to the house and up to the attic, removed a false door and handed him rifles, pistols and a machine gun. The father and his son were then brought back inside; the partisans had fired their guns in the air.

On the way back to the forest, Abba handed out the new weapons. The fighters broke apart the wooden cutouts and left them by the side of the road.

At the end of autumn, the heavy rains blew in from the East and the paths were muddy and dead branches were carried in the swollen streams. In the Russian camp, a soldier, after listening to the radio, would write up reports, which told of the Allied summit meeting in Teheran, of Red Army victories, of the coming winter offensive. The Russians, in quilted coats and felt-lined shoes, were better suited for cold-weather fighting than the Germans, who suffered in paper-thin boots that they called "dice boxes."

One night, Abba, on a visit to the Russian base, heard Adolf Hitler on the radio:

> Of all the Jews of Europe, there will remain only enough to fill an automobile to be driven around as an exhibit.

Abba frowned and said, "The problem is, every Jew in Europe thinks he should be the one to get the free ride in the automobile."

There were over three hundred Jews in camp, and the most important task was keeping them alive. At night, Abba sent partisans to steal food and guns. About twenty fighters went on each mission. The partisans wanted to raid only those peasants who were pro-German, and often walked miles to reach a particular house. If a farmer had two cows, they took only one. A raid might yield a cow, two pigs, a horse, a sack of potatoes. If the partisans found someone helping the enemy, they went out of their way to kill him. If these same peasants helped out the partisans, however, the Germans exacted a far harsher punishment. When a boy in a town near Rudnicki gave information to the partisans, a German unit invaded the town, drove the people into their wooden houses and set the houses on fire. All that remains of the town today is a clearing and a statue of a weeping woman.

The peasants in the nearby villages began to resist the Jewish partisans. It was one thing to be raided by the Lithuanians; being raided by the Jews was something else. The farmers would spit on the Jews, or hide food and guns. Unlike Poles or Lithuanians, Jews had no friendly population to fall back on. Villages organized militias, which were supplied by the Germans. A system of couriers and flares was devised. When Jewish partisans were spotted—some peasants claimed they could recognize Jews at a distance—a rocket was sent above the trees. In the next village, when a sentry saw the rocket, he sent up another, until rockets were going up in town after town. Gathering in dusty squares, the peasants would hand out guns and hide along the road and wait to ambush the Jews.

Yurgis told Abba to disguise his troops. If the Jews wore quilted coats like the Russians or short boots like the Poles, they would be less easy to identify. Like many progressives, Yurgis wanted Jews to look like everyone else. Abba refused, saying that fighting as a Jew meant being hated by peasants; it meant being alone and not being ashamed of being alone.

Abba instead responded with force, meeting every threat with gunfire. If a partisan met a peasant in the forest, the partisan would kill the peasant before he could sound the alarm. On raids, the Jews, taking no chances, shot their way into towns and shot their way out, sometimes even killing civilians, women and children. The War remade the Jews in its own image.

Around campfires, the partisans talked about Jewish rebels captured by the Germans, horror stories that reminded them of the cost of failure. There was the SS soldier in Lublin who hung Jewish partisans by the scrotum; there was a Nazi official named Arthur Greiser who burned Jewish partisans at the stake; there was a baron in Cracow who tortured Jewish partisans with a thumbscrew and an iron boot; there was Fritz Katzman, an SS general who fed Jewish partisans spasmodic poison, then, seated with his guests, watched them die as he ate dinner; there was the German who tossed Jewish partisans into a pit of starving wolves; there was an officer who strapped Jewish partisans to a crude version of the rack; there was Von Herff, an SS lieutenant who blinded Jewish partisans with a hot poker and left them to wander back to their camps as a warning to the others.

Reinhardt Heydrich, the assassinated Gestapo chief, had once explained such behavior as the only way to treat those Jews who had somehow escaped the German apparatus of slavery and death camps. "The remnant that finally is able to survive all this—as this is undoubtedly the part with the strongest resistance—must be treated accordingly, since these people, representing a natural selection, are to be regarded as the germ cell of a new Jewish development."

One morning, as some Jewish partisans returned from a mission, they met a man in civilian clothes, leaning on a tree, studying a map. His skin was as rough as the bark of the tree and he had a broad, steely face. From one look, it was clear that he was a soldier, that he had traveled a great distance, that he had killed many men. He was dressed like a farmer, in a bulky coat, wool pants and boots, and he carried a knife, a pistol and a machine gun. Stick bombs hung from his belt. Like the wolf Vitka had seen in the forest, he had the fierce ease of a creature surveying its territory. One of the Jews asked the man where he was going.

"I'm looking for Yurgis," he said. "Who are you?"

"A Jewish partisan."

"Who is your leader?" asked the man. "Kovner?"

"Yes," said the partisan.

The man said something in Yiddish and the Jewish partisan answered in Yiddish.

The man was Isser Schmidt, a Jewish Communist who had grown up in a town nearby. When the Germans invaded, he fled down the jammed-up country roads. In Russia, he joined the Lithuanian Brigade, 20 percent of which was Jewish. The soldiers trained beneath the winter skies of Gorky, Stuka dive-bombers buzzing overhead. They ate in mess halls ringing with voices, took leave on desolate boulevards, bars and brothels, smoky Russian nights. One afternoon, a Russian general asked the brigade for volunteers, men who would jump into the forests behind enemy lines. Isser raised his hand and was sent to Moscow. He was taught to blow up trains, make bombs and kill Germans.

Isser Schmidt jumped into Belorussia in 1943 on a night so dark he could not see his parachute. There were six other men on the jump, each in civilian clothes. Isser felt his chute yank open as the cold air burned his face and the trees rose to meet him. On his phony papers, Schmidt, who would command the mission, was identified as Davidovski. He led his men through the countryside, recruiting and sabotaging. A few months later, when he reached Rudnicki, he was anxious to join the partisans and put his men under Yurgis, whom he had known as a Communist before the War. Yurgis scattered the new men among various battalions, with Isser sent to the Jewish Brigade.

Isser would be a kind of special agent, a policeman who would examine every word and action, rooting out subversives. He gazed into each face and seemed to know all the secrets, all the dark places. This was a war without fronts; soldiers dressed as peasants and peasants dressed as soldiers; no one was trusted. In camp, Isser questioned new recruits, looking for spies, Poles and Germans who went into the forest dressed as partisans. It might be their uniforms, too new, or their guns, too well kept, or their accents, too perfect, or their hometowns, which they knew nothing specific about—but something gave them away. A trial would be held. When it was over, Isser would lead the man down a forest trail. Neither a Zionist nor a foot soldier, he was the wordless expression of history, the terror of the next fifty years. If he came to dislike you, it was the end of your adventures.

Isser often spoke with Vitka and he was moved by the stories she told of the ghetto, of Jewish policemen who bought their lives with the lives of others. He took to hunting Jews who collaborated with the Germans. He was capable of that brand of sentimentality that is just the other side of cruelty. In the winter of 1943, he grew suspicious of Natek Ring, a Jewish policeman from the ghetto. In the forest, Ring had traded his green uniform for partisan gear. One morning, at roll call, he did not answer to his name. The next day, he returned to base, saying he had been to see his mother hiding in Vilna. Abba asked him why he had not gotten permission to leave; Ring said he did not need permission to see his own mother.

Ring was charged with collaborating. In the ghetto, Jews had seen him lead enemy soldiers to rooms where people were hiding. On his latest venture, he had moved through the city with surprising ease; some felt he was even now working for the Germans. Isser was bareheaded as he led Natek Ring into the trees. Two shots and the birds stopped singing. Isser came back down the trail alone, wearing a fur cap and new boots.

Years later, Natek Ring's mother told the story to an Israeli newspaper. She said that Abba Kovner had sentenced her son to die for going to see his mother. Asked to comment, Abba said only that things were done with haste in the forest, it was war and life-and-death decisions were made quickly. "Unfortunately, in partisan conditions, it is not always possible to see into the soul of a man."

A few weeks after he reached the forest, Isser Schmidt led the Jews on their first sabotage mission, a forty-mile hike to blow up a munitions train. Five partisans went on the raid, four men and Ruzka. It was the first time a woman had gone on such a mission. The few women in the forest were the wives of commanders or prostitutes brought for the partisans. Yurgis believed women would endanger the raids. Abba said the girls, who had faced the same danger in the ghetto, must be given the same chance to fight. Ruzka, not as graceful as Vitka or as farsighted as Abba, was the toughest fighter in the camp. Abba knew she could prove the value of the Jewish women. Yurgis just shrugged, as if to say, "It's your mistake to make."

Isser led the partisans out of camp in the early evening. It was cold and the water in the streams was frozen mid-current. Each fighter had a gun and two grenades. Ruzka, very small, insisted on taking a turn carrying the mine, which weighed over fifty pounds. As she came out of the forest, she could see the cold winter stars, the galaxies turning in their vortexes. Isser led the soldiers south on country roads. They soon reached a frozen river with bubbles in the ice and water moving under the surface. A tree trunk was laid bank to bank. Isser went first, carrying the mine, slipping, catching himself, reaching the far shore. Ruzka crossed slowly, feet apart, one step at a time. Looking down, she could see cracks in the ice. She missed a step and threw up her arms and plunged into the water. She caught the log with her hands but her legs were numb and her boots heavy as she hauled herself up. She got to her feet and crossed the river.

Isser looked at Ruzka, her pants frozen, water dripping from her boots. "We are a short distance from base," he said. "You can be back in less than an hour."

Ruzka stared at him.

"Start back now," he said, "or you will freeze to death."

"I must talk to you alone," said Ruzka.

A few feet down the bank, Ruzka said, "I will not go back."

"I order you," said Isser.

"I refuse the order," said Ruzka. "You will have to put a bullet in my head to keep me from this mission."

Isser looked at Ruzka. Her eyes were clear and she held his gaze. "Very well," he said.

A few miles down the road, the partisans broke into a house and stole dry clothes for Ruzka. These were men's clothes and Ruzka rolled the sleeves of the work shirt and stuffed socks into the toes of the boots.

In the morning, the partisans reached the railroad. Isser could not find the bridge he wanted to mine; he broke into a house, where a young man was sleeping, boots at the edge of his bed. Isser prodded the man with his gun. As he opened his eyes, Isser said, "We have come to blow up the railroad bridge near here. Take us."

The young man said he knew nothing of a railroad bridge.

"In that case," said Isser, "we will shoot you."

The man dressed and led the fighters to the wooden bridge. It was built over a steep ravine and underlaid by a web of supports. Isser carried the mine onto the tracks. He worked quickly, tying the mine beneath the bridge and running a fuse into the trees. The partisans held a gun on the peasant. He would be freed after the blast, when he would be a part of the crime. Just after dawn, Ruzka spotted the train breaking into a turn, smoke rising from its funnel. On the wheels it said: To Victory. When the engine coasted onto the bridge, Isser pulled the fuse. There was a flame and then a blast. The train smashed through the wooden beams and went into the ravine. Smoke drifted from the wreckage. There were shouts and more explosions as the munitions in the train ignited. The partisans ran into the trees, the sky filling with rockets and tracers—scratchy lines in the morning sky.

A few days later, Yurgis got a report from his scouts. Fifty soldiers had been killed and a storehouse of German weapons destroyed in the explosion. Ruzka did not speak of the mission, or of her role in other battles. She felt the stories were too important to be spoken in the voice of one person, that it was the collective fate of the Jewish people that mattered. This was her religion. It is a paradox that a religion that discounts the individual gave her the strength to leave a record of bravery that is a testament to the individual. If Ruzka was forced to speak of herself, if a story hung on some victory that she had achieved, she disguised herself, moving into the third person. Ruzka became a nameless girl from Poland who did what anyone would have done. Only at the end of her life, living in Israel, surrounded by children and grandchildren, did she speak in the first person. Her family knew she was sick, but only Ruzka knew she was dying. One afternoon, her daughter, Yonat, asked about her past.

"You know the story," said Ruzka.

"I know about the group," said Yonat. "I want to hear about you."

"It's not important," said Ruzka.

"To me it is," said Yonat. "It is my story too."

Only then did Ruzka speak of herself, a Jewish girl from Poland, typical in every way, who happened into the worst place in history.

The Russian commander told Abba he wanted to attack Vilna. A raid on the city—a German stronghold—would demonstrate the strength of the partisans, and perhaps convince others to revolt. The Russians had the sophisticated weapons required for such a mission, which was of the into-the-lions'-den variety. But they did not have the couriers, guides who really knew the streets. For that, they wanted to borrow a few Jewish girls. Abba thought it over, then said: "If you want our help, fine. But it has to be a Jewish mission: Jewish soldiers, Jewish orders."

The commander asked what role that would leave the Russians; Abba said, "You will give us the weapons."

On the eve of Yom Kippur, two boys and two girls left the Jewish camp dressed as peasants. One of the girls, in a scarf and a fur coat, carried a battered suitcase, the kind you might see a farmer carrying on the road to town. This was Vitka. In the suitcase were magnetic mines, time bombs which would stick to any metal surface.

The group followed the road through the frozen country and into the hills on the edge of Vilna. Below them, the city dealt in its traffic of trucks and soldiers, the ghosting progress of the occupation. By sundown, the partisans had reached the fur factory, where a few hundred Jews still worked as slaves. Vitka spoke with Sonia Madejsker, a Jewish Communist who lived in a factory house. Sonia, with blond hair and big eyes, was the partisans' only link to the underground that still operated in Vilna. She told Vitka the fur factory would soon be shut down, the Jews sent to concentration camps. A group of these workers wanted to flee with Vitka to the forest. Yurgis had already told the Jews to cut back on the number of people living in their camp as refugees. In most cases, these Jews had no battle experience, could not fire a weapon, did not want to learn. In the forest, they wanted only to wait out the War; still, they had to be fed and clothed.

Vitka Kempner.

Vitka told all this to Sonia, and then said she had come to the city not as a humanitarian but as a soldier.

"These people go to the forest," said Sonia, "or they die."

Vitka said she would make a decision after the mission.

The partisans spent the night in the fur factory. In the morning, Vitka went alone to the city. Wandering the twisting streets, past crowds of soldiers and girls in school uniforms, she closed her eyes and muttered. The stores were open, the newsstands posted head-lines—life went on as before. For a moment, she felt as if she had never been born. On the avenue, down which the Jews had been driven to the ghetto, a normal street coursing with normal weekday traffic, she was overcome with hatred. It was a great reassurance. It proved that she had been born, that she was as much a part of this world as the schoolgirls and the soldiers. You cannot count on the love of your fellow man, she knew that. You cannot count on the decency of your neighbors, she knew that too. Nor can you count on tomorrow looking like today. But hate—you can count on hate. Vitka found herself in the industrial quarter, beneath the towers and smokestacks, looking for targets. Back at the fur factory, she told the others her plan: the boys would hit the waterworks, which supplied the sewers and taps, while the girls hit the electrical transformers, which gave the city light.

After sunset, the partisans drifted into the city. The squares of the city were crowded with soldiers on leave, a current of voices. It was the moment when, a few years earlier, Jews had broken their holiday fasts, sitting down to big, steamy family dinners. The boys left the girls on the street, promising to meet at the fur factory in an hour. The boys let the crowd carry them, past houses and buildings, to the waterworks. In front of the building, there was a manhole. The boys circled the block until the street was empty. Then, one of the boys—his name was Mates Levin and he had been trained as a plumber—lifted up the manhole cover. The second boy climbed in and Levin followed. When his eyes adjusted, he could see the iron ladder stretching below and the pipes going in every direction. It was a great switching station that carried water across the city. Crawling to the junction of the pipes, Levin attached two mines with a click. He set the timer for four hours. He then climbed up, lifted the manhole cover, looked out, saw no one coming, and scrambled into the street.

The girls were on the other side of the city, in the factory sprawl along the river. Tugboats and barges lined the banks and there were foghorns and factory whistles and gulls rising from the dumps. The electrical transformers were spooky grids that hummed in the night sky. They were not protected, not even by a fence. Now and then, there was a pop and a current buzzed up the coils. Vitka put a mine on one of the metal grids; it slid to the ground. The transformer was covered in paint and the mines would not stick. Vitka, in a fury, scratched at the transformer, stripping away the paint, which made her fingers bleed. When German soldiers walked down the street, the girls hid in the shadows, holding their breath, watching them pass. It took maybe twenty minutes, but the girls managed to scrape away enough paint so the mines would stick. They set the timers for four hours.

The boys were waiting in the fur factory. They were tired and wanted to sleep the night and return to the forest in the morning. Vitka said that the partisans must leave at once, before the bombs went off. The Germans would tighten security after the explosions; the roads would be impassable. Every inch of the city would be searched. By staying in the factory, the boys would endanger not only their own lives but the lives of every Jew in the factory. The boys said the Germans would never suspect Jews of such a daring attack. It was a terrific fight, and it went on and on. At last, Vitka, running out of time, gave up. She told Sonia to prepare the Jews who were ready to go; she would take them to the forest.

An hour later, Vitka was leading sixty Jews down the dark road. In the hills, she could hear the explosions, one after another, coming from different points in the city. Turning, she could see the lights go out in the windows and the streets go black and Vilna disappear in the darkness.

The boys left the city the next day. They were picked up by a German patrol and never heard from again. "We made it and the boys did not," says Vitka, "because they were tired and we were tired too but the women were stronger than the men."

The first snow fell. It blew down from the mountains and bent the pine trees. The Germans could follow footprints in the snow and so the partisans learned to be careful. They filled in their tracks, walked on frozen streams, followed circuitous routes back to camp. Each night, Jewish soldiers roamed the frozen valleys, with rifles and grenades, bombing outposts, vanishing in a hail of bullets. Farmers trudging across their snowy fields would see a flash on the hills and then hear the explosion. The partisans were engaged mostly in sabotage, blowing up trains and bridges. At first, they used a mine set off by a long fuse: pull the fuse, bang! But the partisans had to stay very close to the tracks until after the explosion, and the Germans learned to spot the fuse. So Abba, working with the Pensov brothers, who were partisans, invented a new kind of mine, which kept the partisans out of danger. It had a fuse made of pencil lead. As a train went over, the fuse snapped, setting off the bomb.

In 1944, Jewish partisans destroyed fifty-one trains, hundreds of trucks and dozens of bridges. Now and then, the Russians parachuted a newspaper reporter into the forest, and there are grainy photos of trains sabotaged by the Jews. Boxcars lie in a heap, the train rails shot to pieces or rerouted in some unexpected direction, or else the rails hang together but have buckled and warped into corkscrews, like something in a surrealist painting. In some pictures, partisans stand next to the wreckage in the manner of a fisherman showing a catch. When the Russians sabotaged a train, they laid the mine and fled. The Jews waited for the blast. As the train crashed, they shouted, "That is for Ponar."

The Jewish partisans were often short of weapons. What they gathered on raids could never replace what they shot off at night. Yurgis promised the brigade bombs, pistols, machine guns. But when the airdrops came, the Jews were in line behind Russians and Lithuanians; they received only leftovers, or nothing at all. Abba said the shortage would not stop the missions. If the Jews did not have bombs, they went out with pistols. If they did not have pistols, they went out with nothing. Using their bare hands, they tore down telephone poles and ripped up telegraph wires. Sweating through long winter nights, they heaved up train rails and hid the debris. When the train steamed into the clearing, the conductor—too late, too late—would spot the gap in the tracks. The brakes would screech and the train would roll into the soft snow, partisans hollering and running into the trees.

One night a partisan group, led by Abba, broke into a chemical factory and stole drums of fuel, which they hauled to a bridge on the Vilna–Grodno highway, a road frequented by enemy convoys. The partisans tied dead pine needles into bundles, soaked the bundles in fuel and lashed them to the bridge. Abba turned over the drums, spilling the fuel. A partisan lit a bundle of needles and raced across the bridge, spreading the fire. From a distance, you would have seen a frozen river spanned by flames. There was a German outpost across the river. A detachment of soldiers soon reached the bridge. There was no way to cross the river, so the Germans just stood looking at the Jews; and the Jews looked back. After several minutes, Abba shouted the command and his soldiers retreated into the forest.

Rebel bands had begun to appear throughout Europe. During the peak of the fighting, the Germans lost close to a thousand trains a month to partisans, and millions of dollars' worth of equipment. Vast stretches of the East, which lived in open defiance of German rule, were known as "partisan republics." In Lvov, Poland, the partisans surprised a Nazi in bed. A few days later, his head, and the heads of twelve other SS men, turned up on posts on the edge of town. In Czechoslovakia, partisans assassinated Reinhard Heydrich, chief of the Gestapo; in retaliation the Germans destroyed the village of Lidice and killed all the men. For the most part, though, German soldiers met the partisans on dark roads or forest tracks, in quick, brutal skirmishes. Field Marshal Kesselring, a German commander who fought the partisans in northern Italy, commented on the fighting with a stunning lack of self-awareness: "My reading of history and firsthand acquaintance with guerrilla warfare have led me to the conclusion that it is a degenerate form of war," he wrote. "In small groups, [the partisans] ran amok, doing their nefarious work in woods and on roads, under cover of darkness or fog—but never openly. To the work of these bands must be ascribed acts of sabotage to military installations, dumps, railways, roads, bridges and telegraph lines and equally frequent crimes against humanity. Only on a few exceptional occasions did the bands accept a fair fight; once they had stealthily done their mischief, they melted away among the civilian population or as innocent hikers."

By the winter of 1944, there were 250,000 Axis troops fighting in the Partisan War. Most of these soldiers were Ukrainians or Poles or Lithuanians or Estonians or Latvians. But there were also twenty thousand German regulars fighting, which amounted to three divisions of the Wehrmacht. These soldiers, many of them in the Special Police, carried machine guns, grenades, rocket-launchers and flame-throwers. In detachments of forty or fifty, with trucks or half-tracks, they swept through the country, killing an average of two thousand people during each mission. They responded to partisan raids with collective punishment, massacres that often wiped out entire towns.

The Nazi soldier leading the Partisan War in the East was Erich von dem Bach-Zelewski, an SS general born in western Poland. He was dark-eyed and broad-shouldered. His two sisters had each married a Jew, which must have made for memorable family discussions. Fighting for Germany in World War I, Bach-Zelewski was twice wounded and twice decorated. He joined the Nazi party in 1930, and quickly developed into a famed street fighter. In 1942, shortly after Germany invaded Russia, he was sent to a hospital suffering from a nervous breakdown. In a lucid moment, he grabbed a doctor and said, "Don't you know what's happening in Russia? The Jewish people is being exterminated."

Bach-Zelewski, who recovered and continued to battle the partisans, was responsible for thousands of deaths. After the War, he cut a deal, agreeing to testify at Nuremberg against other captured Nazis. One day, while he was on the stand, Hermann Goering, who in Germany had ranked only behind Hitler, jumped to his feet and shouted, "That dirty, bloody treacherous swine! That filthy skunk! Goddamn *Donnerwetter,* dirty son of a bitch! He was the bloodiest murderer in the whole goddamned setup!"

As Bach-Zelewski was led out of the courtroom, Goering spat in his face and yelled, "*Schweinehund und Verräter!*"

In the first weeks of 1944, Vitka went to gather firewood, pulling at dead branches, low on the big trees, until they splintered and cracked, revealing the good sand-colored wood inside. She wore heavy boots and a ratty coat. Her eyes were clear and brown. She had grown strong in the forest. The wind blew dark clouds from the East. It was afternoon but already it felt like night. The skies opened just as she made it back to camp, the snow so heavy it extinguished the campfires. In dugouts, partisans huddled over steel drums, feeding their small fires. When the wind blew into the chimneys, the flames flattened and smoke filled the dugouts. "The night of the storm is etched in my memory," Ruzka later wrote. "It was one of the most amazing experiences in the forest."

In the middle of the night, there was a big gust of wind, a splintering, a crash and screams. Several partisans, wanting to see what had happened, ran out into the blinding sheets of snow. A tree had fallen across one of the dugouts, pinning two girls. The partisans lifted the tree and carried the girls, through the snow, to a dugout where the sick were treated. One girl was covered in cuts; her injuries were not serious. The other girl had been hit in the head, her skull fractured. She was going into shock. The doctor, who had come with the partisans Vitka had led back from Vilna, was not in camp, having gone that morning to treat a man in a village ten miles away; there was little chance of his making it back very soon. The partisans did their best for the girl, warming her hands and making her talk. But she needed real help.

Then, in the early morning, when hope was almost lost, the doctor appeared out of the storm, carrying his bag. His eyelashes were icy, shoulders covered in snow. He examined the girl. A piece of the tree had gone into her skull. He opened his bag and spread out the tools he had smuggled from the ghetto, well-kept and shiny. He needed to operate. In the dugout, the only light came from the fire in the steel drum. Now and then, the wind came down the chimney and blew out the fire. The partisans lit it again and again. For the most part, the doctor had to operate by feel. Sometimes there was a flash of lightning and he could see the girl and how his work was going. The nerves had been severed in her right eye, but he was able to dig the bark from her skull and close the wound. She would survive the War.

When the doctor finished, he stood in the door of the dugout, smoking a cigarette. The storm had blown over and the sun was rising. The snow was piled on the dugouts and the paths were buried and everything was hushed and strange in the snow.

Gum disease, flu, scurvy, lice, stomach pains, scabies, rickets—these were just a few of the ailments from which the partisans suffered. The dugouts let in the bad weather, water dripping through the rooftops, soldiers shivering in the wind or waking in puddles of mud. Some plugged the leaks or looked for a better place, but most just figured to hell with it, rolled over and went back to sleep. Either they were ill, felt an illness coming on, or were just recovering from illness. Many suffered from pneumonia. The diet in camp was the same day after day. Meat and potatoes. Meat and potatoes. Meat and potatoes. Citrus fruit was a memory from another world. There were few vitamins, and so the partisans had sores in their mouths and on their hands. Like deckhands on a whaling ship, they lived and died with the weather.

In the winter, Abba put Ruzka in charge of the health of the camp. She had always been attuned to suffering, one of those people who address their own needs by addressing the needs of others. She set up a laundry. Though some partisans were married and had wives who helped them wash and mend clothes, most were bachelors, and wore a shirt or a pair of pants until it was torn and lice-ridden. Ruzka ordered partisans to bring their clothes, twice a week, to a pit, where they were boiled in water and ashes. When a fighter returned from a mission with frostbite, she pulled off his shoes and examined his black, swollen feet. In severe cases, she sent the fighter to the doctor, who, with his shiny tools, cut off one or two toes, or an entire foot. The partisan would hobble out to the fire and sit cursing into the flames.

There was rarely any bread in camp. If, by some miracle, a partisan returned from a raid with bread, Ruzka cut it into tiny slices, giving pieces to only the sickest people in the camp. Extra rations were stored against emergencies. At times, a sort of hysteria swept through camp. On one occasion, a few partisans broke into the storeroom and stole some loaves of bread. These men were caught, tried and sentenced to death. "This incident caused great anxiety in camp and was a powerful lesson," Ruzka later wrote. "The thefts ceased. What could not be achieved through education, coaxing, and appealing to conscience and justice, was achieved all at once through the trial and the sentence."

A few times a month, transport planes left Moscow, flew across Russia and into enemy territory, dodged German fighter planes and the rackety-tat of antiaircraft guns, then dropped supplies, by parachute, into the dense forests of Lithuania. For partisans, meeting the drops meant waiting all night in the cold for planes that sometimes did not come; it depended on the weather and on the effectiveness of the German air force. Transports were often shot down. Abba sometimes worked the drops himself, pulling on a coat and a fur hat, gathering a bundle of firewood and wandering through the trees to a spot chosen a few nights before. There were no mosquitoes in the winter, and the wind blew along the ground, turning the snow into a hard crust. In a clearing, Abba dug a pit in the soft snow, built a teepee of wood and gathered kindling. He fanned the fire into a blaze to signal the Russian pilots. As Abba waited for the planes, he sat against a tree, rolling cigarettes and writing in his notebook. Some partisans had complained about Abba's writing, saying it must distract him from his duties. On hearing these complaints, Yurgis told Abba to go into the forest when he wanted to write.

Abba would sometimes stop writing and look at the trees, or at the sky above the trees, for the shapes of transport planes. There was a beauty in the forest, but it was a sinister beauty. At last, the planes would appear in the east, a few hundred yards above the trees. The pilots, afraid of being shot down or followed to the partisan camps, flew without lights. As they went over the clearing, Abba could see the narrow cockpits and stubby wings of the double-engined Douglas aircraft. After a few passes, the doors of the planes opened and boxes were pushed out and fell very fast and then the parachutes unfolded and the boxes jerked and drifted to the ground. There were about fifteen boxes in each drop: vodka, chocolate, pistols, machine guns, bullets, grenades and condensed milk from America. A few parachutes would sail into the trees and get hung up in the branches. The partisans cut down some of these boxes, but those caught in the highest trees were left as a kind of monument. As the pilots flew away, they made a last pass over the clearing, banking and flashing their cockpit lights.

In one drop, there were copies of a Free Polish newspaper, which Abba read by the campfire. An article, headlined "Immortal Heroes," spoke of the massacre at Katyn, a town in eastern Poland where 1,300 Polish army officers were found in a mass grave, killed by either the Russians or the Germans. Abba could not figure out who the immortal heroes were. The Poles who had escaped the massacre? The local peasants who hid the Polish officers? Maybe the people who found the grave? Then Abba read the last sentence: "When Poland is liberated, when Warsaw is free, the Polish people will establish a temple of heroism where every one of the sacred martyrs of Katyn will be brought."

Abba read the article a second time, words flashing through his mind: Immortal. Heroism. Martyrs. Sacred. "I was seized by pain and anger," he later wrote. "In our hearts we had only pity and tears for the dead of Ponar. We felt only pain for them—and, secretly, the pain was not just because they were dead but for the way in which they were killed. But the Poles? The Poles are proud of Katyn. Which of us is insane?"

For the first time, Abba felt the force of what he had witnessed: the Jewish Council, the Jewish police, the thousands marching to the trains. In the space of the forest, he could at last see the ghetto, where there was no space; in the light of the forest, he could at last think of the ghetto, where there was no light. "It was not just that they were killed," he wrote. "It is that they were dead even before they were killed. They had given up on the morality of life, and they forgot the holiness of simply being alive. The horror is not in the executions. It is in the life that came before the executions."

Abba carried these beliefs through the War, and it was still what he believed when he made his name in Israel. He came to be known by a single phrase: "Do not go like sheep to the slaughter." He was later criticized for this phrase and for the philosophy it seemed to suggest: that, even for those who died in Ponar, there was a choice; that, in choosing to compromise, they chose to die; that there can be no compromise or trust—that Jews must be hard. In his later years, Abba backed away from this phrase, and from the other proclamations of his youth, but in his heart, where he was never free of the ghetto, he knew he had it right when he was young; there can be a purity in the first reaction that is rougher and less defensible than the polished tones of hindsight, but is still closer to the truth.

Abba walked for hours in the forest, the firelight dancing between the tree trunks. "This time it was not the Cossacks who killed us," he thought. "It was not the mobs from the East or the Black Hundreds. It was the flower of a modern civilization. And when they murdered us, it was a different kind of murder. The victim never faced his killer. It was an anonymous assembly-line killing."

In camp, Abba read some of the other newspapers from the airdrop. In *Pravda*, a Russian correspondent wrote of the partisan missions, including those carried out by Jews. There were the explosions and the wrecked trains and dead bodies, but there was no mention of a Jewish Brigade or of Jewish partisans or of Jewish anything. According to the newspaper, the missions had been carried out by Lithuanians. It was as if the Jews had never existed. Abba, for the first time, thought of what he would do after the War, of how the Jews must seek revenge, answering a crime that could not be answered. "Suddenly I felt something terrible taking form in a faraway place, in some as yet unconquered city," he wrote. "I felt that one day the implications of this story would choke you until tears started and yet you could not cry."

Late one night, a few Jewish partisans, out for a walk, noticed tattered parachutes and broken crates hung up high in the trees, leftovers of a recent airdrop. The Jewish partisans, who often received nothing from the drops and who were forever short of supplies, boosted each other into the trees and climbed, handhold to handhold, to the top branches. As they cut away the cords, the boxes crashed to the ground. There were vodka, chocolate and guns, which they drank, ate and carried back to camp.

A few days later, Isser Schmidt, having just returned from the Russian base, spoke to Abba. The Russians knew about the boxes, said Isser; they wanted to know who had cut them down.

"Those men stole from the War effort," said Isser. "They stole from the people of Russia."

"What makes you think I know who took those things, or even that those things were taken?" said Abba.

"You know," said Isser.

"Even if I did know," said Abba. "I would not tell you."

In the afternoon, a few agents of the Soviet Secret Police escorted Abba to the Russian base. Walking between the Soviets, Abba looked like a splinter of a man, head down, arms at his sides, big hands raw and bloody.

Ruzka and Vitka sat up through the night, worried that Abba had gone to the base, not named names and been killed. Or maybe he had been tortured, named names and would return a different man. At dawn, Abba walked into the Jewish camp alone. He had been forced to stand all night in the snow. The Russians threatened him—"They tried to scare the life out of me," he said—but gave up when they saw he would not break. Abba believed Yurgis had saved him; any other commander would have had him executed. Many times, in the course of the night, he said to himself, "Yurgis is a Jew."

The next day, Yurgis stripped Abba of his command. From now on, the Brigade would serve under a non-Jew and would be known as a Lithuanian Brigade. But the new commander had fought alongside Abba, and respected him. He knew that no matter what you called the Brigade, it was Jewish. He knew that the men would continue to look to Abba as their leader. Therefore, in all but name, Abba continued to lead. Abba thought Yurgis had done this intentionally, making a move that would show he had taken action but choosing a new commander who would respect the existence of the Jewish Brigade.

Years later, Abba's son, Michael Kovner, asked Isser Schmidt about the incident. Isser, who was living in Jerusalem, narrowed his eyes and said, "Oh yes. Why would Abba not tell us the names of those men?"

"He thought they would be killed," said Michael.

"You see, that is why I loved Abba," said Isser. "He was so naive."

It was unclear just what Isser meant: Was it naive for Abba to think the men would be killed? Was it naive to think that such men should not be killed? Or maybe it was naive for a commander to risk his life for the lives of foot soldiers who would probably not survive the War anyway.

On the radio, the partisans learned of victories in the East. In July 1943, the Germans had been defeated in the biggest tank battle in history, at Kursk. By October, the Red Army had reconquered most of the territory that the Germans once occupied in Russia. By the first heavy snows, the Russians had crossed the Dnieper River, the last natural obstacle on the steppe. From the air, the Germans were strafed by huge formations of Stormoviks, two-seated assault bombers with the rear gunner in an open cockpit hammering away with machine guns and cannons. On the ground, the Germans were outflanked by thousands of tanks, one-man T-34s with sturdy little beetle-backs and heavy treads. At night, the German bases were pounded by truck-mounted rockets, Katyushas, a missile flying off the flatbed and hitting the enemy line with an ear-popping concussion.

In the winter, the partisans could see the first evidence of the German defeats. Rudnicki, which had been a remote corner of the War, was starting to feel like a front, a confusing concentration of soldiers, as the roads to the west filled with enemy trucks and transports. Vitka would sometimes stand at the edge of the forest, watching the traffic. The German soldiers returning from Russia looked ice-burned, with red faces and red ears. The partisans called them "Frozen Apples."

In camp, there was a joke among the partisans: "What is the difference between the sun and Germany?"

"The sun rises in the East and sets in the West; Germany rises in the West and sets in the East."

In April, the sun came out and the snow melted. In camp, the Jewish partisans could hear the rushing water. The trees would soon leaf out and the flowers bloom. Vitka was joking with Ruzka, making snowballs. Abba walked over and smiled. It was a sad smile. Before Abba could open his mouth, Vitka asked, "Where am I going?"

Vitka soon left for Vilna to deliver a manifesto, calling the few rebels who were still living in the city, mostly Communists, to revolt. Vitka was also to buy medicine for the sick partisans in camp. The road took her through a flat county into a village of thatch-roofed houses. An old peasant woman stood in a doorway, smiling at Vitka. The sun was low and the fields looked as if they were on fire. Vitka, not wanting to offend the woman or make her suspicious, said hello. The peasant asked Vitka where she was going.

"Vilna."

The peasant asked if she could come along.

Some time later, Vitka and the woman reached a bridge that crossed a river broken by sandbars; in the setting sun, the water glittered like broken glass. There were two soldiers on the bridge—a German and a Lithuanian. The peasant walked over to the Lithuanian soldier and whispered in his ear. The soldier looked at Vitka, then said, "Let me see your papers."

Vitka handed over her forged documents.

"This girl is a Jew," said the Lithuanian. "A partisan."

The German looked at the documents.

"They are phony," said the Lithuanian.

"She has blond hair," said the German.

"The roots are black," said the Lithuanian. "And her clothes are singed from the fires the partisans sit around in the forest. And look at her eyelashes. The tips are white, burned by the fires."

As the soldiers talked, Vitka ripped up the manifesto and threw it on the wind. The peasant gathered the pieces and gave them to the German. He examined the scraps, then told the Lithuanian to search Vitka. He found the list of medicines.

"I need the medicine for sick people in my village," said Vitka.

"Send her to the Gestapo," said the German.

"She is a Jewish partisan," said the Lithuanian. "I have proved it."

"I can't make that decision," said the German.

The soldier made a call and a short time later a horse cart came to the bridge. Vitka was seated in the cart between two Lithuanian policemen—one short and fat, the other tall and thin. The German soldier gave the tall policeman Vitka's papers, the list of medicines, the pieces of the manifesto. "Take her to Gestapo headquarters," he said.

The driver raised his whip, the horses broke into a trot, farmhouses flashed by. "Look at my papers," said Vitka. "I am not a Jew."

The policemen ignored her.

On either side of the cart, fields stretched to the horizon. Vitka spoke of her Christian upbringing, and of her childhood in a small Lithuanian town. Up ahead, the road went into the hills. She would soon be in the city, tortured and killed. Look at me, she thought; this is the moment before my death and I do nothing. The soldiers carried rifles. She thought of jumping from the cart and letting them shoot her in the fields.

The horses strained into the hills. The evening sun lit up the valleys. Vitka noticed the uniforms the police wore, threadbare, frayed at the cuffs. As the cart went over a rise, she could see the steeples of the city. "You're right," she said. "I am a Jew and I am a partisan. That is why you should let me go."

The policemen ignored her.

"You have heard the news from the front," she went on. "You know that the Russians are advancing and will soon be in Vilna. The partisans keep detailed records," she said. "We have the names of every collaborator. If you take me to the Gestapo, your names will be on that list. I guarantee it. If I am killed, you will be killed."

In the city, the cart drifted past dark houses. The streetlights led into the distance. "This is your last chance," she said.

"The Germans are still strong," the tall policeman said.

"That's what they want you to think," said Vitka. "But believe me: they lose every battle...

"Many policemen work for the partisans," she continued. "But, of course, you know that."

The tall policeman looked at the driver and said, "Jews, you cannot believe a word they say."

The cart stopped and the police led Vitka around the side of a building to the door of Gestapo headquarters. The tall policeman shoved something in her hand—her papers. "In future missions, never cross the bridge where you were arrested," he said. "And tell your commander that we hope to meet him soon."

Vitka pieced together the manifesto and wrote out a new copy, which she gave to leaders of the underground in the city. With the help of a courier, she acquired the medications on Abba's list. The medicine came originally from a German doctor, an army captain who traded pills for jewelry, gold or furs. By midnight, Vitka was on a road to the forest, a roundabout route that would skirt the bridge where she had been arrested. The hike led past Ponar. After dawn, as Vitka walked by white tree trunks, a military truck raced down the road. From a hill, she could see soldiers searching the fields. Bloodhounds nosed through the ground fog, scaring up birds. In a house on the road, there was a farmer who, in the past, had sheltered partisans. When Vitka reached the house, she found the farmer in his yard, breaking up sod with a pitchfork. As Vitka talked, the soldiers in the distance turned and looked at the house. "They are coming," said the farmer. "Follow me."

In a barn, the farmer told Vitka to climb under the hay stacked against a wall. She lay there a long time, the hay cold and wet and smelling of summer. She heard voices, someone yelling in German, the words muffled by the hay. Something went into the hay. Thunk.

Thunk. Thunk. A pitchfork passed an inch from her face. A moment later, she heard the pitchfork clatter across the floor. Much later, the hay was pulled back and sunshine flooded her eyes.

"Please go," said the farmer.

Several hours later, Vitka slipped into the cathedral-cool of the forest. She gave Abba the medicine and told him she would no longer go to Vilna. "It is a miracle that I made it back," she said. "How often can a person depend on miracles?"

At the campfire, the partisans were gathered around five men who had just reached camp. They were dressed in rags, with blood and dirt under their fingernails. Each had been given a slice of bread. Vitka found it hard to sit near these men, they smelled so bad. It was familiar and terrible, the odor of dead bodies.

One of the men was named Farber, a Jew who served in the Red Army. In the fall of 1943, he was captured by the Germans and sent to a work camp; each morning, the Germans watched the prisoners shower, looking for those who were circumcised. Farber and six other circumcised POWs were sent to Ponar, the camp surrounded by fences and mines. A sign on the outer fence read, "Entry strictly forbidden, dangerous to life! Mines!" The seventy Jewish prisoners in Ponar were to dig up graves and burn bodies. The Germans, who knew that they would soon be defeated by the Red Army, were destroying the evidence. The officer in charge of the operation was called the Strumführer. "This man, a refined sadist, was about thirty years old," Farber said. "He dressed like a dandy in white suede gloves that came to the elbow. His boots sparkled like a mirror. He smelled of very strong cologne."

"No one has ever left Ponar," said the Strumführer. "No one ever will."

The prisoners lived in an open pit, the mouth covered with logs. There were two ladders into the pit, a "clean" ladder for Germans, a "dirty" ladder for Jews. The prisoners, men and women, were shackled. At dawn, they were counted and marched off to work. In some graves, the dead were clothed, in some, the dead were naked, which meant they were killed during a German clothing drive. One prisoner pulled bodies from the graves with a hook. He was called the hook man. Some of the bodies had been buried for two years, and they fell to pieces, or the skin slid away. SS guards sat at the edge of the grave, making sure no arm or leg was left behind. Speaking of the dead, prisoners were not allowed to say the word "body" or "corpse." They could refer to the dead only as "figures." "How many figures have been burned today?"

Carriers brought the bodies to the edge of the forest, where they were set on a bed of logs. When the bed was full, a second bed was placed on top of the bodies. A layer of corpses was then placed on top of those logs. When a pyre contained five or six layers of logs, or about three thousand bodies, it was soaked in fuel and lit by thermal bombs. The Germans cut air-shafts in the logs so that oxygen was drawn to the bottom of the pyres and the bodies really burned. A fire-master stood by with a spade, making sure the fire never went out. The smoke was thick and black. When a woman who had been pregnant when she died was burned, her abdomen gaped open and the workers could see the fetus on fire. After three days, all that remained of the bodies was ash. The prisoners sifted the ash for metal or coins. In 1943 and 1944, over sixty thousand bodies were burned at Ponar.

When there was no longer enough light to work by, the prisoners were marched to their pit, where they washed their hands in magnesium. There was an electric light in the pit, and, at night, the prisoners wandered through the rooms that had been cut in the soft earth. One prisoner was the daughter of the richest Jewish family in Vilna. "This is Becker's daughter," someone told Farber. "How many stone houses he had!" On Friday nights, a rabbi who had been taken prisoner led some of the Jews in whispered prayer. Farber told the Rabbi he wanted to escape, an attempt that would endanger every prisoner in camp. As there was nothing to lose, the Rabbi gave his blessing.

In the back of the pit, there was a storeroom, a wood board propped up as a wall. On February 1, 1944, a few prisoners pulled away the board and began to dig; a tunnel was the only way past the guards, fences and mines. Each night, as the others slept, one of the prisoners extended the tunnel. A bread saw, found on a corpse, was the favored tool. There was a lot of dirt in the tunnel, which workers put in their pockets and scattered in the pits. Sometimes, a worker tunneled into a grave, an arm or leg falling into the passage. The tunnel was barely big enough to crawl in and there was so little oxygen that matches did not burn. Farber spliced the electric light and ran a bulb into the tunnel. If a guard started down the ladder, a lookout flashed the light. The worker climbed out, replaced the wall, wiped his hands. By April, the tunnel, over a hundred yards long, reached beyond the outer fence.

At 11 p.m. on April 15, which the Rabbi said would be the darkest night of the year, thirty prisoners gathered at the entrance of the tunnel. They went in single file, according to the amount of work they had done. In front was the man who had done the most digging. When he reached the end of the tunnel, he hacked off his shackles with the bread saw, passed it back, then, after a few minutes, dug to the surface. He pushed through the mud and grass. Fresh air rushed into the tunnel. One at a time, the prisoners climbed out. Guard towers stood against the sky. A prisoner snapped a dead branch. A searchlight clicked on. As it swept the grass, Farber could see prisoners caught in the beam. Machine guns rattled. Many of the prisoners ran for the woods, at least fifty yards away. One after another, these men fell. Farber got on his stomach and crawled. Dogs barked and there was shooting in camp. Farber met a few other prisoners in the woods. At the river, they floated on the current, hoping to lose the dogs. Dodging trucks and patrols, they reached Rudnicki in seven days.

A few days after Farber and his men arrived in camp, a kid with blond hair and blue eyes walked into Konyuchi, a pro-Nazi town on the edge of the forest. There was an enemy garrison nearby, and the Germans used Konyuchi as a staging point for sweeps and raids. They built towers around the town and organized a local militia; the militia had recently captured two partisans and tortured them to death. The blond kid, who said he was a member of a pro-Nazi militia from another village, walked through Konyuchi, noting each building and tower. He then returned to the forest to sketch a plan.

Konyuchi was a village of dusty streets and squat, unpainted houses. Crooked trees grew in the yards. There was a market where the farmers sold vegetables. The partisans—Russians, Lithuanians and Jews—attacked Konyuchi from the fields, the sun at their backs. There was gunfire from the guard towers. Partisans returned the fire. The peasants ducked into houses. Partisans threw grenades onto roofs and the houses exploded into flame. Other houses were torched. Peasants ran from their front doors and raced down the streets. The partisans chased them, shooting men, women, children. Many peasants ran in the direction of the German garrison, which took them through a cemetery on the edge of town. The partisan commander, anticipating this move, had stationed several men behind the gravestones. When these partisans opened fire, the peasants turned back, only to be met by the soldiers coming up from behind. Caught in a cross fire, hundreds of peasants were killed.

The next day, members of the Gestapo drove out from Vilna, walked in the smoky streets of Konyuchi, photographing the dead. These pictures were posted across the countryside. They were said to show the barbarism of the "Red Bandits." Of course, the photos actually helped the partisans; for the people in the villages, the massacre was reason to fear the rebels. In the future, the peasants were not so quick to turn over a partisan, even for a kilo of sugar.

For Jewish partisans, the massacre at Konyuchi was a disturbing echo of the first days of the War, when German soldiers destroyed their towns. The rebels sat for hours at the campfire, asking themselves, "Who are we?"

For Abba, the answer was clear.

Who are we? Only this. Not who we were before.

The raids continued through the spring and into the first hot days of June, as the forests thickened with life. Summer in the Baltic is its own country—the days are an endless buzz of electricity and each morning a mist settles in the gullies and creeps on the fields. In the evening, there are storms. The partisans would listen closely to the storms; if the thunder was fast and regular, it was not thunder but a barrage from Russian guns. The shells lit up the countryside. In June, the Russians attacked the German-occupied Baltic States, an offensive that Stalin called Operation Bagration, after a hero killed in the final war against Napoleon. The Russians, following the route Napoleon took out of Moscow, swept north of the Pripet Marshes and into Lithuania. The attack was led by Colonel General I. D. Cherniakhovsky, the youngest commander in Russia, a well-built man with slanted eyes. Asked if he was a Jew, Cherniakhovsky said, "No, my parents were."

Two days before the advance, on June 19, 1944, partisans throughout the Eastern forests, on orders from Moscow, attacked German trucks, trains, roads, bridges. Over a thousand enemy transportation links were destroyed, making it almost impossible for the Germans to resupply their troops or call up reserves. In camp, Abba could hear Russian artillery pounding the line, softening the enemy for the fight. The bombing went on without pause. If it did stop, there was twenty minutes of silence, then the Russians sent up more shells, hoping to catch the Germans out of their bunkers. After forty-eight hours of bombing, everything got quiet and the birds flew up from the trees. The fighting had begun.

The Red Army advanced behind tanks with plows clearing barbed wire and cutting channels through the minefields. They drove on even at night, in trucks fitted with screeching sirens and searchlights to blind the enemy. A correspondent from the *New York Times* watched the army on the move.

London, Saturday July 8—Advancing Soviet troops, nearing the border of Lithuania, drove within twenty miles of Vilna, its capital, yesterday, while 110 miles to the south, other Red army units began an artillery bombardment of the great Baranovichi rail junction.

London, Tuesday July 11—General Cherniakhovsky's army, advancing on both the rail junctions of Vilna and Lida on a sixty-mile front, took Kemelishki, twenty-five miles northeast of Vilna, in an outflanking movement that put his forces within nine miles of the Divinsk-Vilna Railroad.

Soviet soldiers raced down the road, reaching for the next hill, the next valley. If they met an enemy stronghold, they often went right by it, stranding thousands of Germans behind the lines. Trapped enemy soldiers wandered the fields, looking for a way across the front. Partisans hunted the soldiers, cutting them down in brutal attacks. The roles had been reversed; the Germans now found themselves far from home, in a hostile country. On occasion, enemy soldiers were captured by Jewish partisans. When a German realized he had been captured by Jews, he threw up his hands and said, "I am a Social Democrat."

"You have got to be very careful with a German," a partisan told an American reporter. "They shout 'Hitler kaput,' then shoot you in the back."

That summer, units of the Red Army reached Rudnicki. The soldiers wore green side caps or helmets or else were bareheaded, with high-collared tunics and entrenching tools. Their faces were a cross section of a great nation, city soldiers and peasants. The city soldiers wore glasses and spoke well and carried books in their pockets, and these were the men later purged by Stalin. The country boys were big and rough and friendly. The partisans hugged the soldiers and wept. Looking at them, Abba shook his head, saying, "Too late, too late."

A Russian officer stood before the partisans, giving a speech, filled with big words and beautiful phrases, that, in the end, had a simple message: by harassing the enemy and tying up German reserves, the partisans had made the advance possible. "You have done the most dangerous work of the War," he said. "We are grateful to you."

He said the partisans would now fight in the Red Army. Soviet soldiers handed out rifles, machine guns, pistols, rocket launchers, as well as vodka, cigarettes and meat. The Russians, who had been fighting for days, then set up camp. Vitka says the soldiers slept for three straight days.

In the Russian and Lithuanian camps, partisans fired off pistols, danced and drank. Now and then, a drunk partisan leapt through the campfire. For these men, no longer trapped behind enemy lines, the worst of the War was over. Many of the Lithuanians would now return home. But it was quiet in the Jewish camp, with partisans sitting up in their dugouts. After a year in the forest, they would soon return to Vilna; for the first time, many of them thought of what they would be returning to.

On July 7, the partisans, gathered in ranks, marched on Vilna, where units of the Red Army were already fighting. Clouds snapped over the soldiers, their faces shaded by helmets. Now and then, a plane passed by, a C-32 transport flashing in the west. It seemed the entire war was stretched along the road, trucks and half-tracks, blown-out tanks, soldiers looking for their units. The partisans spent days on the road, battling Germans trapped behind the advance. An article in the *New York Times* offers a glimpse of the partisans from the outside:

> Today, well organized partisan brigades are helping mop up the isolated Germans. The mopping up was going on each side of the road. Stormoviks circled overhead and Russian tanks, their tops crowded with infantrymen, set off in wide sweeps across the fields. Long lines of captured transport, much of it horse-drawn, streamed toward Minsk. Mounted partisans passed, sitting on Netherland, German or Hungarian saddles and carrying arms from all the nations of Europe.

In the outskirts of Vilna, Ruzka saw a young woman holding a crying child, a picture as ancient as the world. The child was very thin and it had the face of an old man. The child said something in Yiddish. A Jewish child from some hole in the forest.

Ruzka burst into tears.

"What is it?" asked Abba.

Ruzka tried to answer but only sobbed harder, her face wet with tears. Abba had never seen Ruzka cry, not in the ghetto, not in the forest.

"Tell me," he said.

"I thought I would never again hear a Jewish child cry," said Ruzka.

The Germans had built Vilna into a fortress. It took the Red Army days to breach the defenses. The breakthrough, on July 8, 1944, was reported in the *New York Times:*

London, Sunday July 9—Russian tanks and infantry smashed into the streets of Vilna Saturday in an advance of twenty to twenty-seven miles. Street fighting raged in the city of 200,000 persons.

London, Monday July 10—In Vilna, Russian troops were wiping out a large group of German parachutists landing in the town yesterday morning...Moscow's midnight war bulletin said today that the Germans, recently reinforced by five picked regiments, had been ordered by the Nazi high command to defend the city to the last man.

London, Tuesday July 11—Inside Vilna, Moscow announced that the battle was continuing with "increasing violence" and that Soviet infantry and tanks, frequently fighting hand-to-hand, had driven the Germans from the Eastern and Southern parts of town and penned them in the center. Moscow said the Germans were suffering enormous losses in the first big street battle in the current campaign. Berlin said its troops were fighting behind barricades in the center of Vilna.

From a rise, Abba could see the boxy white buildings of the city tucked into the hills. The red shingle roofs ran together. A Russian handed him a pair of binoculars. Through the lenses, Abba could see signs, transports, tanks. The river shimmered. Bodies filled the gutters. A Soviet soldier was walking down an alley, a German coming up from behind. Abba wanted to cry out. When he put down the binoculars, Vilna fell into the distance. Eight thousand Germans had died in the battle—the Nazis were on the edge of collapse.

Abba led his men down the road, past the train station and into the city. There were skirmishes but the heavy fighting was over. German soldiers waved white flags. The *New York Times* announced the victory:

VILNA FALLS AFTER 5-DAY BATTLE
Russians Win City—Capture 5,000 Germans in Lithuanian Center After Hot Fight

London, Friday July 14—Russian troops yesterday captured Vilna, capital of Soviet Lithuania, after five days of fierce street battles in which 8,000 Germans were killed.

Routed by the sledge hammer blows of the Red Army, the Germans were in full flight along a blazing fifty-five-mile front and Berlin broadcasts indicated that a full-scale withdrawal from the Baltic States was imminent.

A story that ran in the next column gives a sense of the Nazi state of mind:

BERLIN THREATENS TO DESTROY EUROPE
Maelstrom of destruction due if Russian flood spills on 'Holy German Land'

London, July 13—German broadcasts heard in London tonight said that before the Russian "peril" could penetrate the Reich's borders the Nazis would "turn this continent into a maelstrom of destruction where only one cry is heard—the cry of blood."

Abba and the partisans walked through the city. It was deserted. The shadows of airplanes climbed up the buildings. Some houses had been turned into rubble. Others had been hit but were still standing. In a few, one wall had fallen and you could see into the rooms—a bed neatly made, a table set for dinner. Turning a corner, Vitka almost stepped on a young man with open eyes, a corpse. It was the first dead body she had seen close up. In the forest, when she blew up trains, she might hear screams but that was as near as she got. As a result, the people she killed took on the abstract quality of the enemy, a word all in capitals. "In war, many things are acceptable," she later said. "You kill and there seem to be no consequences; but there are consequences—they just come after."

In the afternoon, the partisans walked to the ghetto. There were flower boxes in some windows and laundry drying on lines hung between buildings. After the ghetto was liquidated, some of the poor of Vilna had moved in. But most of the houses were empty and every window suggested a story, the struggle of those who had lived there, the lives they would not lead. Now and then, one or two people, stooped and emaciated, stumbled into the street. These were the ghetto's last Jews, those who, for a year, had lived between walls and underneath floorboards.

A jeep rumbled up the street and a man got out. He had an angular face, an overcoat, a tie and a sweater and he was smoking a pipe. He seemed surprised to find soldiers in this desolate place.

Jewish partisans, including Abba, Ruzka and Vitka, in liberated Vilna.

This was Ilya Ehrenburg, a Jew from Russia, a writer and poet whose dispatches from the front had been a tremendous inspiration for the partisans, who read his columns in the forest. In a sense, he was everyone's hero.

Abba told Ehrenburg that he was a partisan, part of a Jewish brigade. Writing in his notebook, Ehrenburg shook his head, saying, again and again, "Wonderful."

Ehrenburg gathered the partisans for a picture, ten kids, men and women, in mismatched fatigues. Ruzka wears a coat with metal buttons, a hat on the side of her head, a machine gun in her small hands. Vitka looks long and slender in her heavy boots; she holds a machine gun with a casual indifference. Abba stands at the center with his high forehead and wild hair. You can reconstruct a moment from this picture: the fading light, the shock of return, the sense of no victory.

Ruzka, Abba and Vitka.

If you single out one of these people, block out the other features and look at just the eyes, then compare these eyes with the eyes of the same person in a picture taken before the War, you will see what the years of battle took from them.

The next day, the Jewish partisans gathered the bodies of the Jews killed in the street battle, put the bodies on a cart and followed a road into the hills. The trees were green in the valleys. They reached the cemetery where, for hundreds of years, the Jews of Vilna had buried their dead. It was weedy; many of the gravestones had been knocked over. The partisans buried the bodies and said a few words over each grave. It was early evening and the sky was getting dark. Vitka looked at Abba and Ruzka. Beyond them, she could see across the fields to the city, where the smoke was still rising. She thought of the ghetto, the forest, the Jews who had stumbled out of hiding. For Vitka, there would be no peace; the War was not over.

In the summer of 1944, Ilya Ehrenburg published a series of articles about the Jewish partisans in *Pravda* and *Red Star,* official newspapers of the Soviet Union. "In vain did German generals gaze intently into the wide-open spaces, awaiting truce envoys with bread and salt," he wrote. "Instead bottles of incendiary liquid struck German tanks, and women set fire to huts in which transport drivers were sleeping." Above each story ran a picture of the partisans, battle-weary and triumphant. Across Russia, the stories were read by Jews who had fled the Germans and who feared no Jews had survived the War. Many of them were Zionists and they knew of Abba Kovner. The articles sent a current through the community—Abba Kovner is alive! That summer, thousands of Jews, hoping to find the partisans, began hitching rides and boarding trains for Vilna.

The city was part of the wreckage of war. Blocks had been ruined, stores looted. Each day, people wandered back to the city from hiding, slave factories, POW camps. Lithuanians, Poles, Communists and Jews crowded into tiny candle-lit bars, drinking vodka. There were fights in the alleys, rapes. Each morning, blood stained the cobblestones. There were still Germans in the city, would-be tycoons who had once hoped to get rich on slave labor. Trapped by the Red Army, they had fallen from the top of society to the dregs, lower even than the Jews. They were not allowed on the sidewalks, and armbands marked their nationality. Now and then, a German was found on the street, throat cut. The Russians tried to impose a kind of order—if someone got especially out of hand, he was taken into a cellar and shot.

The Russians wanted the Jewish partisans to fight with the Red Army in Prussia. But for the Jews, the War, this part of it, anyway, was over. They wanted only to rescue survivors and heal. In the end, they were helped by a Jew named Ribelsky, a doctor who worked for the Russian high command. "If you find an antique, something valuable and rare, what do you do?" Ribelsky asked a Russian general. "Smash it up?"

"In my line, I would put it in a museum," said the general.

"That's it," said the doctor. "These partisans are antiques, the last Jews in Europe. So what do you do? Take them to war? Smash them up?"

As the Russians staged their advance into Prussia, the Jewish partisans watched the Red Army advance, like a truck dazzling down the highway, taillights going into the night. They had been hitchhikers along for the ride and now they were left in Vilna, bruised but alive, wondering what comes next. In the newspapers, they read about the War. The Allies had landed in France. The Russians were fighting on German soil. General Cherniakhovsky, who led the attack on Vilna, was killed at Mehlsack, marching in front of his soldiers. Auschwitz was still operating in Poland. For the partisans, being out of the fight was like waking in the middle of a dream in the middle of the night. They wanted to make good use of their time.

One afternoon, in a square in Vilna, a few hundred partisans, Jews and non-Jews, were presented the Medal of Valor, the highest honor in the Red Army. It was engraved with a hammer-and-sickle. At the ceremony, a general thanked the partisans for killing over one hundred thousand enemy troops.

Abba, Ruzka and Vitka lived in a house in the city. A window showed empty blocks of crooked buildings. Each morning, Abba walked to the railroad station, where Jews arrived from the East. Before the War, many of these people had thought of themselves as Lithuanians, Poles, Hungarians. By 1944, everyone was a Zionist. The War had destroyed their future as well as their past, corrupting every pleasant memory. Abba helped settle these Jews in vacant houses and ruined hotels. Some, who had known Abba before the War, asked about old friends and relatives. Shaking his head, Abba would say, "All gone." The Jews—those who stayed, those who fled— were like a family of birds, that, separated by a natural boundary, in this case, the Eastern Front, had evolved into two distinct species. Compared to the refugees, the partisans seemed cold and brutal, bled of sentiment. A few of the refugees, who had once been high-ranking Zionists, tried to reclaim authority. But no partisan would take orders from a Jew who had spent the War in Russia. Over time, the returnees came to believe in Abba, in the low-grade insanity that had seen him through the War.

As Abba walked in the crowds of Vilna, listening to voices in Russian, Lithuanian, Polish and Yiddish, he wondered about the other liberated towns. Are Jewish refugees in those cities too? How many? How can we help them?

He met with the Jewish partisans now living in Vilna. Strange to see them out of the forest, not hunted, not running. Some had retreated into everyday life. Abba understood their desire to escape, to slide into a sequence of empty mornings. So much had happened in the last two years. But Abba would not let them forget. "There will be a time for normal life," he said. "But that time is not now."

Abba turned to the couriers, those girls who had gone out from the ghettos during the War. Cesia Rosenberg, the partisan from Narocz, with blond hair and quick eyes, was to walk east, studying Jewish refugees on the road. Vitka was to travel fifty miles to Grodno, observe refugees, search for Zionists and report back.

Turning to Ruzka, Abba said, "You go to Kovno."

THE CITIES

RUZKA FELT STRANGE traveling by railroad. A month before, being caught in the station had meant arrest, torture, death. Ruzka now walked easily through the crowds to the platform. A Russian soldier asked to see her papers. She instead showed him her medal from the Red Army, explaining that she had been a partisan. He saluted and took her aboard. The train was crowded. The soldier ordered a man out of his seat. As Ruzka sat down, the soldier nodded and walked away. Ruzka could feel the people looking at her, this dark-haired girl in partisan rags. There were whispers—someone said, "Yid." A woman clucked her tongue. Ruzka looked up, but no one met her gaze.

The train was soon beyond the city. Kovno was a hundred miles to the west. Even through the train window, Ruzka could feel the chaos in the country. The roads were filled with refugees, farmers returning home, soldiers back from war. The crops were scorched, the fields crossed by tank treads. Now and then, the train went through a valley untouched by the War, passing a barn, a field, a cow. Looking at the scene, Ruzka would shake herself and say, "What do you want, Ruzka? To live on that farm? To milk that cow?" In her bag were some clothes and her medal. She also carried documents and books from the ghetto, a reminder of Jewish Vilna, which already seemed like a phantom.

Kovno rose in the window, a city of dark streets and shattered buildings drifting on the delta between the Niemen and Neris rivers. There is a castle in the city, and churches and an ancient square with a clock tower. During the War, Kovno was bombed by the Germans and the Russians and the beautiful skyline was ruined. The Jews of the city had followed the same basic story line constructed for every Jew in Nazi Europe: ghetto, trains. Most of the Jews died in pits behind the Ninth Fort, a citadel in the fields east of town.

Ruzka walked through the avenues teeming with soldiers and refugees. She saw refugees from Majdanek, the death camp near Lublin where many of the Jews of Vilna were killed. Majdanek was liberated in July 1944. These were the first survivors Ruzka saw, the human ruins captured in Nazi films. She was shocked by their appearance, striped uniforms and shaved heads, faces so sunken that the eyes looked like discs. On each arm was the tattoo of German bookkeeping. Ruzka turned away, then scolded herself: "These are my people."

Around a corner, survivors had surrounded a captured German soldier. A survivor walked up to the German, pushing him, at first with caution, then with real violence. As the German soldier fell back, the survivor hit him. The other survivors raced forward. The German raised his fists to return the blows. A Russian soldier stepped in with a gun. The German fell to his knees.

That night, Ruzka met the Zionists of Kovno, many of whom had fought in the forest. They talked of the survivors: Where would they go? Ruzka said there was no going back; these people had no lives to return to. If the survivors were to live on, they must move ahead. The next morning, she returned to Vilna.

It was the same in every town: empty buildings and rubble, burned-out tanks. Jewish survivors, lost and demoralized, stumbled from the concentration camps. "They are all just awaiting the word, the directive to get up and go," said Ruzka. "No one asks about the dangers." In other words, the surviving Jews, no matter the risks, were desperate to flee Europe.

After questioning each courier, Abba looked out a window of his house. The sun was shining on the church towers. "No matter what it takes," he said, "we must get these people to Palestine."

It was the beginning of what Jews called the "Bricha," the Escape, the mass flight that would smuggle Jewish survivors to Palestine. Bricha. An idea that rose in more than a dozen minds in the same historical moment. It came into the minds of Jews in Palestine, who needed the refugees to build their state; it came into the minds of Jews in Liberated Europe, East and West, where the glorious past had fallen to pieces; it came into the minds of Jews in Occupied Europe, where the promised land was a dream in the camps; it came into the minds of Jews in America, where some wondered why they had not known more or done more; it came into the minds of Jewish partisans like Abba and Ruzka and Vitka, who believed that, even after the War, the Jews would not be safe in Europe. To the partisans, all the deaths must be given a meaning. Some even said, "Hitler has done more for Zionism than any man since Herzl."

Abba Kovner, with comrades, studies a map of Eastern Europe.

Abba thought the survivors should be gathered into cities, from which they could be moved to ports on the Mediterranean, Adriatic and Black seas. They would then sail to Palestine. He spent hours studying papers and war reports and maps, trying to find a way over the mountains. Every path was blocked by a hostile government or by a fighting army. A path finally opened in August 1944, when Romania, which had fought with the German alliance, surrendered to the Red Army.

Abba learned that several Jewish agents from Palestine had been sent to Bucharest, the capital of Romania; they were trying to contact Jewish refugees. He wanted Ruzka to travel to the city, meet the agents and tell them the story of the ghetto and the forest, earning their support, moral and financial. On her way, Ruzka would note every checkpoint and barrier, plotting a route for the survivors. She would then return to Vilna to help plan the Bricha.

Ruzka was being sent as an ambassador, the first partisan to meet the Jews of Palestine, to tell the story. To Jews outside of Europe, the scale of the catastrophe was not yet clear. Some people would no doubt refuse to believe the story, greeting it with the same skepticism that had met Sara, the girl who first spoke of Ponar. That's why Ruzka was chosen. No one could tell the story better. This shy small-town girl had blossomed into a presence, the center of every room; your eyes kept going back to her. Of course, Ruzka did not know this about herself. She had simply gone from one moment to the next. But Abba knew it. "Go to Bucharest," he said. "You will be believed."

Ruzka traveled with Samuel Amarant, a Jewish partisan who had once taught high school. The train was crowded with refugees. People swayed in the aisles and Russian police walked by with guns; they were looking for enemy soldiers, Germans who had traded their uniforms for civilian clothes. Abba told Ruzka she would be back in Vilna in two weeks, but she knew the War had a habit of scattering people. It had been that way with her family. A brief parting grows into a final farewell.

Before the War, Ruzka had loved the railroad. The clang of the bell was romantic. But in the ghetto she had seen the Jews marched to the boxcars, and she could never again think of trains in the same way. Every train was a weapon she had seen used in a murder. Every train had killed her mother and her father. Ruzka never knew what exactly happened to her family, though she was certain that they were dead.

Ruzka and Samuel picked their way from town to town, train to train. Sometimes the train stopped in the middle of the countryside and a Russian soldier walked through the cars, ordering everyone off. The track ahead had been torn up or blown to pieces—the work of partisans. On foot, Ruzka and Samuel crossed hills and valleys, often hitching rides. Trucks drove by, men on bicycles. On paved roads, Russian tanks rattled past.

There were pack-trains on the road, dozens of gypsy wagons pulled by mules. Children sat on tall beds of hay, eating or sleeping, along with Russian women following their husbands into battle. There were sheep in the fields, goats on the red shingle roofs. As the reserve soldiers moved up, they stole livestock from peasant farms and drove teams of cattle before them. In the course of fighting, thousands of cavalry had been killed, their mounts set free. In the valleys, horses, with flared nostrils and hysterical eyes, moved in great silent herds.

Ruzka and Samuel were questioned at the checkpoints. It was hard to convince the Russian soldiers they were not spies. Sometimes Ruzka showed her medal and said she had fought as a partisan; sometimes she said she was a refugee going home to Romania. Each day, as the Red Army liberated the concentration camps, there were more survivors on the road. With their appearance, a new image entered the human catalogue—the walking corpse, the living dead, the breathing void. Russian soldiers let them ride the trains home. If a refugee said he was a Jew returning to Greece, say, the soldier asked to see his tattoo, then waved him aboard.

Ruzka and Samuel stood among the survivors on platforms, crowded into trains, swaying through valleys. They crossed Lithua-

nia, Belorussia and Ukraine; they went through Pinsk, Rovno and
Lvov; they passed over the Niemen, Satyr and Dniester. After ten
days, they reached Romania. The skies were long over the Transyl-
vania Alps. The road wound among the peaks, sometimes passing
through a cloud. Beyond the mountains were the Ploesti oil fields,
wells leading to the horizon.

In November, Ruzka and Samuel entered the outskirts of
Bucharest, the buildings multiplying into crowded streets, warehouses, factories, beer gardens and shops. The city sits on a plain
between the Danube River and the Carpathian Mountains. Early in
the century it was rebuilt to look like Paris, with tree-lined boulevards and manicured parks and a replica of the Arc de Triomphe.
The shadows beneath the trees are gloomy. There are Eastern
Orthodox churches in the city, with domes and narrow, arched windows. Above the doors are frescoes of Jesus, in golden robes and
halos, waving blessings over the congregants. The Jewish quarter was
destroyed during the War, most of the city's 95,000 Jews sent to
Auschwitz. On August 23, 1944, anti-Fascists had staged a coup in the
city, toppling the regime. The new government quickly signed a
peace treaty with the Soviet Union. The Fascists had fallen, the War
was over. The boulevards stirred back to life. There were parades,
parties. For Ruzka, it was strange to be in a city that had survived, a
city of cinemas and cafes. As she walked in the streets, waiting to be
found out, discovered, sent back to the ghetto, she said to herself,
"You do not belong."

After a few nights of asking questions and following leads, Ruzka
and Samuel caught up with a group of Jews who had reached the
city, soon after liberation, from Palestine. One of these men, Meno
Ben-Efraim, had parachuted into the Balkans a month before. At the
end of the War, the Jews of Palestine, sensing the extent of the
slaughter, parachuted thirty-two fighters into Nazi Europe. Twelve
of these fighters were captured, seven executed. Ruzka studied Ben-
Efraim, every shrug and gesture. He was a curiosity, a suggestion of a
world long imagined and prophesied in books. She wanted to tell
him everything. As she spoke, it was as if Vitka and Abba were in the
room. She talked about Ponar, the ghetto, battles in the forest. She

had not come through the War empty-handed, after all. She had the story, and the story was real.

Ben-Efraim wanted Ruzka to return to Palestine to tell her story. "We thought that the people would be heartened by the words of a fighting, self-liberating Jew," one of the men at the meeting later said. "For the first time, the people in Palestine might hear something different than the bitter news that had reached them up to that point."

Ruzka said that her friends expected her in Vilna; she could not leave. Ben-Efraim promised that Samuel Amarant would be sent back to tell the others where she had gone. Ruzka argued, but Ben-Efraim was an important Zionist from Palestine. In a sense, he outranked her. "You must go," he said. "It is an order."

Vilna had changed since the first days of liberation. The Red Army moved out, the secret police moved in—on the hunt for local dissidents, nationalists and Zionists, anyone who did not share the Communist dream. Lithuania was being swallowed by the Soviet Union. Each day, Abba went from building to building, begging Jews to leave before it was too late. One afternoon, he talked to Joseph Harmatz, who had fought in the ghetto and in the forest. Harmatz had taken a job with the new government of Lithuania. His life was comfortable. He wanted to stay.

"What kind of future do you think you face here?" asked Abba. "All of our friends have left and those who haven't are going soon. You've got no family—why on earth do you want to stay?"

Over time, Abba convinced Harmatz, and dozens of other Jews, to flee the city. Abba himself was waiting for Ruzka to return. In the fall, a courier finally brought news of her trip to Palestine; Samuel Amarant, carrying the news to Vilna, had been arrested at a crossing and sent to jail in Russia. Each morning, Abba had to remind himself that Ruzka would not return. It was as if a part of his strength, a muscle or an organ, had been removed. For Vitka, it was a time of sadness and anger. With Ruzka's departure, a part of her life had come to an end, her life in the ghetto and the forest, where three people learned to fight as one. She resented Ruzka for leaving it behind. But when things got difficult, she often thought, "What would Ruzka do?" In this way, at least, the girls continued together through the War.

In the fall of 1944, Germany still occupied western Poland. The Red Army, hunkered in camps across the Vistula River, within sight of Warsaw, looked on as the Polish underground rose up in revolt and was crushed by the German army. Warsaw was turned to rubble. The Russians meanwhile set up a new Polish government in Lublin. The government—it was not recognized by Britain or the U.S.—included dozens of Jews. The Russians, who thought of everyone as a traitor, believed they could trust the Jews; even if a Jew had wanted to, he could not collaborate with the Germans. The Red Cross opened an office in the city, handing out food and blankets. They also compiled lists of concentration camp survivors. Each day, hundreds of Jews streamed into the city, hoping to find a cousin, a niece, an aunt. Lublin soon became a kind of refuge, a room in a storm, where Jews, as if by instinct, came in search of one another.

Abba's soldiers left for Lublin, in twos and threes, at first light, down roads wet with rain. They traveled from Vilna by cargo truck and troop train, some dressed as partisans, riding with soldiers heading to the front; some dressed as refugees, carrying documents forged by Abba. With a fountain pen, he copied the stamps of agencies and nations. Some dressed as bureaucrats, minor officials from friendly governments. If questioned, they threw up their hands and rambled in a foreign tongue—a combination of Yiddish and Hebrew.

Abba asked Cesia Rosenberg, the blond-haired ghetto courier, to travel to Russia in search of the Zionist leaders who, three years before, had fled as Vilna fell to the Germans. She was to look in railroad stations and meeting houses for Mordechai Rosman, who, on the day of the invasion, before boarding a train, had left Abba behind, saying, "There are hundreds of Zionists in Vilna. You will lead them."

By the end of the year, Abba and Vitka were among the only Jews left in Vilna. As they made plans and helped friends escape, Ruzka's absence settled around them. It was the one thing they did not talk about. For the first time, they lived as a couple, perhaps sensing the life they would spend together. "When Ruzka left, these two came together," Gabik Sedlis, a partisan living in Vilna, later said. It is tempting to see this situation in terms of a soap opera tryst: Ruzka goes off, leaving her best friends to find each other. Or, for higher ratings: Abba sends Ruzka on a mission, engineering his moment alone with her best friend, Vitka. In reality, the geometry of their romance, its degrees and angles, had crystallized during the War, where each decision was connected to a hundred others, where, from a thousand possible fates, one emerged, looking inevitable. In such situations, no one can say just why a decision was made, or if a decision was made at all. It happened because it happened. Because it happened, no one can imagine it happening in any other way. For Abba and Vitka, it was the end of the life they had lived with Ruzka and the beginning of something new.

Abba learned he was to be arrested by the Soviet secret police: As a Zionist leader, he was in charge of an outlaw organization. The next morning, he packed a few shirts and notebooks and left, promising Vitka he would meet her in Lublin. He paid a last visit to Shmuel Kaplinsky, the Jewish Communist who had mapped the sewer tunnels, and his wife. In the eyes of Shmuel and his wife, Communists who believed the future was with the Russians, Abba, like all Zionists, was a reactionary. He was also a friend. Sitting in their apartment, leaves turning gold beyond the window, he talked of the adventures and tragedies they had been through. "I could not leave without saying good-bye," he told them.

"You are leaving?" asked Shmuel, surprised.

Abba knew he should not tell his plans to these friends, who, after all, were Communists. Abba was deserting their cause.

Abba thought a moment, then said, "You will not see me again."

"We should turn you in," said Shmuel, who as a party member was obligated to report on Zionists.

Abba shrugged and Shmuel's wife started to cry. She asked Abba where he was going. Before he could answer, Shmuel raised his hand, saying, "Don't tell us."

A few days later, two agents from the KGB, in baggy suits and long black coats, came to the apartment.

"Where are your Zionist friends?" one of the agents asked.

"Who are you talking about?" said Shmuel.

"You had a strong Zionist organization in this city," the agent went on. "Where have they gone?"

"How do I know?" said Shmuel.

"Where is your comrade Abba Kovner?" asked the other agent.

"I don't know," said Shmuel. "You will have to ask him."

In the last weeks of the year, Vitka gathered the loose ends of her life in Vilna, visiting old haunts, meeting old friends. One day, she caught a ride to the airfield, where a French single-engine prop plane waited on the runway. She showed her medal and fake papers and begged her way on board. She was going to meet Abba in Lublin. From a seat in the back of the plane, she looked out the window. At any minute, Vitka expected to see a police car appear on the road, agents coming to take her to jail. A pilot made an adjustment and the plane began to taxi. Vitka, who had refused to go as she was sent, was leaving as she chose, when she knew it was time. The plane gathered speed and climbed into the sky. Her stomach dropped and sweat broke out on her neck. It was the first time she had flown. The other passengers chatted calmly, their voices lost under the noise of the engine. As the plane banked, Vilna appeared in the window, falling into its cup in the hills.

It was an old ship, past its prime, weather-beaten and sooty, sailing under a foreign flag. In the evenings, Ruzka stood on deck, looking at the sky, wild and electric. She was traveling on borrowed papers, as the wife of an official. The Zionists who were also on board did not come to see her: Had she been forgotten? Late at night, she lay in her cabin below the waterline. All her life she had wanted to go to Palestine and now she was on her way and could think only of what she had left behind. "I walk around like a dog without a doghouse," she wrote to Vitka. "I have lost my yesterdays and have yet to find my todays." Ruzka was in her early twenties, a generous, shy, determined girl, her mind full of visions, hopes, abstractions. When she slept, she dreamt of an ancient coast, desert nights, tents, temples, towers, the sad music calling the Muslims to prayer. Each morning, she went up on deck to watch the ship cut through the black water. If she jumped, she would be gone in a moment, sucked away in the wash.

The ship passed by Istanbul on its way through the Bosporus, from the Black Sea to the Sea of Marmara. Stone buildings crowded the shore, mosques and markets. The view changed every moment, alleys and archways on the watery horizon. Each building suggested the long history of the city, the Fall of Rome, the Turkish siege, the Ottomans. In the Middle Ages, European Jews, on pilgrimage, often broke down in Istanbul, fearing to travel on to Palestine. They worried that by returning to Jerusalem, which they knew only from the Bible, they would be ending the exile, and so forcing the hand of God. Some spoke of a rabbi from the Carpathian foothills who was offered a chance to follow subterranean bogs to Palestine; crossing into the depths, his way was blocked by a floating sword. A few years later, when the rabbi reached Istanbul by sea, he was warned in a dream to turn back. His ship was then swept into a terrible storm. Ruzka experienced a secular version of this fear, worrying that she was not yet ready for the new life.

Her ship sailed into the Aegean and on into the Mediterranean, passing Cyprus and Rhodes. In the morning, the sea was rich with brine and the wind blew a mist across the deck. The coast of Palestine was lined with cliffs. The rock was honeycombed, water moving through the caves. Down the coast, the beaches were empty. Here and there, a minaret stood against a flat sky. Jeeps drove along the shore. The ship sailed into Haifa, the city rising in terraces of streets and houses. Buildings rattled in the wind. It was the largest naval base in the Middle East, filled with British sailors and American merchant marine, spies, counterspies. Containers were piled high on the piers, warships anchored the distance. In the ancient quarter, Arabs sat in the shade of grape trees. The water along the docks was oily and blue.

The ship tied up, a gangway was lowered and the decks swarmed with British police. As Ruzka spoke no English, a translator was found. She was questioned: No documents, no one with her, no one waiting, nowhere to go. She still bore the stink of the War, the lean, haunted look of a guerrilla. With a hundred other refugees, she was sent, by bus, into the desert. The windows were open and a hot, dry wind blew through. The bus stopped before a camp, a factory of barbed wire and guard towers, spotlights sweeping the fields. The prison—it was called Atlit—was built for the thousands of Jews who reached the country illegally, with forged papers or on pirate ships. In 1938, when the Jews of Europe most needed a safe haven, the British, in control of Palestine, issued a White Paper, limiting Jews to fifteen thousand immigrants a year. The British did not want to offend the Arabs, who were far more numerous than the Jews, and also had oil.

For Jews liberated from concentration camps, Atlit was a terrible shock. In long lines they were marched past soldiers and machine guns, to a metal building filled with refugees. It looked strangely familiar. In fact, if you set a photo of Atlit alongside a photo of Majdanek, the death camp in Lublin, it is hard to tell them apart. Barracks, fences, guard towers. Which is which? At last, you notice the color of the sky, the shape of the trees. Ah, cypress trees! Atlit! Once inside, the refugees took off their clothes and were given a bar of soap. "You are going to the showers," a guard would say. Now and then, a Jew who had been in a camp in Germany and who knew the word "showers" as a euphemism went howling mad.

In the showers—they were really a hot chemical bath—Ruzka felt the lice which had plagued her in the forest fall from her body. She was given back her clothes and wandered out into the yard, where Jews, hundreds of them, were speaking every language of Europe. Someone gave Ruzka a grapefruit. It was heavy in her hand; she had never seen one before. She peeled off the skin, took a bite, spat it out. It was terribly sour. But it was citrus fruit. In the forest, nothing was more valuable. She could not bring herself to throw it away. She stuffed it in her pocket, where it remained for weeks, rotting into a pulp.

Each day, Palestinian volunteers wandered through Atlit, questioning refugees, handing out food and clothing. If an especially important refugee reached camp, a famous scholar or public figure, the Zionist leaders could usually bribe a British official, securing that person's freedom. A few years later, when the refugees were really suffering—the camp would operate for about ten years—Yitzhak Rabin, who would later become the Prime Minister of Israel, led a daring nighttime raid on Atlit, freeing over a hundred Jews, including a weak-bladdered young boy whom Rabin carried away on his shoulders. "Here it is," Rabin later said, "the future of Israel urinating on my back."

In the afternoon, the mountains beyond the fence grew deep and dark. Ruzka talked to volunteers, explaining who she was and where she had come from. No one was expecting her; there were no orders to get her out. She felt forgotten, shipwrecked. Why have I come at all? she wondered.

On a clear day in Lublin, you could see Majdanek. Shortly after the Red Army liberated the camp, reporters from England and America gave the West its first close look at the German crimes. In photos, the camp looks frozen, as if the guards have stopped working a moment before. The barracks are filled with survivors the Germans did not have time to kill; the ground is littered with bodies the Germans did not have time to bury; the storehouse is crammed with shoes, hundreds of thousands of pairs—orthopedic shoes, baby shoes, loafers, heels—taken from the dead. In camp offices, contracts wait to be signed by Nazi officials and German tycoons, to use the hair of the corpses in clothing and rope. Next to the crematorium, a vast pile of ashes, the last batch from the ovens, waits to be scattered on the fields. The ashes are still there today. A shelter has been built over them and they have aged into a rocky gray mass.

The articles that came out of Majdanek were different in tone from the other newspaper stories. The familiar, hard-boiled, matter-of-fact objectivity of war writing has been replaced by a tone of unbelieving horror, conveyed by words like "massacre," "atrocity," "inhumanity." "We were told that no bodies were accepted for the crematorium unless the chest bore a stamp certifying that it had been searched for gold teeth," W. H. Lawrence wrote in the *New York Times* on August 30, 1944. "I am now prepared to believe any story of German atrocities, no matter how savage, cruel or depraved."

Some of the Jewish refugees, who had flocked to Lublin, walked out to visit the camp. Abba never did make the trip. Perhaps he did not have the strength to go, perhaps he did not need to. Though Abba had never seen Majdanek, he already understood it; he understood it the way Einstein understood the black hole—as a theory, as something the numbers suggested. His calculations, rhetoric and fears had long told him such a place must exist, that somewhere, on the edge of the universe, a hole must have opened, a void that swallowed up all energy, even light. The trains had to be going somewhere—right?

In those days, Abba never left the crowded blocks of the city. Lublin was a frontier town, a settlement without rules. There were homeless Poles driven west by the Russians; soldiers from the Red Army wanting to raise hell before being sent back to the front; slave workers, freed from the Nazi factories, seeking revenge; marked German businessmen; Jews, refugees and survivors, who wanted to kill or vanish or die. When a Jew reached Lublin, he went first to the Red Cross. A refugee would go into a back room with a handwritten list of survivors and return a moment later. There were so few names on these lists that, for many people, the sparse columns triggered a swoon of dread. Lublin was, as an American military governor later said of a conquered city in Germany, "A gigantic sore crawling with people of all lands, tongues and temperaments, a town of drunkenness and murder."

The Zionists, many of whom came to the city from the forests, lived on the top floor of a building in the old Jewish quarter, in bunk beds, two or three to a bunk, fourteen to a room. It was cold in the attic, wind whistled against the windows, rain dripped from the eaves and there was little to eat, but they were not unhappy. In the dim light, these young people whispered and cried, telling their stories—a muttered voice, a pause, a burst of laughter. Many, with skeletal faces and the big, beautiful eyes of the malnourished, had ragged good looks. They shared everything; there was nothing left to share.

One night, as Abba lay in his bunk, he heard someone say his name. He looked across the room. It was Vitka, who had just arrived in Lublin. She told Abba about her plane flight, the clouds from above. Vitka was just past twenty, and she was still fascinated by what she saw and what she learned, for its own sake, whether or not it led to some meaning or vision of the world. It was experience itself— each moment in its place, each place in its time—that drove her on.

In Vitka's memory, Lublin is one long conversation, never stopping, not even for sleep, the sun rising, the sun setting, eyes blurring with fatigue. In the afternoon, she and Abba walked in the narrow streets, between creaky buildings, searching for familiar faces. The winter was coming and there was wood smoke in the air and they often sat in a cafe drinking hot chocolate with whipped cream; their money came mostly from trades, from swapping items picked from the ruins for a few crumpled bills. One day, Cesia Rosenberg turned up in the attic. Cesia had just returned from her mission to Russia, bringing with her the Zionist leader Mordechai Rosman.

Mordechai was twenty-eight, wore a ragged wool coat and had his hair tucked behind his ears. He had dark, hunted eyes. Vitka stared at him—he would not hold her gaze. He said a few words, dropped onto a bed and then, without preliminaries, told his story:

"When we got to Minsk, it was burning," he said. "The people were gone, but there was still food on the tables in the restaurants. We walked all the way to Russia. It took weeks. Sometimes we rode a train. I was arrested in Moscow. They thought I was a spy. I was soon released. I went to an office for the Red Army and asked to join up. I wanted to fight. The soldiers laughed at me. The next thing I know, I'm on my way to a collective farm in Asia. I worked the harvest in the fields. In the winter, some friends and I slipped away at night, following the roads south to Kazakhstan. We holed up across the border from Turkey. There were fourteen thousand Jewish refugees in town.

Like me, they were trying to cross the border to Iran and from there go on to Palestine. Each day, I went to bars and cafes, where I met Zionist officials and the local police. There was no one to bribe.

"In the spring, the newspapers were filled with Russian victories, the march into the Baltic, into Lithuania. I studied every article, looking for the secret stories which can be read between the lines. In the summer, I came across the stories of Ilya Ehrenburg, stories about partisans, you and your group, Abba, and how you marched on Vilna. Right then, I knew I was in the wrong place. I had missed the fight. So, the very next morning, I started north, going from town to town. In Moscow, I camped out in the train station. I wanted to catch the train for Vilna, but a train came only once a week and who knew where it was going? Schedules meant nothing. So I waited. And waited. And waited. Finally, a train pulled in and this young girl gets out"—he motioned toward Cesia—"saying she has come for me, to bring me to Lublin. So, here I am."

Mordechai said he regretted missing the fight in the ghetto and forest, and that he would continue to regret it for the rest of his life. Abba told him not to worry—there would be many more chances to prove himself. In fact, Mordechai had arrived just in time to work on the Bricha, the evacuation of Jewish survivors to Palestine. "A sword is dangling over our heads," Abba explained. "The Holocaust is not a unique catastrophe that is over and done with. It can happen again. It's our duty to warn our fellow Jews and get them out of this slaughterhouse."

Even after the Second World War, Europe remained treacherous for the Jews. Why? Because history does not follow the abrupt changes suggested by the dates in the history books, which read like stage directions: Exit Fascist Germany, Enter Democratic Germany. The massacre did not make the Poles sympathetic to the Jews, nor did it convince most Germans that they were wrong—about the Jews, about anything. Defeat did not turn the Germans into the British, nor did it make them into the French. The decent Germany that appeared so soon after the War was an American construct, a story we told ourselves to get through the Cold War. The sentiments of a people, especially a people as race-conscious and death-haunted as the Germans, flow in deep channels. Freed from the camps, the Jews wandered into yet another wilderness.

The Red Army liberated Auschwitz on January 17, 1945. The British army liberated Bergen-Belsen on April 12, 1945; in the camp, there were forty thousand inmates on the verge of starvation. By the summer of 1945, less than a million Jews were still living in Europe. When these people returned to homes in Lithuania or Latvia or Estonia, they did not get the welcome they might have been hoping for. Arriving at houses in which they had grown up, they were often met by a slammed door or a gun. Again and again, the homecoming of a Jew was marked by violence. In the years after World War II, fifteen hundred Jews died in such attacks, a mind-boggling, post-Holocaust killing spree that culminated on July 4, 1946, in Kielce, Poland.

Before the War, eighteen thousand Jews lived in Kielce. By 1946, just two hundred remained. One night, when a Christian child was found dead in the town, the Jews were accused of the blood libel, of killing the baby so its blood could be used in a religious ceremony. Was it stupidity, insanity, projection? A million Jewish children had been killed in Poland during the War and now, one year later, the people of Kielce were accusing the survivors of murdering a child. Within an hour, the citizens of Kielce were in the street with torches, shouting, waving clubs. The local police and soldiers joined the mob in front of a house where a few dozen Jews lived. The street was awash in orange light. The Jews were burned out, chased, shot, stoned, beaten with ax handles. Forty of them died. Today, Kielce is just another dark Polish town, a crossroads, not a stop, a stain in the window, but, even at eighty kilometers per hour, you can feel the void. In 1946, Kielce was a sign clear enough for every Jew to read: Get out of Europe!

The British controlled Palestine and would not let the Jews enter; they were opposed to any movement of the refugees. So, after the War, thousands of survivors—they had nowhere else to go— remained in the concentration camps, which had been refashioned as refugee centers. The inmates were now called Displaced Persons, DPs, that scourge of post-War Europe, where fourteen million people were on the road: Germans flung out of their homes in the East, French returning to their homes in the West. In some camps, the Jews still wore numbers and stripes. In others, they dressed in whatever clothes they could find. If you were in Bergen-Belsen in 1946, say, you would have been witness to the surreal image of emaciated Jews dressed in the uniforms of the Waffen SS. More DPs came into the camps each day, some of them Zionists, who urged the survivors to go to Palestine. *If the British will not let you in, go anyway: flood the seas, force the gates.*

By the winter of 1945, over a hundred Jewish agents from Palestine were in Europe. Working with local Zionists, they built a labyrinth of contacts and hideouts. Each leader was given a mission—recruit troops, map routes, raise money. Some Zionists found stacks of counterfeit British pounds that the Germans had printed during the War, hoping to sink the UK economy. The Zionists used the money for uniforms, trucks, guns. Some Jews, working for the Bricha, crossed borders with phony Red Cross certificates that identified them as refugees. When Abba needed to travel, he put on a concentration camp uniform—the Russians let the survivors ride the trains home. Other Zionists even carved concentration camp numbers into their forearms, using a hot needle and blue ink. In this way, the partisans took their place alongside the survivors, marking themselves as the Germans never had a chance to.

On one occasion, some of these men found themselves in a room with actual survivors, who whispered and stared at the phony tattoos. A Zionist looked at the numbers on the arms of the survivors and then at his own number. In a flash, he saw his mistake. The Nazis had carved the numbers so they could be read by camp guards; the partisans had carved their numbers so they themselves could read them. In other words, the fake tattoos were upside down. The Zionists ran from the room, afraid they would be mistaken for spies.

On their way across Europe, the refugees followed an underground railroad, which took them from Zionist to Zionist. It was perhaps the greatest voluntary migration since the time of Moses. By word of mouth, DPs were told to leave the towns and camps and gather in abandoned warehouses and factories in the ruins of cities. They were then divided into groups, called kibbutzim. Each group was led by partisans with guns and grenades. They moved down empty roads at sunset, slept in wheat fields, started again in the morning. Reaching a border, they were met by the next group of partisans, the next station on the underground railroad. At night, they built fires and talked of how it would be in Palestine.

Vitka was stationed in Krosno, a town on the border of Poland and Czechoslovakia. In her wool pants and greatcoat, you can almost believe she is border patrol. She stands under the trees for hours, rubbing her hands in the cold. At last she sees headlights appear over a rise, trucks rumbling up the dark road, the faces of the drivers, mouths turned down, serious. Lights flash. Vitka gives a signal. The truck stops, refugees climb out. Looking at them, she sees every face of Europe, a concentrate of towns and farms and cities. They follow her into the fields. Early the next morning, she takes them across in a remote spot along the border, dogs barking, a light coming on in a farmhouse.

Now and then, on the way through Germany or Poland, a group of refugees were attacked. Thugs, spilling from houses, wanted to rob or rape or kill Jews. But the partisans who stood on either side of the refugees were not the same Jews the peasants had known in the past. These were instead the Jews the War had created, fighters and killers, once-gentle boys who had gone brutal in the forests of the East.

In 1945, a group of Jewish refugees camped outside Obernau, a town in Czechoslovakia. During the War, Jewish slave workers built munitions at a Krupp factory in town. The workers slept in dog kennels, and on weekends, the villagers came on excursion to look at the Jews in their cages. A Bricha leader sent ten refugees into town for food. As the refugees walked into the square, a group of Germans, former SS soldiers, spilled out of the police station in their army uniforms. They chased the Jews down the street, shooting. Six refugees were killed, the others got away. An hour later, a dozen partisans came back in trucks. With guns and grenades, they forced the

Germans into the police station, where they were lined up and shot. For three days, the Jews stayed in the town, eating and drinking as they pleased.

At the height of the Bricha, a thousand Jews crossed into Slovakia each day. On the way south, they lived off the land, stealing food and milk. As they often traveled by train, where the refugees were easy prey to local bandits, the partisans rode on the roofs of the railroad cars, straining in the wind, pistols in their pants pockets, a warning to the locals—these people are protected! In those countries controlled by the Red Army, the DPs were robbed by soldiers. Since the partisans could not fight the Russians, they told each refugee to fill a bag with rocks; that way, if they were robbed, they would have something appropriate to hand over.

For the most part, the Russian border guards did not bother with the refugees, letting them drift south, out of their zone and into the path of the British. As a group of the Bricha reached a crossing out in the sticks, a Russian soldier, his feet propped in a window, would squint and ask, "Zhid?"

"Da," a partisan would answer. "Zhid."

The Russian would then wave the Jews on ahead.

The refugees walked over mountains, across steep passes and into cool valleys, eventually reaching Italy, where American soldiers, each of whom had been required by General Eisenhower to visit a concentration camp, were especially friendly, smiling, joking, handing out gum. Never did they stop the refugees, who shambled off to the seacoast, where rusted ships waited to take them to Palestine. When the boats were loaded, the partisans turned back to the border and the next group of refugees. In the three years that followed the German defeat, 140 ships filled with Jewish refugees sailed from Europe to Palestine.

Late one afternoon in the spring of 1945, as Abba stood on a border in Eastern Europe, he watched a group of Jewish refugees walk into the forest. It was amazing to see. The Jews moved as naturally and easily as water going downhill. Abba stood for a long time, the sun falling behind the hills. He buttoned his coat. "Maybe they will survive," he thought. But a part of him knew it was too late to survive. Too many people had died. It was a question now only of heeding the dead. With the refugees on their way to the ships, and hundreds of people working on the Bricha, he knew it was time to return to the struggle that he had begun in the ghetto and now hoped to carry into every home in Germany.

Atlit, the internment camp where Ruzka was held in Palestine, was dry and dusty. Most days, the temperature went above a hundred degrees. It was like nothing Ruzka had ever experienced. She could feel sweat bead on her neck and race down her back. Now and then, gulls swept over camp, dragging their shadows. The sea, less than a mile away, was the memory of another world. The refugees, hundreds of whom had been in the camp for years, were back-numbers in the British bureaucracy, filed and forgotten. They wore cotton pants, shorts, boots, sandals, loafers, floppy hats. In their eyes, which reflected deserts and mountains, was the restless energy of the next fifty years. Standing under the palm trees, in lanes of barbed wire, they could see the hills of Haifa shimmering in the heat.

After several weeks in the camp, Ruzka met a Palestinian relief worker who listened to her story. His name was Benjamin Greenbaum. He was just a few years older than Ruzka, and his father, Yitzhak Greenbaum, was on the executive committee of the United Jewish Agency. That night, Greenbaum, who lived on a nearby kibbutz, Gan Shmuel, told his father about Ruzka, "a partisan who has arrived directly from Lithuania."

Over the next few days, members of the United Jewish Agency, in cars and trucks, with sad smiles and handshakes, came to meet Ruzka. They were surprised by her youth, simplicity, size—this tiny girl in rags, baggy pants and dusty fatigues, cuffs singed by partisan fires. Her very existence seemed a kind of miracle. Once, as Ruzka told officials that emissaries must be sent to Vilna with money for her friends, the treasurer of the United Jewish Agency took notes. Looking at him, Ruzka wondered if there would ever be a way to tell these people what she had lived through, what had happened, what was to come.

Vera Weizmann, the wife of the Zionist leader Chaim Weizmann, drove to Atlit to see Ruzka, who had begun to feel like a display item, a desert curiosity. Weizmann asked if it was true that six million Jews had been killed by the Germans. She herself considered this number impossible—"too large," she said—and guessed that no more than three million Jews had died. Ruzka was quiet for a moment, said something under her breath, then ran off. It was the first time she had heard the number—six million—that would become a drumbeat in the head of every Jew: six million, six million, six million. It stung Ruzka when she heard it, and it kept on stinging her for the rest of her life.

It was Yitzhak Greenbaum who freed Ruzka from Atlit, telling the British she had come down with tuberculosis and needed to be treated in a hospital. He then drove her to Gan Shmuel, which is fifteen miles south of the jail. The coast road took them through boxy towns and settlements, white houses spilling across the hills. In Caesarea, a Roman ruin once home to Pontius Pilate, the stumps of archways and columns ran to the sea, warm and blue and full of jellyfish. In such terrain, the past lives alongside the present; the past, in fact, is more present than the present. The hills are full of shadows, of figures from the Bible, the Crusades, the Ottoman Empire. Working together, these images—past and present, then and now—have an effect not unlike that of an old stereoscope, where two pictures, viewed side by side, merge to give an illusion of depth. For the first time, Ruzka knew she was in Palestine. The car, turning from the sea, sailed through plowed fields and shanties into Gan Shmuel, a kibbutz protected by a fence and a guard tower.

There were few trees on the kibbutz and the residents took turns sitting in the small scraps of shade. Ruzka stayed in a guest cottage—a window, a bed, a sheet. It was too hot to sleep with the sheet. One day, she was driven to a nearby kibbutz to meet Meir Ya'ari, the leader of her Zionist youth group, The Young Guard. Ya'ari, an important Jewish leader, a man of vision and eloquence, attracted a cultlike following. He had wild black hair and his face was sharp and austere. People were affected by his eyes, which were deep and black, and by his words, which were grandiose and courtly and mannered, beautiful sentence following beautiful sentence, like fashion models coasting down a runway.

Ruzka and Ya'ari, sitting alone in his room on his kibbutz, spoke for hours. There was real warmth between them. He asked Ruzka if Abba and the others had received his telegram.

"What telegram?" asked Ruzka.

"When the Germans invaded," said Ya'ari, "I sent a telegram."

"What did it say?"

"Save yourself."

Save yourself. In Vilna? It was like telling a man in a burning house to save himself. Great idea. How?

"We received no telegram," said Ruzka.

She thought a moment, then added, "Even if we had, it would have made no difference. For us, the idea of revolt and saving ourselves were the same thing."

In coming weeks, Ruzka met several leaders of the Jewish community, intellectuals who had left their families in Europe to build a new life in the old land. Heeding the call of Zionist writers like Moses Hess and Theodor Herzl, they moved, before the First World War, to Palestine, then a sleepy outpost of the Ottoman Empire. There were already Jews living in the country, ancient communities in Jerusalem and Safed, communities that, dating to the days of Ancient Israel, survived the destruction of the Temple and the Expulsion. But the pioneers were different from the Jews of these old communities—the pioneers returned with the learning of Europe, science, medicine, politics. By refusing to accept tragedy for the Jews, these men changed the plot, opening a new chapter in Jewish history. Using modern farming techniques, they brought water to arid regions and, in a famous phrase, "made the desert bloom."

In person, these pioneers were simple, slump-shouldered, gray-haired, bright-eyed old-timers. To Ruzka, they were heroes, names she had read in books in the dreamy days before the War. They crossed Palestine to hear her story. She spoke to groups, individuals, anyone who made the trip. In Tel Aviv, she told Shaul Avigur, a Zionist official, that hundreds of agents must be sent to Europe. "Those who survive will emigrate to Palestine," she explained.

He disagreed, saying only Zionists would want to leave Europe.

"There are no longer Zionists and non-Zionists," said Ruzka. "There are now only Jews and they have nowhere to go."

She paused, then said, "Can you imagine here what happened there?"

One day, Ruzka met David Ben-Gurion in Tel Aviv, in his house a few blocks from the sea. Ben-Gurion, the leader of the Jewish community, would become the first prime minister of Israel. At sixty, he was short and solid, with a strong chin, high forehead, stubby legs, no neck, pink skin, blue eyes. His hair, a white cottony mess, started on either side of his head and grew straight up. In every situation, in open-collar shirts and baggy pants, he seemed rumpled, slapdash, blown-together. Whatever he wore looked like pajamas. With him a new style was born, the studied indifference of Israeli leadership. He would be followed by a string of statesmen who seemed to revel in a lack of polish, an earthiness of manner: if naked is good enough for God, a stained shirt is good enough for you, mister. For a long time, Israel was perhaps the only nation where a politician could honestly say, "Looks have nothing to do with it."

Ben-Gurion sat across from Ruzka. Looking at her, he must have seen a dozen girls from his own youth, from the Polish town which he left in 1906, where he was called David Grien. "Where have you been?" he asked Ruzka. "Why have The Young Guard hidden you from me?"

To Ruzka, David Ben-Gurion was Jewish Palestine; talking to him was talking to the promised land that had sustained her in the ghetto. In him was the power to acknowledge her story, raise it up, give it meaning. She watched his eyes as she spoke, noticing his impatience. Ben-Gurion did not think it his role to worry over the fate of those Jews who stayed in Europe. His job was to lead the Jews of Palestine. Besides, what could he have done to help the Jews of Europe? On occasion, the Jewish Agency had bribed Nazi officials, buying the freedom of a few thousand Jews. But was this a smart action? By offering bribes, weren't the Jews of Palestine just giving the Germans more money to kill the Jews of Europe? As Ruzka spoke, Ben-Gurion interrupted her with questions that suggested the drift of his mind. "What about the Russians," he asked. "Are they very anti-Semitic?"

To Zionists like David Ben-Gurion, some kind of Jewish massacre had been inevitable. For a Jew, a life in Europe could end only in ruin or death. It was one of the motivations of Zionism, one of the reasons Jews must quit the Continent. Some cynics later suggested that Ben-Gurion welcomed the Holocaust, which, they say, he saw as the last violent shudder of the Old World that would make way for the New World. In other words: no Holocaust, no Israel. But this is terribly unfair. Even someone as smart as Ben-Gurion could not have foreseen such a massacre. After the War, on a visit to the European refugee camps, where he met a cousin, Ben-Gurion was shocked. "The best British propaganda for Zionism is the DP camp at Bergen-Belsen," he said. "[The British] behave like Nazis there."

For Ben-Gurion, there was only one answer—a Jewish state. In this way, he was not unlike Jacob Gens, obsessed with a single vision of the greater good. The Ghetto before all else; the State before all else. If Ben-Gurion met a Jew obsessed with the old struggle, with punishing Nazis, he accused him of wasting energy. He resented even those bits of European culture (language, food) that some Jews tried to preserve in Palestine. To Ben-Gurion, Ruzka's passion was a relic, an example of "ghetto thinking."

As Ruzka left the meeting, she felt disillusioned, lost.

A few months later, in February 1945, in Tel Aviv, Ruzka addressed a meeting of the Histadrut, the Zionist general labor federation. The hall was filled with Jews, born in Europe or America, who lived in settlements in the Galilee and Negev. In a soft, insistent Yiddish, she told her story to the hushed crowd. People leaned forward, gasped. Some of the young women walked up the aisle and stood at Ruzka's side, touched her, took her hand.

When Ruzka finished, Ben-Gurion stepped to the podium. "You have now listened earnestly to words spoken to you in an unpleasant language," he said. "It is the language of those who have died."

The hall filled with boos and catcalls. Ben-Gurion tried to continue but was shouted down. He said his words had been taken the wrong way: he was insulting the language, not the speaker. Ruzka ran outside. It was too much, too fast. It was as if she had the bends, had come from the depths too quickly. She said it again to herself: "The language of those who have died."

Ruzka moved to Eilon, a kibbutz in northern Palestine. Out her window were dusty hills. On the other side of the hills was Lebanon. The sea was a mile to the west. People who lived on the kibbutz remember her as a sad, lonely refugee walking by herself at night. Ruzka had slipped into a hole and wondered if she would ever find her way out. The War was still raging in her head; she could not stop fighting. To her, the idea of a normal life was something you tell children. She had seen the real world.

Locked in her room, shades drawn, scribbling note after note, Ruzka fell into a trance of letter-writing. The only people she cared about were her friends, and her friends were on the other side of the War. Sometimes Ruzka wrote in Polish, sometimes in Hebrew, sometimes in Yiddish. Her letters to Vitka had the desperate, shaken, uncertain energy of someone who has been abandoned.

Eilon, August 1, 1945

Dear Vitka,

I had begun doubting I would ever hear from you. I have hundreds of thoughts, one more gloomy than the next. How could I explain your silence? How is it possible to understand, that the people who are closest to me—after all, you know what you mean to me—do not write even a word?

Maybe I shouldn't start this way, but understand, so much anxiety has accumulated in me that it is no wonder I vent it so. Yesterday I received a letter from you. The first letter, Vitka, surely you will never understand what it meant to me. Just the fact that you wrote . . .

You know perfectly well that I would prefer to be with you, it would be so much easier for me, my girl, if these months were not separating us . . .

It is a difficult time for me. I went through a lot and endured a lot and there isn't a day I do not think about all of you and miss you and wait for you. I don't know if any of you can understand the intensity of my anticipation, the endless waiting for something that has to happen, like in the Ghetto.

You probably know that I am alone here, and that I suppress all my thoughts and feelings. I am not looking for an opportunity to share them with anyone. In my thoughts I speak with you, tell you things and wonder what you would do in my place.

Occasionally I think of the bond that exists between us and its intensity terrifies me. You see, I still live in the past; tomorrow is a fog.

I thought that when all of you come, we will form one Kibbutz, our Kibbutz, that will reflect everything that is inside of us. Now, I don't know anything, Vitka. You write that you are afraid it will be hard for me when you all come. Do you really think that our paths have separated?

This would be the most painful blow I could ever sustain! You surely understand how difficult it is for me to grapple with these thoughts—and I keep waiting, as for salvation, for your arrival.

Ruzka Korczak alone in Palestine, on the shore of the Sea of Galilee, in 1945.

I could write much more, Vitka—however it's enough for today. I will end, so that in a few days I can write again. I am waiting for letters. Vitka, write everything. I *must* know everything.

Ruzka

In the fall of 1945, Ruzka left Eilon and toured Palestine, traveling from kibbutz to kibbutz. It was the only way out of the past—tell the story. By telling the story, she refused to remain the silent object of history. By telling the story, she showed other young Jews just what was possible, the best and the worst. East from Jerusalem, into the stony hills of Judea, the wasteland of the Bible, deserts where the prophets went for visions, the road followed in spring-like coils, each turn affording a glimpse of rocky hills or the Dead Sea. Across the Sea are the heights of Moab, from which Moses viewed the Promised Land. The mountains look bare at first, but if you study them you see that they are covered with life, Bedouin chasing herds of sheep, goats perched on a narrow, impossible-to-reach ledge, standing in a patch of shade. When the sun dips to the horizon, the desert looks like a rough pink sea.

Hard cactus plants grow in bunches along the road, green and fleshy, covered with thorns. At the center of each plant a fruit blooms, a sabra. Sometimes, as you drive in that hot, dry country, you pull to the shoulder and pick a sabra. If you are not careful, you catch a handful of thorns. On the outside, the fruit is tough and sharp but beneath the skin it is juicy and sweet. It is after this fruit that the Jews of Palestine, those born in the country, call themselves Sabras. Prickly skin, sweet core. Arab farmers planted the cactuses at the edge of their fields, where they acted as a fence. In the future, after years of War, the plants would mark those places where an Arab farm or town had once stood, a melancholy reminder that the beginning of one dream was the end of another.

It was to the Sabras that Ruzka was speaking, Jews who represented the first generation of that new race that had been promised by the Zionist intellectuals of Europe—Jews who would never know life as a minority, or pogroms, or a day without guns. To them, Ruzka was an emissary from their friends caught in the War. She spoke in dining halls and steamy cottages as workers came in from the fields, hands rough and bloody, mud on their boots, skin parched and brown.

Ruzka had arrived in Palestine as the War was still raging, so she was the first person to bring a description of the slaughter to such farm workers; years later, Israelis still remember her as the first messenger. In Palestine, the rumblings of Europe had always seemed distant and unreal. When Hitler came to power in 1933, a homemade Nazi flag was raised above the German embassy in Jerusalem. A Jew scampered to the roof and tore it down; for a long time, that was as close as the fighting came. A few years later, as the Germans were chasing the British across Egypt, there was, in Palestine, a fear of invasion. Tel Aviv was bombed by the Italian air force and British soldiers were seen gearing for retreat. If Egypt fell, it was said, the German army would march through Palestine and Turkey, on into Russia, where they would join with the Axis soldiers fighting on the road to Stalingrad. Moshe Dayan was in charge of Jewish defense; he hid radios and weapons and drew up a wonderful, Masada-like, end-of-the-world scenario called the Northern Plan: If the Germans invaded, the Jews, the entire community, would retreat to Mount Carmel, where they would fight to the last person. Such memories of war—outrageous reactions to invasions that never came—compared with the stories Ruzka told, well, they were like something from a book by Robert Louis Stevenson, where the scrappy kid gets away in the end.

Ruzka spoke—hands at her sides, in lilting Yiddish—of the decisions each person was forced to make in the ghetto, of Ponar, how the bodies were burned, how the stomachs of the pregnant dead gaped open, the fetuses on fire inside, which, she said, symbolized how the Germans destroyed even the unborn generations. She also spoke of the Partisan War, afternoons of exhilaration, of love. She taught the words to the partisan songs. She told audiences not to judge or value the fighters over those who did not fight. "Not only would our judgments be unfair," she said, "they would be wrong." She instead asked them to remember a Jewish town from which not a single person survived, a town as lost to us as those ancient civilizations of which we know not even the name. Then she spoke of hate, which she said kept her alive in the War, a thirst for revenge: the desire to kill one more German, blow up one more train. Though the need for revenge, she said, would never go away, she had come to see, while traveling through Palestine, that the nature of revenge could change: "We can now think of revenge with a plow as we once carried automatic weapons and grenades."

Meir Talmi, who saw Ruzka at kibbutz Mishmar ha-Emek, said: "The dining hall, a large woodshed, was filled end to end. We listened to the tale told in simple straightforward Yiddish, in a quiet voice, and, at the end of her account, the entire audience stood on its feet and sang the Zionist hymn."

One afternoon, Ruzka met Chaim Weizmann, a Zionist pioneer, the head of the World Zionist Congress and, later, the first president of Israel. By this time, Ruzka had grown weary of such leaders, who seemed to regard hearing her story as just another experience to acquire. Obsessed with the creation of a Jewish state, these men— and they were almost always men—were not much concerned with her struggle. To them, the Partisan War was a storied but irrelevant part of the past. Chaim Weizmann was different. Of all the prominent Zionists, he was perhaps most haunted by the Old World, by Motol, the town in the marshes outside Minsk where he grew up. In his memoirs, Weizmann called Motol one of the "darkest and most remote corners of the Pale of Settlement," and went on to describe the desperation of its people. Motol was the lens through which he continued to view the present. Looking at Ruzka, he saw not just a wounded refugee; he saw the fate he had escaped.

Weizmann was a chemist by profession and spent his days in his laboratory in Rehovot, a small town up the coast from Tel Aviv. There was therapy in science, the cool certainty of numbers—a thesis proved, a reaction achieved. Weizmann continued this work until he was very old, wandering among test tubes as other old men trudge the back nine. Ruzka met him in his office in Rehovot. He told her of his youth, streets where he grew up. He then asked about her hometown, schooling, parents. Without realizing it, she was telling her story. Her face had the terrible beauty of burning wood. Weizmann listened carefully. In Yiddish, he asked questions that brought out the exact points she wanted to make.

"How was the idea of revolt born?"

"What did the partisans think of Palestine?"

"Did they understand why no help came from Palestine?"

"Did the Jews maintain a human demeanor to the very end?"

Weizmann had been a charismatic young man, and though this charm could no longer be seen in his face, it could be read in his ease, his confidence. He had a way of seeing through causes to the people behind each event, and he always saw these people, not as groups or ideologies, but as individuals. He had a great talent for listening, not getting in the way of the speaker. Though Ruzka was telling a story she had told many times before, Weizmann seemed to her the first person to truly understand the weight that she was carrying. Speaking with him was cathartic; she later called it one of the great events of her life.

When Ruzka finished her story, Weizmann said, "You experienced all of that and witnessed all of that? How are you able to go on living?"

Abba discussed the Plan in the spring of 1945, at a dinner of survivors and refugees in Bucharest. Fittingly, it was Passover and the fighters must have thought of the Hebrew slaves, not yet Jews, waiting in that brief pause in Egypt, after Pharaoh said go but before he gave chase. Standing at the head of the table, hair pushed back, his voice climbing, Abba said Yes, the War is over, but No, not for the Germans; it is time for Germany to suffer; the Germans, who killed the Jews, must now pay with their own lives. He quoted Psalm 94, in which God is called upon to take revenge on the enemies of Israel.

> *Can wicked rulers be allied with you,*
> *   those who contrive mischief by statute?*
> *They band together against the life of the righteous,*
> *   and condemn the innocent to death.*
> *But the Lord has become my stronghold,*
> *   and my God the rock of my refuge.*

He will repay them for their iniquity
and wipe them out for their wickedness;
the Lord our God will wipe them out.

Abba was a deeply religious thinker who did not believe in God. He thought in terms of the Old Testament, vengeance and justice, an eye for an eye. Where was God when the tanks rolled east? Where was God when the ghetto was built? Where was God when the ghetto was destroyed? And what about today? The War is over, but where is God? Is he with the Poles as they kill Jewish refugees who return to their homes? Is he with the Germans as they pass out flyers: "Bring back Hitler and we will have bread"? Is he with the Nazis as they strip away their uniforms and resume normal lives? If there is no God, if the prayers go unanswered, then Jews must answer the prayers of the Jews. Germany must pay. "We will do it for ourselves," said Abba. In that moment, the eyes of the room on him, his jaw twitching, Abba was the leader of a new religion.

He asked the people at the table to join his *new* brigade, Avengers. *We will repay them for their iniquity and wipe them out for their wickedness.* In one motion, the room was on its feet. "Everyone wanted revenge," said Avidav, a Jewish leader who was at the dinner. "No doubt we were taking the action that God himself, were there a God, would have taken."

The Jewish fighters, ragtag soldiers who would have followed Abba to the ends of the earth, had reached Bucharest from Lublin, on trains, on foot, in trucks covered with canvas. They were there in May, when Germany surrendered, VE Day, Russian and American soldiers meeting on the Elbe River. Bucharest filled with crowds that night, cheering and shouting; it was like Times Square, with sailors and soldiers and girls in bars cadging off the same old drunks and everyone hugging and smiling—but not the Jews, who kept with them the cold serious fact that their war was not over, would never be over, that they had merely moved into a new stage of combat.

In the morning, the streets were full of garbage and the girls exhausted by the sailors and the Jews in their rooms talking, day and night, about camps, refugees, Americans, British, Russians and always the one thing they could not forget, the Plan. Were they already calling it the Plan? Plan A? Plan B? Or was it still a vague idea to be assembled piece by piece, stitch by stitch? It was all some of them were living for.

Vitka wrote Ruzka and it was there too, in the words she did not say, in the sentences she left as fragments, in the cool wind that blew up from the page: *You are gone, we are here; you are no longer one of us.*

The young Jews who joined Avengers—within a few weeks, there were perhaps fifty members—were organized into cells and divisions, which took orders from five leaders, including Abba and Vitka. The battalion was made up of believers and atheists, intellectuals, partisans, survivors. Why did they join? Because their families were dead, because they had nothing to live for, because they wanted to kill, because the War was over and still not over, because they believed Germany would not be punished, because, as bad as the War had been, they could not face a life outside of war. "The destruction was not around us," Abba said. "It was within us. We did not imagine we could return to life, that we had a right to have families, to get up and go to work as if accounts with the Germans had been settled."

To those who did not want to join Avengers, who wanted to move on, Abba knew just what to say. He spoke to Gabik Sedlis, who had forged documents in the ghetto, as he packed for America. Gabik wanted to go on with his life. "Why do you think you survived?" asked Abba. "Because you are smarter than those who died? Because you are better? No. You survived for one reason: you were lucky. So now your life does not belong to you. It belongs to us."

"I had to join them," Gabik said years later, in his apartment in New York, where he made a name as an architect. "I was the forger. I wanted to say no. But no one said no to Abba."

Asked what Abba was like in those years, Gabik smiled and said, "He wanted to be the revolutionary who built the resistance. Two thousand years from now, he wanted people to talk about Judah Maccabee and Abba Kovner. He told me six million Germans will be killed and he will be arrested and at the trial he will speak to the world."

Abba believed the revenge should be anonymous. He did not approve of those Jews, mostly from Palestine, who traveled in Europe hunting Nazis. These agents had acquired a list of SS officers, names and addresses, and would, dressed as British soldiers, drive to some house, ask the man inside to ride with them to headquarters, then, beyond the city lights, say, "We are Jews," and shoot him. Abba thought such attacks too personal: they acknowledged the Nazis as individuals, allowing them to face their accusers, a luxury the Germans had never offered the Jews. For the same reason, Abba was also not satisfied with the work of international trials and military tribunals or, a few years later, the courts of West Germany. The Germans, he said, must be killed in the same inhuman, factory-like manner in which they had killed the Jews.

Over time, Abba sketched out the Plan. Just where it came from or who thought of it first, no one seems to know. It was almost certainly discussed in the forest, around the campfires; it was carried to Vilna and Lublin; by the time it reached Bucharest, the details were largely in place. The soldiers of Avengers would scatter, traveling to a handful of cities near concentration camps or else of symbolic value to Nazi Germany. Munich. Berlin. Weimar. Nuremberg. Hamburg. Using forged papers, they would take jobs in the city waterworks, learning the sewers of each town. At the given moment, the Jews would shut off the valves to those neighborhoods where foreigners lived, then fill the pipes with poison. Death would flow from the faucets, killing without discrimination, young and old, healthy and sick. Five cities in an instant. An eye for an eye. Plan A.

Plan B was the fallback. Captured Nazis, just the highest-ranking officers, were being held in the former concentration camps, awaiting trial for war crimes. Plan B was to poison the bread these men ate with each meal. Both plans, A and B, relied on the chaos of Liberated Europe, a babble of languages, a stream of refugees, confusion on the roads, a land with no one in charge, where a saboteur could vanish into a column of DPs. "We must try to take revenge," said Abba. "We must put it in the books, even if we fail. The Jews tried to do something; the Jews tried to avenge their dead."

The squares of Bucharest were bright and windy. Peasants and refugees sat in the cafes, and pilgrims streamed out of the churches. One day, as Vitka walked amid the summer crowds, she saw a few soldiers in raisin-colored boots and berets. Their uniforms looked comfortable and well worn, and they had the jaunty confidence of army officers among the vanquished.

As the soldiers reached their truck—a green flatbed, with muddy tires and dirty windows—they were surrounded by Jewish refugees, shouting and clapping. On the bumper was the tricolor flag of Palestine and over it a blue Jewish star. The soldiers shook hands with the refugees. One of them extended a hand to Vitka and she took it but could say nothing. She had heard of such men, Jews from Palestine serving in the British army. To see them with her own eyes, well, it was a thrill. In the ghetto, where Jews were outcasts, wearing the star as a badge of shame, Vitka had thirsted for such an image; she never thought she would live to see a day when Jewish soldiers walked the streets of a European city.

The soldiers had traveled from Ponteba, a town in northern Italy where the Palestinian Jewish Brigade had a base. In Bucharest, the men hoped to contact refugees and help them on their way to Palestine—work carried out on leave, against British orders, with the help of Americans, at the risk of court-martial. The Jewish soldiers, whose base had become a crossroads, a gathering place on the way to Palestine, were totemic figures, saviors who offered survivors a sense of protection. "If the soldiers had told [the refugees] to walk into the sea," a member of the Jewish Agency said, "they would have gone with the certainty that the water would part before them."

Abba decided the members of Avengers would travel to Ponteba, where the soldiers from Palestine might supply them with money and equipment. But it was more than that. Abba, who spent years in the wilderness, fighting alone, wanted to feel once again a part of a bigger project; more than anything, he wanted the Jews of Palestine to understand his need for revenge.

The road to Italy went through forests and villages, the fields shadowed by crows. The members of Avengers traveled two at a time, on foot, by truck, with fake papers, Russian medals, concentration camp tattoos. On trains, the Russian soldiers drank vodka and shoved their way down the aisles, stealing rings and tossing refugees out of the train and into the flashing countryside—Hungary, Serbia, Croatia, rocky slopes in the distance. Strange hangover days, victorious armies carving up Europe among them. Abba and Joseph Harmatz, a friend from the ghetto, were held up on their way into the British sector. A Russian border guard asked the men to hand over their watches. Abba said something and the soldier put his finger on his gun. Abba took off his watch and handed it over. It wasn't losing the valuable that bothered him. It was the way the soldiers treated him, as if he didn't count as a person. When the Russians were far behind, Abba turned and spat.

Harmatz was shocked. Abba, how can you feel that way? The Russians are the liberators.

Abba spat again.

On the way, they picked wild grapes, and they were dark and silky and sun-baked and delicious. The water in the streams was cool and refreshing. They crossed from Austria to Italy in the high alpine country, the wind sharp and cold, snow on the hills. American armored cars went by, each with its gun and its silent gunner in back. The road filled with refugees. Under a dome of sky, across the peaks, you could see the Jewish base. It was about two hundred miles north of Venice, where Austria, Yugoslavia and Italy meet. A picturesque town of steep streets and wood houses, ski trails in the winter, wood smoke and frozen streams.

The soldiers were camped along a great river in the shade of the hills. It was the Third Battalion of the Jewish Brigade, five thousand soldiers who had emigrated to Palestine from fifty-two nations. These men enlisted with the British Army, partly to fight Germans, partly for military training, which would prove crucial in their war with the Arabs. The Brigade would eventually supply thirty-five generals to the Israeli army. Though the British, not wanting to offend the Arabs, at first resisted it, by the end of the War the soldiers were serving under a Jewish flag.

The Brigade fought with a kind of fanatical bravery. When straws were drawn to see who would go on a suicide mission, the loser would often break into a hora dance. One unit was commanded by a British Rothschild, Major Edmund de Rothschild, who, after serving in France and Tunisia, asked to be transferred to the Brigade. He was wounded at Cassino. The Jewish Brigade saw action on the Po River in 1945, where they faced the Austrian 42nd Jaeger Division. In their tents at night, the Jews tuned their radios to a German station, the announcer talking of the soldiers across the line as an Asian horde set loose by the British. Before dawn, the Brigade attacked the Austrians with bayonets, driving them off in hand-to-hand combat. The Australian pilots giving air support flew in the formation of a Jewish star. Storming into houses where Germans were hiding, a lance corporal named Levy, who was from Germany, would shout, "Swine! Come out. The Jews are here."

After the armistice, the Brigade was stationed in Ponteba, on the ruins of a munitions dump. In town, Jewish soldiers found Nazis who had ditched their uniforms and were hiding among the sick at the local hospital. These Germans were arrested by the Jewish soldiers, taken to a synagogue and forced to clean the wreckage. Over time, the Jewish soldiers turned their attention to the streams of DPs. In headquarters, there was a map with pins marking the location of each concentration camp. When a refugee arrived on base, he or she was questioned and one more pin was stuck in the map. Soldiers built barracks to house the refugees, handed out clothes, served meals, held religious services. Children were taught Hebrew. Jewish holidays were like festivals.

There were about fifty members of Avengers living in barracks on the base. Each night, as the sky filled with stars, they went into the hills to talk strategy: How do we get the poison? Where will the money come from? Who goes to which cities? Some members of the group went to Austria to trade Italian currency, where it was more valued, making a few deutsche marks on each trip. Vitka spent her days reading newspapers, trying to make sense of the new borders of Europe. Now and then, she received a letter from Ruzka, brought to Italy in the pouch from Palestine. The letters were desperate and needy and Vitka, not knowing how to respond, responded with no response. "Your silence, together with the rumors coming from there, puts me in a terrible position," Ruzka wrote. "There are times when I fear that an abyss has opened between us; if this is true, everything is over."

One afternoon, Abba heard that an old friend had arrived on base. It was Lebke Distel. The last anyone had seen of Lebke, he was being marched out of the Vilna ghetto to the trains. On the base of the Brigade, in torn shirt and pants, he looked the same as ever—dancing blue eyes, blond hair, tough grin, stubs for fingers. Out in the field, a hawk lazing high overhead, he told his story.

From Vilna, Lebke had been sent from prison camp to prison camp, a death march, always one step ahead of the Red Army. In Kortla Java, he worked on the roads in the swampy country. At night, he could hear shelling and rifle shots. He was then sent down the Narva River to Suski, where he built the German railroad. The temperature dropped to twenty-five degrees below zero; prisoners carried the dead to be counted and burned. The snow was to his waist in Koromej, where he was locked up with Jews from Holland and Kovno. He then marched west to a half-remembered foundry of red flames and smoky chimneys. He worked in the metal shop. One day, a door opened and in walked his brother, whom Lebke had last seen in Vilna. Their mother had been sent to Auschwitz or Ponar, her good hiding place given away by a Jewish policeman. Lebke's feet were bloody in Tallinn, the snow-covered capital of Estonia, houses serene beyond the boxcar door. A boat took him to Stutthoff, outside Gdansk, the blue-black port. It was summer. Lebke was shaved, put in uniform and marched to Stuttgart. He dreamt of bread.

On a road to Dachau, the Germans caught the panic of collapse. When the guards were distracted, Lebke grabbed his brother and ran into the trees. Hiding behind the trunks, he watched the column vanish in the distance. In the evening, Lebke and his brother walked in the moonlight, east to the Russian lines. The country was deserted and spooky and surreal. The peasants were hiding or had fled, houses empty and animals in the roads. Lebke told a farmer, "If you don't hide us, our friends will burn you down."

In the morning, Lebke found two bicycles in the barn.

"We will ride these bicycles to Palestine," Lebke told his brother.

They set off, wobbly at first, but soon flashing past fields and farms, straining up hills, leaning into valleys, down roads of refugees, past lakes and over mountains, the kind of excursion Americans now pay top dollar for. In Austria, they met a soldier from the Jewish Brigade. Lebke told his story and the soldier said, "Oh, I have met some people from Vilna. They are on our base in Ponteba."

"Who?"

"Zionists," said the soldier. "The leader is named Kovner."

The soldier drew a map, and a few days later Lebke and his brother coasted down the pass into the base, spokes gleaming. His brother traveled on to Palestine. Lebke stayed. "Everyone was so wound up," he now says. "They talked only of Nietzsche and suicide. I had come from the camps and I wanted nothing to do with suicide. I knew what it was to be alive."

Abba told Lebke he was needed for Avengers. Lebke had blond hair and blue eyes. In Germany, he would not be trailed by whispers. Since he had nothing else to do, Lebke agreed to stick around.

In the summer of 1945, Abba addressed the Jewish Brigade. A photo of the meeting shows hundreds of soldiers seated on the grass in their khaki uniforms, a sea of caps, boots and legs. Abba stands before them in civilian clothes, hair wild, arms waving. In a voice filled with anger, he spoke of the ghetto, the forest, of lessons learned. He mentioned vengeance only in vague outline, using words such as "anonymous," "random," "poison." He knew the plan might frighten those who had not lived through the War. "If we do not take our revenge," he asked, "who will take it for us?" Perhaps, for a moment, he saw himself as he must have appeared to many of the soldiers: a reckless young man, eyes dancing, daring, half-cocked. Some of the soldiers cheered for Abba, this romantic figure from the

East. "I cannot promise you the Jews will be safe from another slaughter," he said. "But I can promise you this: Never again will Jewish blood be spilled unavenged."

In September 1945, at the urging of the leaders of the Jewish Brigade, Abba decided to travel to Palestine, partly for support, partly for the poison needed to fulfill Plan A. It would be safer to buy the poison in Tel Aviv. In Europe, such a purchase might raise suspicions. Abba would travel, with a borrowed uniform and fake papers, as a soldier in the Brigade, another grunt on his way home for leave. Vitka wrote Ruzka, telling her when Abba's ship would arrive.

During his last days on base, Abba assigned each member of Avengers a mission, telling them where to travel when he left. Some would go to Berlin, some to Munich, some to Nuremberg. Vitka would be stationed in Paris, a base from which she would travel city to city, coordinating the troops. If all went well, Abba would return with the poison in less than a month. The members of Avengers told Abba, "All our hopes ride on you."

Vitka was sorry to see Abba go. Through Abba, she had again come to value her life—a young girl waking after an endless fever dream. She followed him down the road that curved along the sea to the waiting ship. It was a hulking gray transport, rising and falling under the long skies. He said good-bye and stepped aboard. As the ship steamed out, he could see the lights of Italy disappear, his last vision of the Old World.

Ruzka was living in Eilon, a kibbutz in northern Palestine dotted by fig bushes and almond trees. A few miles to the west, the land falls in steep cliffs to the sea. The coast is honeycombed with rocky inlets. In the afternoon, the boys of the kibbutz would walk to the shore. On a dare, the most reckless of them would swim into the caves, where the current was strong enough to dash them on the rocks. To swim into the caves and out again was a show of strength. By the time the boys returned home, the adults would be sitting down to a dinner of fruit and sliced cucumber, or else food from the old country—sardines, sausage, brisket, wine. Afternoons on the kibbutz were hot and muggy, but the nights were clear and cool.

Ruzka received Vitka's letter saying Abba would soon arrive in Haifa, and a few days later, she hitched a ride down to the port. Ruzka was at first excited, then gloomy. For seven months, she had lived with a memory of Abba. She wondered if he had changed, if he was the man she had known in the forest. Would the real Abba destroy the memory? The British policed the coast of Palestine for refugee ships. Gunboats and destroyers scattered to the horizon, an optical trick in the deepest distance. Abba's ship docked. The decks filled with soldiers and sailors. Ruzka let her eyes drift from face to face. She spotted Abba in a British uniform. He crossed the dock, dropped his bag, smiled.

"When I heard Abba was coming, I was seized by fear and uncertainty," Ruzka wrote Vitka. "I wondered whether we would rediscover each other—our way of thinking, our rapport, our plans. After our first talk, I felt like laughing at myself for thinking that time could sever the bloody ties we all have. We have grown into a common fate. Now, with Abba's arrival, a certain period has ended—of psychic strain, of lack of perspective, of waiting ceaselessly for you."

When Abba talked about Avengers, Ruzka was shocked by the brutality of the plan. She had already moved beyond the violence of the War. "To do this, to think about it all day, to plan, you really have to be focused on death," Ruzka's daughter, Yonat, later said. "That was not my mother. To her, why chase the dead when the living are here to be cared for?" And still, Ruzka believed there was a kind of inevitability to the plan. The fighting had turned a certain number of the survivors into killers: it was the only thing they knew how to do. "[Revenge] is a cold decision not influenced by sentiments or emotion," wrote Ruzka. "This is fate. And since it is so, there is not much to ponder. Had Abba not come up with the idea, some Mr. Everyman would have done so."

Ruzka said she would do what she could to help. As she knew most of the Jewish leaders in Palestine, she made introductions and set up meetings in which Abba explained his plan and asked for help.

He needed poison. For Abba, these days, passed in offices and corridors outside of offices, were a blur of storytelling and heated arguments. Though his life had been directed toward Palestine, he saw almost nothing of the country. What he did see—a hill racing past a window, the sea at the end of a street—had little impact. His thoughts were less in Palestine than with the men and women who, at this very moment, were fanning out across Europe: Berlin, Munich, Nuremberg, Paris. In his hands was their only hope for justice.

Early in his visit, Abba went to see Meir Ya'ari, the leader of The Young Guard who had met with Ruzka shortly after her arrival in Palestine. Speaking to Ya'ari, Abba felt as if he were talking into a dead phone—ideas, plans, none of it getting across. For the first time, he could see his intentions through the eyes of another, how different the plan looked outside of Europe. When Ya'ari asked for details, Abba softened his tone, speaking only of Plan B, which sounded less apocalyptic than Plan A. Abba said he needed money and poison.

"I fear for you," said Ya'ari. "You will never give up the War. You will never live a normal life. You will never trust. We have much to learn from you about how to die like a hero. But please allow us to teach you how to live a life we can give to our children."

Abba then met the leaders of the Haganah, the underground defense force that would ultimately become the Israeli army. One of these men, Shimon Avidan, was a fair-haired, hollow-cheeked, mustache-wearing soldier from Germany. In the thirties, Avidan had fought in the Spanish Civil War, serving with the Republicans. A few years later, when Jewish Palestine was threatened by Nazi invasion, he formed a special unit for the Haganah, a division made of light-skinned German Jews which was to operate behind enemy lines, committing sabotage, spreading havoc. After the armistice, Avidan traveled through Europe with members of the Jewish Brigade, hunting Nazis. On one occasion, he captured and strangled a high-ranking German officer who, for years, he believed to have been Adolf Eichmann.

Of all the men Abba met in Palestine, only Avidan, with his childhood memories of Germany, supported Avengers. In fact, Avidan was prepared to travel with Abba to Europe, where together they would bring off the plan. For the most part, however, the Jews of Palestine, focused as they were on the struggle in their own country, were against Abba's revenge. They were, after all, engaged in a public relations war, trying to win support for a Jewish homeland—an issue that would eventually be decided by a vote in the United Nations, where the Jews would need the support of at least thirty-five nations. The slaughter of thousands of Germans, even if they had served in the SS, would not help this cause. For many, it seemed that Abba, consumed by hatred, stuck in the last war, was blind to their real priority—the establishment of a Jewish State.

In October, after Abba had been in Palestine a month, he wrote to Vitka in Paris. He was discouraged, and said no help would come from Palestine. The Avengers would instead have to fight on alone, as the partisans had done during the War.

Before returning to Europe, Abba had one more meeting, this time with Chaim Weizmann, the Zionist leader who had listened to Ruzka's story with such empathy. They met in Weizmann's office in Rehovot. Weizmann was a scientist, a rationalist, a man of moderation, of compromise. He was one of the early Jewish defenders of Arab rights and he had close relations with Arab leaders. He believed the Jews could rely on the decency of the West, on the humanity at the heart of the modern state. But with each dispatch from Europe, the picture filling in, his sense of the world had collapsed. In those weeks, Weizmann became an old man, tired, defeated, half-blind. After hearing Abba's story, he said, "They who did this to thousands and millions, who applauded or allowed it to happen, shall they not pay? That which they sowed, shall they not reap?"

Abba spoke about Avengers, about Plan B, a brutal program that seemed opposed to every ideal Weizmann had lived for. After a long silence, Weizmann, sunk in his chair, said, "If I were you, having lived as you have lived, I would do what you will do."

Weizmann wrote out the name of a chemist and a letter of introduction. "Go see this man," he said. "He will help you."

.   .   .

On December 14, 1945, Abba traveled to Alexandria, Egypt, where he
boarded a British ship for Toulon, France. Friends from the Haganah
had arranged the trip. Abba traveled with a fake name and fake
papers. He wore the uniform of the Jewish Brigade, hair cut short.
He was escorted by a Jewish soldier, a young man who had once been
shot in the face, a bullet going in one cheek, coming out the other.
Abba knew him only as "Jacob of Two Holes." In his rucksack, Abba
carried cigarettes, a notebook and two canisters of poison.

On the fourth day, the ship skirted the towns of the Riviera,

Abba Kovner, second from top, returning by ship to Europe, with poison.

weathered buildings curving along the shore, wintry beaches. A cold spray blew across the deck. The smoky port of Toulon came into view. The soldiers began to stir, ready to resume life on land. A few hundred yards offshore, the facades of the buildings clear and discernible, a voice came over the loudspeaker. It was saying a name. At first, Abba hardly noticed. Then, all at once, the name was familiar. He took out his papers. It was his name. The fake name he was traveling under. He was being called to see the captain. Since no one knew who he was, where he was traveling, or why, and since panic was in his nature, Abba thought the worst. *Someone has betrayed me.* He walked to the rear deck, which was deserted, took a canister of poison from his bag, spilled the liquid into the sea. Gold dust on the wind. He was about to empty the second canister, then thought better of it.

He handed the container to his escort, saying, "Keep this."

He then took out his pad and wrote a note; he gave it to the soldier. On the back of the note was the address where Vitka was living in Paris.

Abba walked across the deck, through the buzz of soldiers, up the metal stairs. British military police were waiting with the captain. Abba showed his papers. He was arrested. No one seemed to know why. Just orders. He was brought back to Egypt in chains. Throughout the crossing, locked belowdecks, he was tortured by one question: Who turned me in? Only a few people knew about his mission and he kept going over the names: officers in the Haganah, Ruzka, the chemist. Years later, a Haganah veteran talked of the case, saying Abba's arrest had been engineered at the highest level, perhaps by Ben-Gurion himself. When the Jewish leaders realized that Abba had left the country with the poison, they tipped off the British. They did not want Abba punished—just detained. His plan might greatly damage their cause. For this reason, the military police were not told why Abba must be arrested, only that he was a threat. He was locked in a military prison in Cairo.

A few days later, a messenger reached Vitka in Paris. Abba's escort had dumped the rest of the poison, but he made certain the note was delivered. It read, "Arrested. Proceed with Plan B."

Vitka had left Italy in the fall of 1946, riding a freight train into the Alps, the tracks cutting the yellow fields, mountains black in the distance. She was traveling with Lebke. There were hundreds of refugees on the train, feet dangling from boxcars, hunched in the wind. If anyone asked, Vitka said she was a survivor going home. At night, the stars came out and the train wound through the passes, heaving up slopes, sighing over plateaus. In the early morning, they went through Brenner, a treacherous crossing built by the Romans. A few lights shone in the windows of the town.

At each checkpoint, Vitka showed her phony papers. Now and then, she was arrested, but she was always back on the road by morning. Who had the means to feed a prisoner? She split up with Lebke in Innsbruck, Austria. Lebke went through Munich and on to Nuremberg. Vitka went west to the sea and then north. By October, she was in Paris. A fallen city, like Jerusalem after the Siege or Moscow after Napoleon. The body was intact—the roofs along the Seine, the avenues at sundown—but the soul had been carried off. Vitka could see it in the faces of the people on the street. She took a room in a cheap hotel in St.-Michel on the Left Bank. She asked for a room on the fire escape: in a pinch, she wanted a getaway. Each morning, sitting at a narrow desk, she wrote to the members of Avengers, keeping in touch with every development. In letters to Ruzka, who acted as a go-between, Vitka referred to the poison as "medication": *Without medication, we cannot treat the disease.*

That winter, Vitka traveled through Germany itself, checking on the soldiers in Avengers. On passenger trains, without a ticket, she dashed from car to car, sometimes hiding in the toilet, a step ahead of the conductor. In Berlin or Munich, in a cotton dress and fur coat, her skin the color of straw, she looked everyone in the eye. Not a German in the world could make her look away. She was disgusted by the Germans, convinced that they felt only self-pity in the wake of defeat. In some cities, American soldiers made Germans dig up mass graves. In one photo, you see a German in a suit holding a scorched baby as if it were a piece of roadkill. Vitka especially hated the German women, who, she said, would sell themselves to an American GI for a piece of candy. An hour later, these women would be back on the corner, complaining about the quality of the chocolate.

The members of Avengers lived in the cheapest rooms of the cheapest buildings in each city. Vitka was troubled by the mood in such rooms, by the desperation and despair. For these Jews, it was very hard living among the Germans. Each of them carried his or her own War movie, which flashed through their heads on a tight loop. A thousand times a day, as some rainy ghetto street or dank forest trail jumped into view, they buckled under the weight of the memory. Most of them were now working side by side with the Germans, with fake identities, awaiting the word from Abba. When Vitka arrived, these people demanded information. She told them to be patient. Some broke into fits of yelling, others dissolved into tears. As Vitka left each city, she worried that most of these people, especially those who had been in the concentration camps, were too impatient, too emotional, too crazed to carry out the mission.

It was different in Nuremberg, where Lebke lived with Joseph Harmatz and a partisan named Pinchas Ben-Tzur. During their first days in the city, these men, cool-thinking and determined, wandered out into the countryside, scouting camps where former Nazis were being held by the Americans. A member of Avengers, a young girl, took a maid's job at Stalag 13, formerly a German prison camp. Pinchas was hired by the Nuremberg waterworks, quickly learning the run of the pipes, treatment plants and shut-off valves. Lebke raised money through a series of odd jobs. Harmatz gathered news from the outside. Vitka left Nuremberg with the image of these men walking alone after dark, memorizing the maze of getaways—alleys, markets, bridges.

Vitka was back in Paris when Abba's note arrived: "Arrested. Proceed with Plan B." Apparently, Plan A required more poison than the group could safely acquire in Europe. Plan B, which called for smaller doses of poison, was still feasible. Over the next few weeks, Vitka plotted a way to poison the bread at camps where the Nazis were under arrest. If all went well, the plan would be carried out in five cities on the same day. When couriers reached members of

Avengers with the news, some cursed Abba, wondering how he could let himself be captured. For many, he had become a kind of father. Now they felt helpless, leaderless, alone; they were in no shape for contingencies. Only in Nuremberg did the men, who had been hardened in the forests, receive the news with the soldierly determination that Vitka was counting on.

Lebke, sitting in a bakery in Nuremberg, told the owner why he wanted a job. "My name is Julian Brooklyn," he explained. "I am a Pole just freed from a work camp. I will stay in Nuremberg only until my visa arrives. Then I will move to Canada. My father owns a bakery in Montreal. I want to learn the business. If I can learn each part of the operation, I will work for free."

Through a window, Lebke could see armed guards examining packages. Each day, the bakery delivered bread to Stalag 13, where eight thousand Nazis were being held prisoner, guards from the death camps and members of the Einsatzgruppen, the killing squads that had operated in the East. This information came from the Jewish girl who was working as a maid inside the camp. After looking Lebke over—stubs for fingers, hard blue eyes—the bakery owner said, "Sorry, no jobs." The next morning, Lebke came back with a bottle of vodka and a carton of cigarettes. He started work that afternoon.

Nuremberg was then just miles of debris, vistas of ruin, here and there a building that had escaped the bombs towering above the wreckage. In the outskirts, the world started up again, debris forming into buildings, buildings into streets, streets into neighborhoods, neighborhoods into towns. In Furst, a village just beyond the city limits, Lebke shared a flat with Pinchas Ben-Tzur and Joseph Harmatz, the local commander of Avengers. Each night, when these men returned from work, the apartment filled with resentment. "The Germans were taking their children out in little prams, they had milk to feed them and still complained that the level of fat in the milk was not high," Harmatz later wrote. "They, on the other hand, grabbed our children by the legs and threw them against telephone poles and into furnaces."

At night, these men argued in cafes, a newspaper folded back, an article read out loud. They spoke of the courtroom in the city where twenty-one top-ranking Nazis were on trial. For a time, the leaders of Avengers considered sending a partisan to disrupt the trials. A Jewish presence would be a way of saying, "You tried to kill us, but we are still here." A scout, who said the courthouse was very well guarded, discouraged the mission. In the end, most of the accused were condemned to death anyway. On hearing his sentence, Hans Frank, who had once ruled Occupied Poland, compared himself to a martyr of the early Church. The newspapers said he was reading *The Song of Bernadette.* Julius Streicher, an early leader of the Nazi party, complained that he could hear the gallows being built. "It is all right to hang a man," he said, "but why torture him?" On his way to the scaffold, Streicher, referring to the Jewish festival which celebrates the downfall and execution of Haman, an ancient prince who tried to kill the Jews, shouted, "Purim, 1946." The bodies of the executed were burned in the crematoriums of Dachau.

Every day, Lebke learned a new part of the bakery business, firing ovens, cleaning pans, frosting cakes. He often worked with the women, in a hairnet and gloves. He soon bribed his way into a kitchen job baking bread. The work went on all night, kneading and pounding. Five minutes into a shift, Lebke was covered in flour. He could hear the cooks talking in the other parts of the kitchen, baking pastries and cakes, which they set to cool on long metal tables. Now and then, one of the cooks slapped Lebke on the back, saying, "My friend, Julian Brooklyn!" Lebke, trying to hide his disdain, smiled at their friendly small talk. As far as he was concerned, every German had killed his family. As the nights went on, he noted each variation in momentum and shift change, trying to figure out the perfect scheme. He thought of kneading poison into the dough or else of pouring it into the flour. No good. When the bread went into the ovens, the heat might kill the poison. In the end, he decided to paint the poison directly onto the loaves as they cooled.

Just before dawn, the owner of the bakery would stand next to Lebke, sway back on his heels and say, "Fine work, Julian. Fine work!" He would then hand Lebke the keys, telling him to lock up on his way out. In those hours, when Lebke was alone in the bakery, he lost himself in the simple pleasure of work, of a job well done. If he stayed too long, a guard walked upstairs to see if everything was all right. The night guard stayed on until Lebke went home. By the time Lebke walked into the pale morning, the street was filled with delivery trucks. Each day, ten thousand loaves of bread were shipped to Stalag 13. Nine thousand loaves of black bread for prisoners. One thousand loaves of white bread for their American guards. The average American cannot stand black bread.

On his way home, Lebke sometimes walked by the stadium where the Nazis had held their rallies. It was ghostly in the dawn, a ruin from another age. Lebke was trying to decide the best time to poison the bread. Probably in the morning, in that brief period when he was alone in the bakery, before the trucks arrived. To fool the police, he would leave work, say good-bye to the guards, then sneak back in.

After spending several months in the bakery, Lebke told Harmatz, "If you want to go ahead with the mission, fine. But do it soon." Living in Germany, working with the enemy, leading this phony life: it was destroying him.

Harmatz announced the date. Saturday, April 13, 1946. Fewer guards would be working at the bakery on a weekend and there would be a full moon that night, giving Lebke much-needed light. On April 11, the members of Avengers living in Nuremberg, those not involved in the actual poisoning, were ordered to leave for Lyon, a city in France where Vitka would be waiting. The poison had arrived a few days before—arsenic purchased on the black market from French chemists who had tested it on a cat. The arsenic was smuggled to Nuremberg by a Palestinian soldier from the Jewish brigade, who strapped it to his body in hot water bottles. The soldier, soaked in sweat, walked into Lebke's flat, took off his shirt, pulled away the bottles and collapsed.

Over the next few days, Lebke sneaked the poison into the bakery, hiding the bottles beneath the floorboards. On April 13, before anyone had arrived at work, he used his keys to let in Pinchas—up the stairs, past the tables and the ovens, to a back room where flour drums stood against the wall. "This one is empty," said Lebke. "Get in." From inside the drum, Pinchas could hear Lebke walk away. Over the next several hours, he tuned in to every noise—a mouse in the walls, a shout in the street, a plane in the sky, ovens opening and closing, the clatter of trays.

That night, Lebke showed up to work with two men. In the end, he was only able to sneak one of them into the bakery, a former partisan who hid in a storeroom. As he worked, Lebke, acting as if this were just another night, was swept away by worry: would three men be enough? In a brief window of time, he hoped to poison nine thousand loaves of bread. This moment—Lebke planning and fretting—was very much the moment of Abba and Vitka and Ruzka. It was the moment they had so long been working toward: Jews acting out the vengeance of God.

Who rises up for me against the wicked?
Who stands up for me against evildoers?

Like most big moments, though, it was lost in the little moments that surrounded it. Is there enough poison? Will there be enough time? Will I make it back into the bakery? This nitty-gritty is what protects soldiers, the consequences of the big picture lost in the hustle of the little pictures. Before Lebke knew it, the boss was throwing an arm across his back, saying, "Fine work, Julian. Fine work!"

He handed Lebke the keys and went out.

A few minutes later, Lebke went downstairs, said good-bye to the guard and walked around the block. From the shadows, he watched the guard go off duty; it would be a few minutes before the morning guard came on.

Lebke rushed to the front door, fumbled with the keys and let himself in. Once upstairs, he stood among the ovens, catching his breath. He went to the back room. Pinchas had been hiding in the drum for fifteen hours. When he climbed out, his knees buckled. He massaged his legs and followed Lebke through the rooms. The second man came out of the storeroom. Lebke then slid into a crawl space under the floorboards. He emerged with the bottles of poison. He mixed it in big metal bowls. It was clear and there was no smell.

Pinchas spread the black bread, still warm from the ovens, across the long metal tables. Outside, a strong wind was blowing. The men worked quickly, in a kind of assembly line, one setting out the bread, one painting on the poison, one returning the bread to the tables. Each noise set Lebke's heart racing. After two hours, using small brushes, the men had painted three thousand loaves with poison.

Then, bang! Something smashed into the building. Lebke looked up, poison dripping from his brush. He swallowed hard, crossed the room and looked out the window. A shutter. A shutter had come apart in the wind and banged into the building. It did not matter. The guard would still come up to check. He would search the bakery and find the poison.

"Let's give him something else to find," said Lebke.

He tossed several unpoisoned loaves of bread into a bag and set the bag next to an open window. The guard, coming upon the bread, would assume there had been a robbery. There were severe food shortages in Germany, and such thefts were not uncommon.

Pinchas climbed into the empty drum and the other man went out the window—his work was finished. Lebke quickly hid the bottles of poison and slid under the floorboards. A few minutes later, the floorboards creaked as the guard walked through the room. A flashlight danced on the walls. Taking no chances, the guard called for a policeman. The policeman found the sacks of bread by the open window, sighed and said, "Robbery."

When the guard and the policeman left, Lebke climbed out from under the floorboards. The sky in the window was turning gray. The delivery trucks would soon arrive. Lebke made certain the bread was arranged on its trays. He hugged Pinchas. The men then went out the window, over the roof and down a drainpipe. Delivery trucks were idling in the distance. People were already in the street, men going to jobs, construction workers, cars, buses. A taxi crawled by. Lebke flagged down the driver. He said he wanted to go to the border of Czechoslovakia.

The driver looked at him.

"Don't worry," said Lebke. "I have money."

The next afternoon, a girl walked alone on the road out of Nuremberg. She looked like a military wife in leather shoes and a high-
collared dress. Her eyes were green and her brown hair hung to her
shoulders. It was spring, the road filled with the clatter of American
trucks, soldiers hanging from the back in the sunshine. Country
houses hunkered in the distance. Wooden signs pointed the way to
Stalag 13. Across the fields, the prison camp loomed in a geometry of
barbed wire, walls and towers. The streets near the camp were lined
with small, single-family houses, rooms for rent. Most of the rooms
were taken by the wives of prisoners, young women awaiting the
outcome of the war trials. The girl went house to house, knocking on
doors. She asked to talk to the wives of prisoners. If such a woman
came out to the porch, the girl turned sad and weepy. Her German
was awful. "I've heard the most terrible stories," she said. "An illness
in the camp. Men sick. Is it true? Please, my husband is in the camp.
A Nazi from Poland. We are both Poles. Please. Is he alive? Tell me.
Please."

Some of the wives put an arm around the girl, brushing her face
with a handkerchief. Yes, it is terrible. Many of the men are in the
hospital. Some are deathly ill. The Americans say it is food poisoning. Nothing is certain.

As the girl walked down the street, head down, shoulders
slumped, she looked devastated. On her face, hidden beneath her
hair, was the glimmer of a smile. She was a Jewish girl from Vilna,
Rachel Glicksman, the girl whom Abba had turned away from the
sewers. With her mother, she had survived the camps and gone on to
work for the Bricha. Her mother had gone ahead to Palestine. Rachel
stayed behind, hoping to join Avengers. She was sent to Nuremberg
disguised as the wife of a Nazi to scout out what happened when the
bread reached camp. In the course of the day, walking block to block,
she learned that yes, something terrible had overtaken Stalag 13. She
could sense it most in the American guards, in what they did not say,
how they turned away when she asked questions. The night before,
hundreds, perhaps thousands, of Germans had been rushed to the

hospital. There was a panic. No one knew just what was happening. Before sundown, Rachel was back on the road to Nuremberg. By midnight, she was on a train for France.

A few days later, the story turned up in the newspapers. Members of Avengers would sit together, reading the articles, discussing each sentence. On April 24, 1946, it appeared in the *New York Times.*

POISON PLOT TOLL OF NAZIS AT 2,238
Arsenic bottles found by U.S. Agents in
Nuremberg Bakery That served Prison Camp

Nuremberg, Germany, April 22 (AP)—United States army authorities said tonight that additional prisoners of war have been stricken with arsenic poisoning, bringing to 2,238 the number taken ill in a mysterious plot against 15,000 former Nazi Elite Guard Men confined in a camp near Nuremberg.

It was never clear just how many people were killed in the attack. Like a story from mythology, it varies with each telling. The *New York Times* said no one died, that all the German prisoners were saved in the hospital. To this day, the members of Avengers believe this to be a self-serving fiction, a story created by American officials charged with guarding the Nazis. Other papers said thousands of the Germans died. In *America's Achilles Heel,* a 1997 book about nuclear weapons and chemical terrorism, the writers (Richard Falkenwrath, Robert Newman and Bradley Thayer) claim that "The most lethal chemical poisoning ever, outside of the Nazi gas chambers, appears to be the arsenic poisoning of several thousand captive German SS soldiers in April 1946 by the Jewish reprisal organization Nokmim [Avengers]."

But does it matter how many Germans were killed? If you are a certain kind of literalist, if you save receipts and keep box scores, if you need charts and statistics, then I suppose it does matter. But to those of us looking for the stories that cannot be converted into statistics, the passions moving beneath the surface, it is not ultimately important if one or one thousand men died in Stalag 13. It is not the Germans we are concerned with, after all; it is the Jews. And to Abba, it was never really a matter of leaving corpses behind, but instead of leaving a story behind. He played for the future, for the next generation and the generations after that, for the thrill a kid feels fifty years later when he stumbles across the story in the stacks of the public library. After a war in which the Jews were starved and degraded, in which millions of them were killed in factories, this ragged group, led by a fanatic named Kovner, fought on. Their mere existence was their victory. More than anything, they left the legend of their struggle, a way to look back at history and say, "Here there was a fight."

Each morning, when Abba woke up, he had to remind himself that he was in a jail in Cairo. He had been there for four months, a dusty cell that looked out on a clear blue desert sky. In the morning, the wind carried the smell of markets, spice and incense. Abba in chains in Egypt; the symbolism was not lost on him. Most of the men in the prison were Germans, soldiers captured by the British in North Africa. As he lay in his bunk, Abba, who was isolated from the other inmates, would listen to the soldiers speaking German. There was nothing else to do but sweat and think. In his mind, Abba wandered through the hours just before his capture—the ship, the soldiers—trying to discover who had betrayed him. He also thought of Avengers, wondering if his note had got through, if Vitka had gone ahead with Plan B. Now and then, he lost track of time. He did not know if he had been in jail for a week, a month, a year. He felt the world had left him, he had been forgotten. At night, he could hear camels bellowing in the desert, ships at sea.

Then, a little more each day, his thoughts turned to Palestine. Like a gift, his youthful obsessions were returned to him, plans and dreams—only now, touched by the melancholy of experience. He thought of life on a Jewish settlement, crops planted and harvested, children born. The fury of the War had loosened its hold, like the unclenching of a fist. All at once, revenge was in his past. It was as if

Abba were a diver swimming up from the ocean floor to the warm water where the sun shines.

In the spring of 1946, Abba—probably owing to the influence of the Jewish leaders in Palestine—was transferred to Jerusalem. There are pictures of the city in every Arab home in Palestine and in thousands of Jewish living rooms in New York. It is seen in etchings and engravings, each showing the same sweep of stone, walls and towers. The city has been looked at so many times it can hardly be seen. It is approached only through a tangle of expectations. Your only hope is to come on it by surprise, in a brief moment when the stream of thought has been shut off. Or else you can see the city the way Abba did, through the barred windows of a prison truck. For Abba, the walls and churches were like a greeting at the end of a long journey—Jerusalem as it is seen through the eyes of the exile. "Without the Jerusalem of Lithuania," he said, "there is no Jerusalem at all."

The British jail was in the Old City just inside Jaffa Gate. It was built of the same dusty stone that makes up the Western Wall. Beyond the windows of the jail, which were covered with barbed wire, were the hushed, secretive streets of the Armenian Quarter. After just a few weeks, Abba was released. No one told him why.

In those early days of freedom, Abba had his first good look at Palestine. It was not as he had imagined—in the old Zionist literature, Palestine is called "A land without a people for a people without a land." Now, whether or not he chose to admit it, Abba must have seen that there *were* people in the land, Arabs. He could feel tension in the towns, the electricity of a coming war.

One night, he sat down and wrote Vitka. He wanted her to bring the members of Avengers to Palestine. The fight would continue. The battlefield would change.

Each afternoon, Vitka, who reached the French city of Lyon in the spring of 1946, waited at the train station for the members of Avengers. The fighters arrived with the news: Nuremberg was the only city where Plan B was carried out. In Dachau, someone had tipped off the police; the agents had barely made it across the border with the authorities in hot pursuit. In the other cities, there were mistakes, near-misses, getaways. Always something. This failure only confirmed what Vitka had believed from the beginning—that it takes a special kind of soldier to lead a secret life, plotting and planning, never losing sight of the prize. Most of the fighters, especially those who had been in the concentration camps, were just too brutalized to carry out the mission.

Within a few days, over fifty members of Avengers reached Lyon. Vitka called them to a meeting. Most of the fighters were anxious for another shot at revenge. They had come to Lyon expecting new orders: Plan C. To them, the city was just a way station, a place to lie low until everything cooled down. Vitka took a piece of paper from her pocket. Abba's letter. She read it out loud. In it, he asked the members of Avengers to travel to Palestine and join him on a kibbutz. The letter did not go into great detail, but its tone suggested that the revenge was moving into a new phase. Abba seemed to be saying, "Come home."

When Vitka finished reading, there was a moment of silence and then the room filled with voices.

What does it mean?

Is Abba calling off the revenge?

People who had relied on Abba, his strength and leadership, now turned on him viciously. Some called him a traitor.

A few months later, when Ruzka learned about the meeting, she said: "If I met people who thought in such a way, I would spit in their faces. If someone, in a period of four months, can turn a man they idolize into a traitor, that is the end of the world."

The argument went on for days. In the end, the members of Avengers decided to talk to Abba in person. Perhaps he had called them to Palestine to plan another mission. Perhaps in a month or two, he would lead them back to Germany.

The group traveled to Marseilles, where they blended in with the crowds of Jewish refugees on their way to Palestine. For days, they waited for a ship. At night, they slept on the beach. Vitka spent much of her time with a young blonde woman named Lena who, for Avengers, had worked as a maid in one of the concentration camps.

Somehow, Lena had gotten hold of a camera. She took dozens of pictures, documenting the trip to Palestine. In one photo, the ship sits at the dock in France, the crew waiting on deck. Most of the sailors were Americans, former officers in the US Navy who had been moved by the destruction of the War. Many thought of themselves for the first time as Jews. They volunteered to run the refugees through the British blockade. In Lena's pictures, they look like the Americans in war movies, clean-cut with high cheekbones, naive, happy, untouched by the stink of history.

In one photo, Vitka stands on deck, her hair tossed in the wind. Refugees stare out at the horizon. Vitka could tell a partisan from a survivor at twenty feet. The partisans were soldiers—giving orders, taking orders. The survivors were in some way crippled, sitting until told to move, moving until told to sit. On deck, the many refugees blended into a single refugee, a wreck in need of repair. With them was a strange man. He asked questions, then stood in a passageway to scribble down notes. Vitka asked a sailor who the man was.

"The American author Irving Stone," said the sailor. "He is writing about the refugees."

Vitka was shocked by Irving Stone. After a few days on the ship, she says, without food or space, he seemed to be suffering as much as a man who had spent two years in Auschwitz.

As the boat traveled south, the wind turned warm and the color of the water changed. Birds followed the ship in formations that Vitka recognized from the Russian air force. Sometimes, one of the birds dove into the choppy wake, feeding off the garbage thrown overboard. In one photo, Vitka looks into the wind as the birds fly above, forming a halo around her head.

One afternoon, a sailor told the refugees to be ready—the lead ships of the British blockade were just over the horizon. The refugees and some of the crew moved into a fishing boat that had been brought out from Palestine. The sailors did not want to chance losing the big ship, which was needed to ferry thousands more refugees. There is a picture of Vitka stepping into the fishing boat, smiling at the camera—a summer adventure. There are more pictures taken hours later, when the boat, overflowing with people, was surrounded by British warships. As the British move in, tightening the noose, the photos grow darker and darker. In one shot, the deck of a cruiser looms high above, like an eclipse of the sun. In another shot, British sailors have come aboard. Some Jews grapple with the sailors. At the edge of the photo, Vitka leans back, looking skeptically at a young English officer.

The British towed the boat to Haifa. The docks were crowded with Jews, the faces of Poland, the ghetto, the forest. Vitka could hear them shouting out the names of vanished towns.

THE DESERT

ABBA AND RUZKA met the ship, standing on the crowded pier as the boat was towed in. Ruzka could see the refugees on deck. In the center of the crush, set apart by the deep calm of her eyes, was Vitka.

The refugees climbed onto the dock. British soldiers formed a barricade with their rifles, holding back the crowd. Some Jews cursed at the soldiers. A week before, the Irgun, an underground Jewish army, had bombed the King David Hotel in Jerusalem, where the British had their headquarters. In response, the British had arrested the leaders of the Jewish Agency, a roundup that the Jews were calling the Black Sabbath. When the refugees walked by, some of the Jews tried to push aside the soldiers. Others shouted out the names of towns, or held out water and food: grapefruit, oranges, bread. The soldiers threw back the crowd and shoved the refugees onto the buses that would take them to the internment camp in Atlit. As Vitka crossed the dock, a British soldier took her wrist. A moment later, she was standing next to Abba and Ruzka.

Abba, who had already collected a few debts from the Jewish leaders in Palestine, was able to secure Vitka twenty-four hours of freedom. That afternoon, Ruzka, Abba and Vitka drove into Haifa, which climbs from the sea like bleachers in a stadium, each turn opening new vistas of skyscape and light. There was so much to say that they said nothing, swimming in all that dusty silence. They ate dinner at a seafood restaurant in the hills.

In the morning, they drove into the flat country, where Vitka was due in Atlit. Alone now, she stood in a line of refugees, British guards blinking in the glare. Her day of freedom only made it more difficult. In a clammy metal warehouse, the women were separated from the men. Vitka was stripped and showered, lice falling from her body. That night she slept in a clean hard bed. The barracks were crowded with Jews from Europe, including the members of Avengers. The rooms were hot and steamy. From the rafters, people hung bags filled with shirts, letters, books. There was a record player in one of the bunks and a single recording of Mozart, which had been passed, for years, from outgoing inmates to the new arrivals. For many Jews, the symphony became a sound track of their days in camp—drums crashing like the boots of the guards, horns running together like the voices of the prisoners, strings rising like the hills beyond the fence. And the silence between the notes, the things they did not say.

Because an official had been bribed, Vitka was soon released from Atlit. That afternoon, she caught a ride to Ein Hachoresh, the kibbutz where Abba and Ruzka were living. Ein Hachoresh is fifty miles south of Haifa, a tidy kibbutz of neat yards and cypress trees with paths running between the white, low-slung houses. Dogs laze beneath the trees and muddy tools sit beside front doors. There is a dining hall where, after dinner, tables are pushed back and discussions begin, sometimes going all night. From the yards, you can see groves and vineyards and, in the distance, the scrubby brown earth of the Jordan Valley. In those days, there was a constant threat of Arab raids, so the settlement was surrounded by a high fence. Each night, farmers took their turn walking the perimeter, rifles across their backs.

The kibbutz was founded in the 1920s by eighty Jewish families, mostly from Poland, all of them members of The Young Guard. These people—they called themselves pioneers—promised to build a society without classes or restrictions; in the process, they would create a new kind of Jew, a renaissance figure free of fear, an intellectual who plows his fields in the morning, writes his books in the afternoon. In the fields, the pioneers dressed like Russian peasants, in open-collared shirts and heavy boots. They were not religious. To them, the rituals of the synagogue were products of the Diaspora. In Palestine, speaking Hebrew, working the land, Jews would again be Jews by birthright. In even the most laid-back of these pioneers, you would find a strong utopian streak, a promise to cast aside the old divisions: rich and poor, male and female. All property was shared, even children, who were raised away from their parents in a community house. The boys and girls showered together. "Perhaps we shall be the first torrent of youth to remain forever young, humanity's first chance to escape failure," reads an early statement from The Young Guard. "Let us go between far mountains and deserts to live in simplicity, beauty and truth."

In Israel, these men were not trying to reestablish a relationship with an ancient homeland; they were instead acknowledging a relationship that they believed had been there all along. The covenant of Abraham exists at all times, in the present tense. Some of them quoted the Bible: "The Lord made the covenant not with our fathers alone, but with us, even us, who are all of us here alive this day."

Abba had been sent to the kibbutz by leaders of The Young Guard, who had promised there would be enough room to settle his entire partisan army. Ruzka had moved from Eilon, where she had lived for almost a year. When Vitka arrived, she lived with Abba in a house that belonged to a longtime resident—a gift, a homecoming. A month later, she and Abba moved to a temporary shelter, a shanty that cooked in the sun. As it was too hot to spend the afternoons inside, they napped in the yards. Every few days, another member of Avengers turned up.

In the early mornings, the members of the group worked in the beet fields. At night, they met under the rising moon. In whispers, they talked of revenge. Several of the fighters wanted to buy poison and return to Europe. Some spoke of killing six million Germans. Abba urged caution. Such plans could have been successful only in a certain historical moment, after the War and before the peace, when Germany was in chaos—no police, no rule, no borders. That moment was now over. Winston Churchill was talking of an Iron Curtain descending across Europe, and West Germany was being remade as a bulwark against Communism. The Cold War had begun; the members of Avengers would not stand a chance in this new Europe. "You can fight for your revenge right here," said Abba. "And here you will fight for the future, not the past."

Abba convinced most of the members of Avengers. Even those who disagreed with him were too tired to go back to Europe. They wanted only to lead normal lives. Over time, many of these men and women simply drifted apart. Those who were survivors could not stand the life of the kibbutz; rising before dawn to a world of fences and towers reminded them of the camps. Others missed the lights of a big city. The countryside of Palestine, where Arabs went by the lunar calendar and Bedouin traveled by the moon, was still dominated by the night. Several members of Avengers moved to Haifa or Tel Aviv, where they would sit on balconies, watching the great ships sail for Europe.

There were a few members of Avengers, however, who could not be convinced, who called Abba a traitor and said his mind had been ruined in jail in Egypt. Behind every argument, they sensed a trick. In the fields, they shouted, "A German for every Jew." For the most part, these were not the partisans who had fought in the ghetto or the forest; these were survivors of the concentration camps. In Palestine, such survivors were made to feel ashamed, were accused, in Abba's words, of going like sheep—the nameless, endless, bulldozed dead. In other words, these were people with something to prove. And now here was Abba, trying to take from them the one thing that might mean deliverance—revenge.

It fell to Ruzka, the small girl whom everyone trusted, to convince these people to start a new life in Palestine. She spoke to Rachel Glicksman, who was now living on the kibbutz. Ruzka told Rachel that it was time to move beyond revenge. "Your existence cannot be based on negation," she said. "You cannot live only with death."

"How can you ask me to give up the struggle?" asked Rachel.

"Every kibbutz, every village, every individual, is an underground, is a struggle," said Ruzka. "In this country, the struggle is over life, not death."

One afternoon, ten members of Avengers told Abba they were returning to fight in Germany.

"It is too late for revenge," said Abba.

They cursed Abba, promising never to speak to him again—a promise they kept. They were gone by the evening.

Rachel Glicksman was the last member of this renegade group to leave for Europe, where she would join her husband, a survivor whom she had met in Ponteba after the War. On the way to the airport, Rachel was pulled over by a policeman; he had been tipped to the scheme. He gave her a choice. Go to jail or go home.

"So you know what I did," Rachel says today. "I went home."

Within a few months, the German police caught up with the rest of the group. It is unclear just what went wrong—no one in the group talks about it. They instead shake their heads, saying, "Very bad. Very bad." A few members were arrested while robbing a bank; they needed money for guns and poison. Rachel's husband spent three years in a German prison. By the time he made it back to Tel Aviv, Israel had become a state—the war was over. "He missed it," says Rachel. The events leading up to the arrests remain a mystery. When one of these fighters dies, a shiver goes through the group. Another keeper of the secret is gone, the story lives in one less mind; soon it will be just another strange tale lost in the sweep of history.

Each day, before dawn, Abba and Vitka and Ruzka worked in the fields with the kibbutzniks, some from Europe, some born in Palestine. As they picked grapes, the farmers talked over the swaying vines. They talked about the political situation in Palestine, about the Haganah and the other underground Jewish armies struggling to drive out the British. For the British, who had a hundred thousand troops in the country, Palestine was growing too expensive to rule. One night, to terrorize the authorities, the Haganah blew up sixteen bridges. On other nights, Jewish soldiers repulsed Arab raids, protected settlements and went on raids of their own. As Vitka worked, she could sometimes see an Arab tending his fields in the distance, wearing a white headdress and moving along the horizon, an echo of the ancient life of the land.

Now and then, the workers took a break from the vines. Sitting under the trees, they drank from jugs with water beading down the

Vitka Kempner working in the fields of the kibbutz.

side. The former partisans, stretched on the grass, lost themselves in old arguments: the ghetto, the forest. The kibbutzniks hung on each word. Sometimes, when Abba stood and said, "Back to work," an old-timer shook his head. "No. Finish about Wittenberg." One of the kibbutzniks had wavy blond hair and beautiful blue eyes. His name was Avi Marle, an immigrant who had come to Palestine from Austria before the War. He spoke of the life, the culture and tradition, he had left behind. He was aware of his luck. To him, the partisan stories held the fascination of a tragedy he had narrowly escaped. In the fields, he arranged it so he could work alongside Ruzka. Avi was a man she could talk to, trust, care about, love. They were soon married.

Around this time, Abba and Vitka, though not actually married, began to speak of each other as man and wife. They did not believe in marriage, the convention of it, standing before a rabbi so he could tell them what they already knew to be true.

The couples moved into houses twenty yards apart. After sundown, Ruzka would sit in her yard, watching the bats that flew from the east to feed on the wild figs that grew in the trees. Their clumsy dives filled the night air with energy. A mist spread on the fields. Ruzka could sometimes see the light go out in the room where Vitka slept with Abba. Was she amazed by the way things had worked out? Did she look at the other house, so much like her own, and ask, "Which house is my house? Which life am I living?" Ruzka was sensible. If such thoughts ever crept into her head, she would have told herself, "Yes, it is all very strange—but compared to what?"

In 1947, the British government announced its decision to withdraw from Palestine. The international community would be left to sort out the mess. On November 29, the United Nations voted to partition the land into two states—Arab and Jewish. The Arab state would be on the West Bank of the Jordan River and would include Bethlehem and Hebron. The Jewish state would run along the Mediterranean coast and the Sea of Galilee—a sliver of land, but the first sovereign Jewish nation in over two thousand years.

On the kibbutz, workers came in from the fields to listen to the vote on the radio. It was like an image from an old American painting, farmers crowded into a small room, floorboards sagging under heavy boots, pitchforks and shovels in the doorway, faces in the glow of the dial. Now and then, the station would fade and a farmer would turn the dial, chasing voices across the night. Abba noted each buzz in the chamber, mumble of voices, shuffle of papers. Every few minutes, a delegate, in Spanish or French or Chinese or Arabic or Portuguese, in a voice filled with happiness or anger or no emotion, would cast a vote—*The sovereign state of Brazil votes for partition.*

Votes were bargained for, traded, reversed. On the kibbutz, even the most educated could not predict the outcome. Most of South America voted for partition, as did many of the nations of Europe. When the final vote was counted, a clamor went up in the chamber.

The next generation—the Kovners and Marles on the kibbutz.

Over the radio, a man said, "The General Assembly of the United Nations, by a vote of thirty-three in favor, thirteen against and ten abstentions, has voted to partition Palestine."

The farmers spilled outside, ran in the fields, muddy shovels in the air, cheering, trailed by dogs.

The next morning, a Jewish bus was fired on by Arabs. Five passengers were killed. In the coming weeks, there were dozens of attacks. The road to Jerusalem, which runs beneath cliff-top Arab villages, was under siege. When a Jewish bus or truck climbed the road, guerrillas rained down bombs. By the end of the year, the one hundred thousand people living in the Jewish part of the city were surviving on rations. Now and then, the British tried to open the road. For the most part, though, they were just killing time until the spring, when their soldiers would pull out. But the Royal Navy still blockaded the coast, preventing the shipment of weapons. Jewish soldiers, who fought back as well as they could, were allotted just a few bullets apiece. Zionists in Europe and America stockpiled equipment to be sent to Palestine when the British withdrew. In Tel Aviv, the Jewish Agency, headed by David Ben-Gurion, was preparing for war. Officers of the Haganah were told to train new immigrants and create fresh military brigades. There was not much time.

One afternoon, a young officer from the Haganah came to the kibbutz, looking for Abba. His name was Shimon Avidan, the German Jew who had once supported Abba's call for revenge. Avidan was stocky with dark eyes and fair hair. Like many Jewish soldiers, he had a thin mustache in the manner of an Arab warrior. For Jews in Palestine, the Arab was the enemy but also a kind of model, a mysterious part of a holy landscape. In battle, more than a few Jews wore headdresses. Avidan had been impressed by Abba's leadership, speeches, use of language. He asked Abba to be one of the staff officers of a new unit, the Givati Brigade, which would consist of three thousand soldiers, many of them immigrants.

Abba would serve as a cultural commissar, an office that does not exist in the American army. He would educate recruits. When war started, he would publish a battle sheet to inspire the soldiers, reminding them who they were and why they were fighting, spelling out the cost of defeat. It was not unlike the work he had done in Vilna, with the release of each new manifesto.

Abba talked about the assignment with Vitka and Ruzka. The women told him that he must serve his country. A few days later, he jumped onto a truck and went down the coast road to an army base. Within weeks, he had moved from the front line of the partisan war to the heights of the officer corps. In the weeks ahead, he would stamp each recruit with his all-or-nothing rhetoric, inspiring less with actions than with words. It was a shift from youth, the tatters of which still clung to him, to adulthood, to life as a poet, to a time when Israeli soldiers would carry his books into battle.

On the kibbutz, Ruzka and Vitka lived the traditional life of women in time of war, waking each morning to the same houses and jobs in the fields. A few weeks before Abba left, Vitka had learned she was pregnant. She did not tell Abba, afraid he would not join the Brigade. Only Ruzka shared her secret. As Vitka worked, perspiration shining on her face, she looked like sculpture, something made in the fields. She talked with Ruzka about the stories from the newspapers, ambushes and raids, the coming British withdrawal. In the Middle East, there were over fifty million Arabs and fewer than six hundred thousand Jews. The women spoke of such things with a singsong calmness, believing that the way to speak of what you fear is to speak of it lightly.

On May 15, 1948, the day the British withdrew from Palestine, the people on the kibbutz again gathered before the radio. David Ben-

Ruzka Korczak after the War.

Gurion was giving a long-anticipated speech. "Impelled by a historic association, the Jews strove throughout the centuries to go back to the land of their fathers and to regain statehood," he said. "By virtue of the natural and historic right of the Jewish people and of the resolution of the General Assembly of the United Nations, we hereby proclaim the establishment of the Jewish state in Palestine called Israel."

As his first order of business, Ben-Gurion annulled the British White Paper, which limited the number of Jews who could emigrate to Palestine. It was a brisk, defiant gesture, a scornful rebuke of the hated policy that had closed the trap on the Jews in the months before World War II. *The law is terrible? OK. Create a nation and revoke the law.* Those Jewish refugees still trapped in Europe, or in internment camps on Cyprus, could now emigrate legally to Palestine. As Ben-Gurion spoke, explosions filled the background—the Egyptian air force bombing Tel Aviv. At midnight, as the last British ships left Haifa, Jews stood on the docks, watching them trail away in the dark, turbulent waters.

The next morning, on May 15, 1948, six Arab armies invaded Israel: Syria and Lebanon from the north, Jordan, Iraq and Saudi Arabia from the west. The biggest threat was in the south, where Egypt sent forty thousand soldiers, supported by planes and tanks, into the Negev Desert. Israel's largest city, Tel Aviv, was a short march from Egypt. If it fell, the Jews would lose the war. The Givati Brigade was sent to meet the invasion. Some questioned the choice. Unlike most of the other brigades, which were largely composed of Palestinian-born Jews, Givati included immigrants and recruits. It was green.

The ranks of the Brigade marched, or else went by truck, through towns and settlements along the seacoast. At low tide, they could see the remains of ancient civilizations. People lined the roads, cheering. Fog pooled in the flats. The soldiers moved in and out of the mist. Within a few weeks, Israel would have sixty thousand citizens in uniform. If you were not in the army, then your son was, or your daughter or granddaughter. Now and then, as the troops went through a town, a soldier would spot his mother, jump from a truck, race through the crowd, kiss his mom, whisper a few words, then dash back, the boys pulling him up into the slow-moving vehicle. Egyptian bombers passed overhead. At night, the windows of the towns were blacked out.

In the afternoon, as the soldiers sat over mess tins, Abba walked before the Brigade, thin and unshaven. In a voice filled with passion,

Abba Kovner marching alongside David Ben-Gurion (left) during the 1948 war.

he told the soldiers that they must never give up, no matter the odds, that defeat would mean the end of the Jewish people. He quoted statements from the enemy camp. Azzman Pasha, of the Arab League, had promised "a war of extermination and a momentous massacre which will be spoken of like the Mongolian massacres."

"We did not want this war," said Abba. "But we will finish it."

.   .   .

Egypt had declared war on May 11, three days before the British withdrawal. The Egyptian soldiers, on the way out of Al Arish, a town in the Sinai desert, marched past King Farouk, the nation's twenty-eight-year-old monarch. Farouk, with his dark eyes and racing stripe of a mustache, was a man in search of a nightclub. He usually wore dinner jackets. On this occasion, he dressed like a German field marshal, and he issued a stamp to commemorate the invasion. A few days before, Prime Minister Nokrashy Pasha had told him, "There will be no war with the Jews. It will be a parade without risk."

On the way to Israel, the Egyptians marched past rocky peaks and across burning red plateaus where the wadis run like cracks in fine china. They paraded through towns of flat-roof houses and spiky gardens. Girls threw flowers from balconies, boys cheered. When the army crossed the border, a small battalion headed for the center of Israel. A large battalion continued up the coast, in and out of villages with biblical names. Gaza, Majdal, Beersheba. By the middle of May, the Egyptians had cut off dozens of Jewish settlements. In a dispatch to King Farouk, the Prime Minister wrote, "We will be in Tel Aviv in two weeks."

The Egyptians first met resistance in Kfar Darom, a kibbutz defended by thirty Orthodox Jews. When Egyptian soldiers reached the settlement fence, the kibbutzniks fired rifles. When the Jews ran out of bullets, they filled their velvet religious bags with TNT and hurled them like hand grenades. The Egyptians, who favored head-on attacks and open-field assaults, fought in the manner of a textbook published no later than 1812. They were unnerved by night fighting, which quickly became an Israeli specialty. When Kfar Darom could hold out no longer, the Jews withdrew, at night, in trucks without headlights. The next morning, the Egyptians bombed the kibbutz for several hours before realizing it had been abandoned.

On May 19, the Egyptians reached Yad Mordechai, a kibbutz above the Gaza Strip. Founded by Polish immigrants, the settlement was named after Mordechai Anielewicz, the leader of the Warsaw Ghetto revolt. Tel Aviv is just forty miles north of the settlement. The Givati Brigade was not yet in position; the soldiers needed a few more days to form a defensive line. For the moment, the kibbutz, defended by just a handful of determined men, was the only obstacle between the enemy and the big cities of Israel. Trenches were dug into the fields. The settlers met the Egyptian army at the fence and fought hand to hand. The Egyptians sent waves of tanks and artillery; each attack was thrown back by desperate, hard-fighting, counterattacking Jews. At night, enemy planes bombed the small cottages of the kibbutz. In the end, the Egyptians were simply too numerous and too well equipped. On May 24, Israeli commandos evacuated the surviving settlers. The next day, King Farouk had his picture taken in the ruins of Yad Mordechai. In Egyptian newspapers, it was said to be the scene of a great victory. But in the five days it took Egypt to capture the kibbutz, the Givati Brigade formed their defensive line.

Ashdod is a dusty southern town of muted colors and boxy houses, streets ending at the sea. The Egyptian army found it deserted, empty alleys opening on empty plazas. The Egyptian soldiers reached a bridge in the center of town. A bomb went off. The bridge crumbled. Shells whistled across the ravine. Soldiers of the Givati Brigade appeared on the opposite bank, firing guns. Four planes flew in from the north, Messerschmitts sweeping over the buildings, strafing the Egyptian line. The planes, the first of the Israeli Air Force, had been bought as scrap and rebuilt in machine shops. The Israelis cheered the pilots, most of whom had served during the Second World War in the Royal Air Force. For the Egyptians, it was a shock. They were no longer alone in the skies.

As the armies battled, members of the United Nations shuttled from camp to camp, trying to broker a compromise. After weeks of back-and-forth, the UN arranged a cease-fire, which went into effect at sundown on June 11, 1948. For Israel, the most precarious days of the

War of Independence were over. With few weapons and little ammunition, they had held back attacks on every border. Only in Jerusalem, where they faced the well-trained army of Jordan, did the Israelis suffer a major setback; they were forced to abandon the Jewish Quarter of the Old City. Now, in the few days before fighting was to resume, the Israelis were able to bring in the equipment they had stockpiled in Europe and America—bullets, machine guns, cannons, airplanes, tanks. They also drafted and trained many of the one hundred thousand refugees who had reached the country since the war began. In the field, Israeli soldiers would now outnumber Arab soldiers. "I knew we had won," Ben-Gurion later said. "They could not conquer us. It was only a question of how far we could go."

In the spring, the Iraqi army had passed within a few miles of Ein Hachoresh. At night, standing in the fields, Ruzka and Vitka could see the mortar shells flash like heat lightning. There was diesel in the wind and the smell of burning crops. Vitka gave birth during the cease-fire; she had told Abba of her pregnancy a few months before. When a former partisan girl gave birth, it seemed miraculous. In the forest, most of these girls had stopped menstruating. They thought the War had left them barren. By having children, they believed they were undoing the work of the Germans. Abba saw the baby two weeks later, during his leave. When he held the child, the sleeves of his green uniform rolled back, something inside him broke. They named the baby after Abba's brother Michael, who had been killed by Polish peasants in the Narocz forest.

When the cease-fire ended, there were ten days of fighting, then another cease-fire. When the second cease-fire ended, the Givati Brigade turned south, determined to roll back the Egyptian army and relieve Jewish settlements behind the line. There were commando raids and firefights, fog rolling in, guns flashing. The Israelis captured towns and cities, including the ancient caravan stop of Beersheba. By the summer of 1948, the Egyptians had been pushed into the Faluja

Pocket, a valley shadowed by desert hills. Though beaten to a stand-still and surrounded, the Egyptians refused to retreat.

Each night, in the silky sway of his tent, Abba wrote manifestos which were translated into Arabic, printed on flyers and dropped, by plane, into the Faluja Pocket. The manifestos were written in the classic style of propaganda: *Why are you fighting? You have no quarrel with us! You are fighting only for the amusement of the rich men in Cairo, while these same rich men make love to your wives!* Speaking of Abba's fly-ers, one of the Egyptian officers said, "It is not the guns of the Jews that kill us—it is those terrible words."

The Israelis arranged a meeting with "The Tiger," the top-ranking Egyptian general, whose real name was Said Tasha Bey. The Tiger was a slight stump of a man, with bright eyes and a face like an exclamation point. In the meeting, Yigal Allon, an Israeli general, urged Tasha Bey to surrender, saying, "You have lost everything but your honor. There is nothing dishonorable about surrendering after a hard fight."

Tasha Bey said he would not surrender until he had fired his last bullet.

On each front, the enemy had been beaten back. Only southern Israel and the disputed Old City of Jerusalem were under foreign control. The United Nations would soon force a third cease-fire, and then a permanent settlement with borders determined by the final position of the armies. If the Egyptians remained south of Ashdod, the Israelis would lose the Negev desert, dozens of Jewish towns and access to the Red Sea. But the only way south was down the coast road, which was fortified by Egyptian regiments. A head-on attack would mean thousands of Israeli deaths. Jewish leaders were desper-ate to find a way around the enemy.

Weeks went by. The wind turned sharp and cold. Abba loved the desert nights—desolate, windswept, endless, empty. He went out walking, an officer inspecting troops. These nights were very different from the forest nights of Europe. In Europe, the trees crowded out the sky and the wind rustled in the leaves overhead. In Palestine, the landscape was without shade and there was no relief or windbreak. From a rise, Abba could see the Brigade camped below. The tents shimmered in the moonlight. A Jewish army poised for the final battle. It was the culmination of his struggle. No matter what happens now, he told himself, the future will be better than the past.

Across the wastes, in a military planning room, an officer came upon a solution to the Egyptian riddle. It was like a twist in a South American novel, a solution that brought the past into the present, or, better yet, proved there really is no past, that what people call the past is where we have been living all along. While studying aerial photographs of the Negev desert, the officer, who just happened to be a respected archaeologist, noticed a ghostly structure winding beneath the sand. He held the photos up to a light. Yes. A road. He did some research and found out that the Romans had built a road through this desert two thousand years before. Yigal Allon sent soldiers to investigate. Here and there, the road was exposed. In most places, it was about two feet deep in sand. Over the next three nights, hundreds of Israeli soldiers, working in the chill, uncovered forty miles of road. It went from Beersheba to El Aluja, bypassing the Egyptian army. The Israelis laid wire on the road so that the treads of their tanks would not get caught in the ancient bricks.

On December 25, the Israeli Navy—a few ragged ships bought as scrap—shelled the Egyptians hunkered on the coast road. By firing from the sea, the Israelis distracted the enemy, causing them to turn away from the desert, where the Israeli soldiers were creeping down the ancient road. In the morning, the Israelis attacked the enemy from behind. The Egyptians, taken by complete surprise, fled down the beach into the Sinai desert. Passing through towns where, just a few months before, they had been greeted with parades, the Egyptians were pelted with stones. The Israelis followed in hot pursuit, a development that took the international community by surprise. Until now, the Israelis had waged a defensive war, never straying beyond their borders. They had now crossed into the territory of a sovereign nation, advancing as far as Al Arish, the desert town where the Egyptians had begun their advance.

The British government sent a message: If Israel did not withdraw, the British would honor the military pact they had signed with Egypt before World War II, which obligated Britain to defend Egypt's borders. A few hours later, the Royal Air Force sent six jets into the Negev. Jewish pilots met them in the desert sky. All six British planes were shot down. The British quickly issued an ultimatum: Israel had twenty-four hours to pull out of the Sinai. Over the next several hours, the Jewish soldiers, riding on tanks and trucks, went back across the border. Though an official armistice would not be signed for months, the fighting was over. It had been terribly costly for the Israelis. Six thousand Jews had been killed—one percent of the new nation's population.

On a cool, cloudless afternoon in late autumn, Abba made his way north, walking, hitching rides. Every soldier he met had a story to tell. He listened with his eyes closed. Sometimes, he looked at the road moving fast beneath his boots. He smoked. He saw trucks and tanks, men standing in the shade, a pretty girl soldier with a pink shirt showing under her drab green uniform. Drivers waved and honked. Now and then, an Israeli plane went across the sky. The sea glittered. There was less traffic beyond Tel Aviv. A few European cars heading toward Haifa. A truck broken down on the side of the road. A soldier at a crossroads waiting for a ride home. In each face, Abba could see the features of a friend who had been lost. He got down from the truck and walked. The road was warm. He turned from the sea, a rifle slung across his shoulders. The last of the sun was in the valleys. As he came through the tall grass, he could see the kibbutz, its vineyards and paths, the lights coming on in the red-roofed houses. The wind moved in the fields.

Afterword

I N THE SUMMER OF 1998, I flew to Israel, where I would stay in Jerusalem and spend my days meeting with those former partisans who still lived in the country, tracking down the war stories I first heard on childhood visits to the kibbutz. On the flight, I read books about the country and thought back to the times I spent with Ruzka and Vitka and Abba: Ruzka at our house in Illinois, driving her to Lake Michigan, her amazement at the inland sea, her curiosity, how everything she looked at remade her; Vitka in New York, eating Chinese food on the Upper West Side, talking of the jazz she had heard in Greenwich Village; Abba, a distinguished man with gray hair, walking me through the National Gallery of Art in Washington, D.C., carefully noting the drama of light in each painting. And later, Abba, sitting with my family in his hotel room, tired but not wanting us to leave, taking a pillow to the bathroom and catching a nap in the bathtub. Twenty minutes later, he returned to the discussion well rested.

Abba died in 1987, after a long battle with throat cancer. When my father and mother went to see him in the hospital in Israel, he insisted the nurse carry him across the room to a chair, though it was painful. He did not think it proper to meet with a visitor while sitting in bed. A few weeks before, in Memorial Sloan-Kettering Hospital in New York, the doctors had removed his vocal cords. This man, who lived on the power of his voice, who stood before partisans in the ghetto, before soldiers in the desert, shouting angry words, spent his last days in silence. By this time, Abba was a national hero in Israel, a symbol of defiance. His poetry had won the nation's highest honors and his own history had become part of the national history. Several years before, he had designed the Diaspora Museum in Tel Aviv, one of the most important institutions in the nation. In the museum, there are pictures of the Jewish towns and synagogues of Europe. To

Abba Kovner in the 1980s, near the end of his life.

Abba, it was not enough to know just about the slaughter of the Holocaust. *How can you know what we lost, if you do not know what we had?* To him, the various fields of study—the Jews in Europe, the tragedies of war, the triumph of Israel—were scenes from a single epic.

In the museum is my all-time favorite exhibit. I call it: "I can't believe it's a Jew!" A television screen flashes the names and faces of famous people. These celebrities, alike in no other way, are all Jews. Jackie Mason. Amedeo Modigliani. Marcel Proust. As the images flicker, you say to yourself, "Well sure, just listen to the last name." Or: "Freud! Who doesn't know that!" Or: "What? No way! I can't believe it's a Jew!" I like the exhibit partly because it is funny, partly because it gets to the heart of a Jewish need. Well, I suppose I can speak only for myself, and maybe for my Aunt Renee. We, me and my Aunt Renee, need to know that one story is not every story, that there are as many kind of Jews, as many possibilities, as there are kinds of people. To me, Abba is an example of the variety of human experience. He is a man who lived outside the standard narrative. In America, in the part of it where I grew up, anyway, there is an accepted version of what happened to the Jews in the Second World War. It is the story of boxcars and death camps. It is a story sanctified by Hollywood in the work of Steven Spielberg and also of that incorrigible Italian funnyman, Roberto Benigni. Yes. This is an important story; maybe the most important. It is what happened to the vast majority of Jews in the War. And yet: It is not the only story. Sometimes, when I look at a picture of Abba in the forest, his eyes cold and hard, a gun in his hands, I think, "I can't believe it's a Jew."

When my plane landed in Israel, I was met at the airport by Michael Kovner, Abba and Vitka's son. He was wearing torn jeans and a faded work shirt. I looked at him in a way that made him say, "How do I look? Very proletarian, no?" Michael is handsome, with warm brown eyes and a sunburned face and the kind of smile you work to see. I have told many bad jokes just to see that smile. Michael had just turned fifty, which meant Israel had also turned fifty. He was born during the first cease-fire—the son of the nation. Also at the airport was Michael's sister, Shlomit, who was born nine years later. She was waiting to meet her in-laws, who were arriving on the same flight. We spoke to her for a few minutes, and then we went out to Michael's truck.

In the back of the truck were a dozen paintings, beautiful loopy renditions of fields, hills and valleys. Michael is a painter. I have three of his paintings in my apartment in New York. They show the dusty houses of Jerusalem, or the sunny groves of the kibbutz. On the way to Jerusalem, I was surrounded by landscapes, out the window, in the car.

Michael says it is his mission to paint Israel, not as the tourists make themselves see it, but as it really is—a place where people wake up and go to work. Lately, he has been painting haystacks. When he was a kid on the kibbutz, he would get girls to go with him into the hay. "So you see," he says, smiling, "these are not just pictures of life on a farm."

Michael served in an elite unit of the army, a behind-the-lines battalion that rescued hostages from Entebbe. It was the unit in which Ehud Barak and Benjamin Netanyahu served. Being the son of Abba and Vitka requires the occasional daring act. I have met some of the men he served with; I was with them as they walked through the Old City of Jerusalem, shoulder to shoulder down the narrow streets, like football players in a high school hallway. And I have heard stories of courageous things Michael did with his unit, which I know he would not want me to mention. He prefers the simple memories of his days in the army. Once, as we were driving through the Hudson River Valley in New York, I asked him if it was scary going behind enemy lines on missions into Lebanon or Jordan. "Only when you first cross over," he told me. "That is when you can get shot. After that, it is like camping." A story he once told me—caught in a freak snowstorm on the Golan Heights, trapped for a week in his tiny tent, with canned food and time to kill, he read *The Magic Mountain*—caused me to read that entire book, trying hard to imagine myself as a snowbound commando.

During his service in the army, Michael refused to be stationed on the West Bank. He was excused from service there but in return had to stay on active military duty for an extra number of years. When Michael speaks of his views, which are to the left of his mother's, Vitka shakes her head and says, "Michael, you are so naive. You have never been anything but the majority. You know so little of the real world."

In Jerusalem, I rented an apartment in the old German Colony. Each day, I would drive a rented car to the home of some former partisan, or some member of Avengers. Now and then, Michael went with me on interviews. If someone could not speak English, he translated. At night, we went to a cafe where the waiter served us watermelon so green it was blue, and the fruit was red and delicious and we ate it in slices with cheese. On my birthday, Michael gave me a small painting of an orange grove on the kibbutz.

In August, Michael and a friend of his, a historian, took me on a tour of the battlefields where Abba served in the War of Independence: Ashdod and Yad Mordechai and Iraq-Sudan, a police fort occupied by the Egyptians. It was a key position and it took the Israelis many battles to capture. The facade is bullet-scarred. Inside the building, which is now a museum of the Givati Brigade, there are pictures of Abba. When I was there, a unit of recruits came through, boots pounding the stone floor. They were very young. In another room, they watched a film about the history of the Brigade. I could hear them cheering.

On the way back to Jerusalem, we drove through fields of sunflowers. Michael told me to get out of the car and pick a flower. The tops of the flowers were black from the sun and the stalks were as rough as rope. When I pulled, the flower seemed to pull back. My hands started to bleed. In the car, Michael set the flower on the dashboard. As he drove, he picked at the seeds. I realized I had never before seen a sunflower reach its proper conclusion. The seeds were in perfect rows, as if arranged by a pastry chef.

"It's like a miracle," I said.

The historian, dozing in the backseat, sat up and said, "A miracle? It is no miracle."

"Yes, a miracle," said Michael. "All of it is a miracle."

I spent a few weeks on the kibbutz, sleeping in a guest house under the trees. My bed was surrounded by fans. Each morning, I met Vitka in her garden. She wore a straw hat and a sundress. As I came up, she put her hands on her hips and smiled. She had just returned from an office she keeps on the kibbutz. After the War, Vitka went back to school to become a psychiatrist. She pioneered a system, used around the world, in which troubled children communicate with colors. As she speaks of her work, I remind myself that Vitka was a child when the War began, and that by helping these children she might be helping herself heal as well. We talked in her living room. As she spoke, she would often walk to the refrigerator and return with slices of melon. "Grown on the kibbutz," she would say. It was very sweet. She told her stories in wide-eyed amazement, as if she could hardly believe them herself.

Some days, she took me to other settlements to meet former partisans. In one house, I saw the work of a survivor, who, using toothpicks, had built replicas of dozens of synagogues destroyed in Poland. The models were hung on the wall, and they were strange and delicate and beautiful.

One morning, Lebke told us how, with most of his fingers gone, he was still able to poison the bread. As he spoke, he gave me a shrug that I recognize from my own grandmother. It means, "You would have done the same."

At night, I ate in the dining hall of the kibbutz. The food was often served by Ghadi, Ruzka's youngest son, who was the general secretary of the kibbutz. In Ein Hachoresh, leadership means the opposite of privilege. Ghadi has gray hair and lively blue eyes. He would wink when he saw me coming and slap down an extra piece of chicken or fish. The food on the kibbutz is no more and no less than you need to put in a good day's work. Ruzka's oldest child, my cousin Yehuda, was then living in Toronto, where he worked for the kibbutz movement of Israel. I went to see him there when I decided to write this book. I asked for his blessing and he looked at me like I was crazy. "What is this, a Victorian wedding?" he said. "Ruzka would want you to tell it—so tell it."

Sometimes, as I spoke to Vitka, Michael would come into the house, closing the door softly. He had been out in the fields with his easel, painting the groves. When Vitka finished talking, he would take me in his truck, from back road to back road, down to the beach.

It was a beautiful curving shore with the posts of a long-gone pier stretching into the surf. "I grew up here," he said. "This is my beach."

I asked Michael how he felt about the stories of his parents.

"Sometimes, I just think about the people who were living in Vilna at the time," he said. "Those who helped and those who did nothing. It tells you about life."

Looking out at the horizon, he then said, "It is like Jesus. He carries the cross. He falls. Some people spit on him. Some give him water. It will not help. He knows where he is going. Still, it is nice to have water."

I also spent time with Ruzka's daughter, Yonat, who looks like Ruzka without the damage of war. Yonat runs Moreshet, an archive established by Ruzka to collect the stories of survivors. Ruzka believed that people find help by telling their stories. She was a historian, a writer, an activist.

Ruzka died in 1988. Though she had been very ill, her children never knew it. She kept her symptoms hidden. "She would not admit she was sick," Yonat says. "She was too busy caring for Abba. It was like this her entire life. When he died, I think she decided, 'OK, now I can be sick.' "

Abba had his funeral, and Ruzka had hers less than a year later.

On one of my last days in Israel, Vitka spread a map of Eastern Europe out on a table in her living room. "I will show you where you must go," she said. As she circled each street or town, she made a comment: "Some of the people here were good, but most were like dogs."

A few days later, I left Israel. At the airport, I was questioned by a security guard, a young woman soldier who asked me why I was in the country. I told her that I was writing a book. She asked what the book was about and I mentioned Ruzka. The woman leaned back and said, "Ruzka, the partisan?"

And then I was in Vilna, in a hotel a few blocks from the Jewish ghetto. Air travel leaves you no time to bridge the psychic distance. Across the street, a museum was showing pictures by Goya called "The Disasters of War." There were sketches of rapes, beatings, torture. The sidewalk in front of the museum is paved with tombstones from the old Jewish Cemetery. If you look closely, you can see the eroded Hebrew letters, the spread fingers of the high priests, dates of birth and death.

With the help of a guide, I went all over the city—to the poorhouse where Ruzka and Vitka met, to the flat where they lived in the ghetto, to the entrance of the sewer tunnels. The ghetto streets have not changed; they are like an old theatrical set that has never been taken down. It is not hard to imagine the actors going through their parts: Ruzka recruiting fighters, Vitka bleaching her hair, Abba crouching in the sewers. When you know the stories of the fighters, you cannot see these shabby blocks in quite the same way.

I went to visit Shmuel Kaplinsky, the man who had mapped the sewers in Vilna and led the Jews out of the ghetto. He lives with his wife in the same apartment where Abba said good-bye to him on his last day in the city. It is a cinder-block building, a run-down flat at the top of a dark stairwell, one dim light flickering high overhead. His wife was very sick, perhaps dying, and Shmuel sat on the edge of the bed, holding her hand. He wore thick glasses. When he looked up, his eyes appeared huge and strange, like something seen through a microscope. He spoke only Polish. He seemed to believe, if he spoke it loud enough and slapped me on the knee, he could make me understand. His wife, in perfect English, told me of her contempt for America and her belief in the inevitable triumph of Communism. When I disagreed, she scowled, saying, "You know nothing of the dialectic." Before I could reply, my guide shot me a dirty look. The woman was really quite ill.

One evening, I went to Ponar, the forest pits where most of the Jews of Vilna were killed. It was dark when I got there. The trails were narrow in the trees and then opened onto the pits in a reeling vertigo. Overhead, the branches of the trees, black against the black sky, seemed stained by thousands of dying looks. I also went to the Rudnicki forest, where the Jewish partisans had their base. It was a gloomy swamp with mushrooms growing along bug-ridden paths, a miserable place. Some of the partisan dugouts have been preserved. As you step into the soft rooms, you can feel the earth breathing all around you. A plaque identifies these dugouts as the home of Communists who fought the Fascists. The Jews have been written out of history.

In the forest, I met a Jewish woman who had served as a ghetto courier. She was a Communist who chose to stay in Lithuania. She had grown old, with white hair and stooped shoulders, but you could still see how pretty she must have been. She was in the forest with a group of Israelis who had come to see where the Jews fought back. I drove her home to Vilna. We stopped at a meandering river. I had an apple, which I offered to share.

"How will we share it?" I asked.

She reached into her purse and took out a huge hunting knife. Opening it with a snap, she said, "This will do the trick."

Over the next several days, I drove across Lithuania, through towns and cities, and into Poland. Sometimes a hay cart would back up an entire highway of traffic. As you passed by, the little man on the cart would wave his whip and curse. Way out in the country, without a town for miles, prostitutes in spiky heels and fur coats stood by the road. While flipping through the radio dial south of Kielce, I heard Zero Mostel singing, "If I Were a Rich Man." I thought to myself, What is wrong with Poland?

You killed all your Jews.

My friend Todd was with me. He is a friend from college, and on the way, we made jokes about many things—but not everything.

One afternoon, we went to Majdanek, the death camp in Lublin where over a million Jews died. As we slogged through the overgrown fields, in and out of the ghostly barracks, I could see couples with Frisbees, kids with soccer balls and dogs fetching sticks.

Turning to Todd, I said, "What do they think this place is?"

He looked at the crematorium in the distance, then said, "They seem to think it is some kind of a park."

This got me thinking of Abba, and how important his story is. All my life, I have heard people say that the proper attitude toward the Holocaust can best be summed up with the phrase "Never forget." Jews must never forget what happened, but they must also see to it that the world never forgets. If the world remembers, then it will not happen again. In this way, some people believe, the future is under control, knowable. But generations live and die, leaves fall and bloom and fall, everyone living will soon be dead—people forget. Even now, when there are still living survivors, some crazy people deny the Holocaust. What happens when the last survivor is gone? What happens when the Holocaust is as far in the past as the Napoleonic Wars? Who really talks, in a passionate way, about the Spanish Inquisition? Right now, we are at that key moment when the event moves from the recent past into history. Maybe that is why Abba, Vitka and Ruzka's story is so important. It proves that you can fight, no matter what people remember or forget. After all, Abba did not need the example of the Holocaust to resist the Holocaust. He had only his sense of dignity, his strength and his belief that if you struggle, then

Abba and Vitka in Israel.

win or lose, you win. With this belief, he convinced many people that they too could resist, which, in the end, saved their lives. One message of his story is this—those who fought often survived.

When Abba died, an Israeli television reporter caught up with Ruzka on the street. He asked her, in Hebrew, what Abba Kovner meant to her.

Without hesitation, she said, "He gave me a reason to live."

BIBLIOGRAPHY

Ainsztein, Reuben. *Jewish Resistance in Nazi-Occupied Eastern Europe*. New York: Harper & Row, 1974.

Arad, Yitzhak. *The Partisan: From the Valley of Death to Mount Zion*. New York: Holocaust Library, 1979.

Arad, Yitzhak. *Ghetto in Flames: The Struggle and Destruction of the Jews in Vilna in the Holocaust*. New York: Holocaust Library, 1982.

Azcarate, Pablo de. *Mission in Palestine, 1948–1952*. Washington, D.C.: Middle East Institute, 1966.

Barnouw, Dagmar. *Germany 1945: Views of War and Violence*. Bloomington: Indiana University Press, 1996.

Beckman, Morris. *The Jewish Brigade: An Army with Two Masters 1944–1945*. Rockville Centre, N.Y.: Sarpedon, 1998.

Bernstein, Burton. *Sinai: The Great and Terrible Wilderness*. New York: Viking, 1979.

Black, Ian, and Benny Morris. *Israel's Secret Wars: A History of Israel's Intelligence Services*. New York: Grove Weidenfeld, 1991.

Bridgman, Leonard, and Bill Gunston. *Jane's Fighting Aircraft of World War II*. New York: Random House, 1998.

Browning, Christopher. *The Path to Genocide: Essays on Launching the Final Solution*. Cambridge, England: Cambridge University Press, 1992.

Buber, Martin. *Israel and Palestine; the History of an Idea*. London: East and West Library, 1952.

Clark, Alan. *Barbarossa: The Russian-German Conflict, 1941–1945*. New York: Quill, 1985.

Cohen, Israel. *History of the Jews in Vilna*. Philadelphia: Jewish Publication Society of America, 1943.

Conot, Robert E. *Justice at Nuremberg*. New York: Harper & Row, 1983.

Dawidowicz, Lucy S. *The Holocaust Reader*. West Orange, N.J.: Behrman House, 1976.

Duffy, Christopher. *Red Storm on the Reich: The Soviet March on Germany.* New York: Da Capo Press, 1993.

Dupuy, Trevor N. *Elusive Victory: The Arab-Israeli Wars, 1947–1974.* Dubuque, Iowa: Kendall/Hunt, 1992.

Eckman, Lester, and Chaim Lazar. *The Jewish Resistance: The History of the Jewish Partisans in Lithuania and White Russia During the Nazi Occupation 1940–1945.* New York: Shengold, 1977.

Ehrenburg, Ilya. *The Black Book.* Tel Aviv: 1981.

Ehrenburg, Ilya, and Konstantin Simonov. *In One Newspaper.* New York: Sphinx Press, 1985.

Elkins, Michael. *Forged in Fury: A True Story of Courage, Horror and Revenge.* London: Judy Piatkus Publishers, 1971.

Falkenrath, Richard A., Robert D. Newman, and Bradley A. Thayer. *America's Achilles' Heel: Nuclear, Biological and Chemical Terrorism and Covert Attack.* Cambridge: MIT Press, 1998.

Foxman, Abraham. "The Resistance Movement in the Vilna Ghetto," in Yuri Suhl, ed., *They Fought Back: The Story of the Jewish Resistance in Nazi Europe.* New York: Crown, 1967.

Friedländer, Saul. *Nazi Germany and the Jews, Volume One: The Years of Persecution, 1933–1939.* New York: HarperCollins, 1997.

Friedman, Philip. *Roads to Extinction: Essays on the Holocaust.* New York: Jewish Publication Society of America, 1980.

Gilbert, Martin. *The Holocaust: A History of the Jews of Europe During the Second World War.* New York: Holt, Rinehart, and Winston, 1985.

Gilbert, Martin. *Atlas of the Arab-Israeli Conflict.* New York: Oxford University Press, 1993.

Glantz, David M., and Jonathan House. *When Titans Clashed: How the Red Army Stopped Hitler.* Lawrence, Kansas: University Press of Kansas, 1995.

Goldberg, David J. *To the Promised Land: A History of Zionist Thought.* New York: Penguin, 1996.

Gordon, Harry. *The Shadow of Death: The Holocaust in Lithuania.* Lexington, Kentucky: The University of Kentucky Press, 1992.

Greenbaum, Masha. *The Jews of Lithuania: A History of a Remarkable Community 1316–1945.* Jerusalem: Gefen Books, 1995.

Grubsztein, Meir. *Jewish Resistance During the Holocaust: Proceedings of the Conference on Manifestations of Jewish Resistance.* Jerusalem: Yad Vashem, 1971.

Gutman, Israel. *Youth Movements in the Underground and the Ghetto Revolts in the Holocaust.* Jerusalem: Yad Vashem, 1987.

Gutman, Israel. *Resistance: The Warsaw Ghetto Uprising.* Boston: Houghton Mifflin, 1994.

Guzenberg, Irina. *Vilnius Ghetto: Lists of Prisoners, Volume Two.* Vilnius, 1998.

Halevy, Yechiam, ed. *History Atlas of the Holocaust.* New York: Macmillan, 1996.

Harel, Isser. *The House on Garibaldi Street: The First Full Account of the Capture of Adolf Eichmann, Told by the Former Head of Israel's Secret Service.* New York: Viking, 1975.

Harmatz, Joseph. *From the Wings: A Long Journey, 1940–1960.* Sussex, England: The Book Guild, 1998.

Hashomer Hatzair. *The Massacre of European Jewry.* Israel: World Hashomer Hatzair, 1963.

Herzog, Chaim. *The Arab-Israeli Wars: War and Peace in the Middle East from the War of Independence Through Lebanon.* New York: Random House, 1982.

Hilberg, Raul. *The Destruction of the European Jews.* Chicago, 1961.

Keegan, John. *The Second World War.* New York: Penguin, 1989.

Kesselring, Albert. *The Memoirs of Field-Marshal Kesselring.* London: William Kimber, 1953.

Konstanin, Rachel. *Green House: The Jewish State Museum of Lithuania.* Vilnius, 1996.

Korczak, Ruzka. *Flames in Ashes.* (In Hebrew). Tel Aviv, 1948.

Kovner, Abba. *A Canopy in the Desert: Selected Poems.* Translated by Shirley Kaufman. Pittsburgh: University of Pittsburgh Press, 1973.

Kovner, Abba. *Scrolls of Fire: A Nation Fighting for Its Life: Fifty-two Chapters of Jewish Martyrology.* Paintings by Dan Reisinger. Translated by Shirley Kaufman with Dan Laor. Jerusalem: Keter, 1981.

Kowalski, Isaac. *A Secret Press in Nazi Europe: The Story of a Jewish United Partisan Organization.* New York: Central Guide Publishers, 1969.

Kowalski, Isaac, ed. *Anthology of Armed Resistance 1939–1945.* Brooklyn: Jewish Combatants Publication House, 1985.

Larkin, M. *The Six Days of Yad-Mordechai.* Jerusalem: Keter, 1965.

Library of America. *Reporting World War II.* Vols. I and II. New York: Library of America, 1995.

Lorch, Carlos, and Netanel Lorch. *Shield of Zion: The Israel Defense Forces.* Charlottesville, Va.: Howell Press, 1991.

Merritt, Richard L. *Democracy Imposed: U.S. Occupation Policy and the German Public, 1945–1949.* New Haven: Yale University Press, 1995.

Near, Henry, ed. *The Seventh Day: Soldiers' Talk About the Six-Day War.* London: The Trinity, 1967.

Porat, Dina. *The Blue and the Yellow Stars of David: The Zionist Leadership in Palestine and the Holocaust, 1939–1945.* Cambridge: Harvard University Press, 1990.

Porat, Dina. "With Forgiveness and Grace: The Encounter Between Ruzka Korczak, the Yishuv and Its Leaders, 1944–1946." *The Journal of Israeli History,* vol. 16, no. 2, 1995, pp. 101–32.

Rudashevski, Isaac. *The Diary of the Vilna Ghetto.* Tel Aviv: Ghetto Fighters' House, 1973.

Bibliography

Segev, Tom. *The Seventh Million: The Israelis and the Holocaust.* New York: Hill and Wang, 1993.

Sereny, Gitta. *Albert Speer: His Battle with Truth.* New York: Random House, 1995.

Shirer, William. *The Rise and Fall of the Third Reich.* New York: Simon & Schuster, 1960.

Sutzkever, Abraham. "Never Say This Is the Last Road," in Leo Schwarz, ed., *The Root and the Bough: The Epic of an Enduring People.* New York: Rinehart, 1949.

Tec, Nechama. *When Light Pierced the Darkness: Christian Rescue of Jews in Nazi-Occupied Poland.* New York: Oxford University Press, 1986.

Tenenbaum, Joseph. *Underground, the Story of a People.* New York: Philosophical Library, 1952.

Wasserstein, Bernard. *Vanishing Diaspora: The Jews in Europe Since 1945.* Cambridge: Harvard University Press, 1996.

Weizmann, Chaim. *The Letters and Papers of Chaim Weizmann: November 1917–October 1918.* Jerusalem: Israel Universities Press, 1977.

Werner, Harold. *Fighting Back: A Memoir of Jewish Resistance in World War II.* New York: Columbia University Press, 1992.

ACKNOWLEDGMENTS

The stories in this book derive from my conversations, over the course of twenty years, with Abba Kovner, Vitka Kempner-Kovner and Ruzka Korczak-Marle. I am also indebted to those former Jewish partisans, living in Israel, the United States and Lithuania, who told me about their lives in the ghetto and in the forest. Specifically, I want to thank Isser Schmidt, Pinchas Ben-Tzur, Rachel Glicksman, Cesia Rosenberg, Mordechai Rosman, Shmuel Kaplinsky and Lena Hamill. Gabik Sedlis, a wonderfully decent man who lives in New York City, was a special inspiration. I also want to thank Itzhak Rogalin, Mira Verdin and Lebke Distel, whom I met at Yaqim, a kibbutz in Israel. In addition, I am grateful to dozens of other partisans and Holocaust survivors who shared their experiences with me. I am also indebted to the children of the partisans, mostly my cousins, who shared their memories, photographs and artifacts. Here, I am thinking of Avi Marle, Yehuda and Rina Marle, Yonat and Yossi Rotbein, Ghadi and Ayala Marle, Shlomit Kovner. I owe special thanks to Michael Kovner, who took me under his wing during my stay in Israel, who served, on occasion, as my translator and adviser, and who is always my friend. I am indebted to Meir Turner, a student of history and an excellent linguist, who translated large sections of Ruzka's memoir, *Flames in Ashes*, as well as the wartime letters of Ruzka and Vitka. I am grateful to Aviva Kempner, for her friendship and advice as well as her wonderful documentary movie *Partisans of Vilna*. Lovers of Americana should not miss her film on Hank Greenberg. I want to thank my editor, Jordan Pavlin, my agent, Andrew Wylie, and Jeff Posternak at the Wylie Agency. For their help I am also grateful to the following people: Dorothy Medoff, William Levin, Lisa Melmed, Alec Wilkinson, David Lipsky for his invaluable contribution, James Albrecht, Renee and Ralph Blumenthal, Robert Blumenthal (as promised), C. S. Ledbetter III. I want to thank my sister, Sharon Levin, and my brother, Steven Cohen. Special thanks go to Jessica Medoff for her advice and constant encouragement. Also to Jessica's father, Allan Medoff, who gave me a beautiful old book about Jewish Vilna and whom I wish I had the chance to know better. As always, I am most grateful to my mother and father, and they know why. Most of all, I want to thank Vitka Kovner, who took me into her house, into her life and into her past, and who is the best living argument I know for the simple bravery of good people.

R.C.

INDEX